Wittgenstein on Thought and Will

This book examines in detail Ludwig Wittgenstein's ideas on thought, thinking, will and intention, as those ideas developed over his lifetime. It also puts his ideas into context by a comparison both with preceding thinkers and with subsequent ones. The first chapter gives an account of the historical and philosophical background, discussing such thinkers as Plato, Descartes, Berkeley, Frege and Russell. The final chapter looks at the legacy of, and reactions to, Wittgenstein. These two chapters frame the central three chapters, devoted to Wittgenstein's ideas on thought and will. Chapter 2 discusses the sense in which both thought and will represent, or are about, reality; Chapter 3 considers Wittgenstein's critique of the picture of an 'inner process', and the role that behaviour and context play in his views on thought and will; while Chapter 4 centres on the question "What sort of thing is it that thinks or wills?", in particular examining Wittgenstein's ideas concerning the first person ("I") and concerning statements like "I am thinking" or "I intend to do X".

Roger Teichmann is Lecturer in Philosophy at St Hilda's College, University of Oxford, UK.

Wittgenstein's Thought and Legacy

Edited by Eugen Fischer, University of East Anglia, UK and Severin Schroeder, University of Reading, UK

1 Wittgenstein on Thought and Will
   Roger Teichmann

Wittgenstein on Thought and Will

Roger Teichmann

LONDON AND NEW YORK

First published 2015 by Routledge

2 Park Square, Milton Park, Abingdon, Oxfordshire OX14 4RN
711 Third Avenue, New York, NY 10017

Routledge is an imprint of the Taylor & Francis Group,
an informa business

First issued in paperback 2018

Copyright © 2015 Roger Teichmann

The right of Roger Teichmann to be identified as author of this work has
been asserted by him in accordance with sections 77 and 78 of the Copyright,
Designs and Patents Act 1988.

All rights reserved. No part of this book may be reprinted or reproduced or
utilised in any form or by any electronic, mechanical or other means, now
known or hereafter invented, including photocopying and recording, or in any
information storage or retrieval system, without permission in writing from
the publishers.

Notice:
Product or corporate names may be trademarks or registered trademarks, and
are used only for identification and explanation without intent to infringe.

Library of Congress Cataloging-in-Publication Data

Teichmann, Roger, 1963–
    Wittgenstein on thought and will / Roger Teichmann.
        pages cm. — (Wittgenstein's thought and legacy)
    Includes bibliographical references and index.
    1. Wittgenstein, Ludwig, 1889–1951.   I. Title.
    B3376.W564T39 2015
    192—dc23
    2015000228

ISBN: 978-1-84465-859-6 (hbk)
ISBN: 978-1-138-34676-5 (pbk)

Typeset in Sabon
by Apex CoVantage, LLC

Contents

Abbreviations		vii
Preface		ix
1	The Philosophical Context	1
2	Thought, Will and World	29
3	The Inner and the Outer	60
4	The Subject: Grammar vs. Metaphysics	101
5	Aftermath and Legacy	125
	References	161
	Index	165

Abbreviations

BB   *The Blue and Brown Books*, Oxford: Basil Blackwell 1958.

CV   *Culture and Value*, trans. P. Winch, ed. G.H. von Wright with H. Nyman, Oxford: Basil Blackwell 1980.

OC   *On Certainty*, trans. D. Paul and G.E.M. Anscombe, ed. G.E.M. Anscombe and G.H. von Wright, Oxford: Basil Blackwell 1969.

PG   *Philosophical Grammar*, trans. A. Kenny, ed. R. Rhees, Oxford: Basil Blackwell 1974.

PI   *Philosophical Investigations*, trans. G.E.M. Anscombe, ed. G.E.M. Anscombe and R. Rhees, Oxford: Basil Blackwell 1958 (2nd ed.).

PO   *Philosophical Occasions 1912–1951*, ed. J.C. Klagge and A. Nordmann, Indianapolis, IN: Hackett 1993.

PR   *Philosophical Remarks*, trans. R. Hargreaves and R. White, ed. R. Rhees, Oxford: Basil Blackwell 1975.

RPP   *Remarks on the Philosophy of Psychology* (two volumes), trans. G.E.M. Anscombe, ed. G.E.M. Anscombe and G.H. von Wright, Oxford: Basil Blackwell 1980.

TLP   *Tractatus Logico-Philosophicus*, trans. D. Pears and B. McGuiness, London: Routledge & Kegan Paul 1961.

Z   *Zettel*, trans. G.E.M. Anscombe, ed. G.E.M. Anscombe and G.H. von Wright, Oxford: Basil Blackwell 1981 (2nd ed.).

Preface

Thought and will are two fundamental, and complementary, aspects of the human condition. Our thought strives to represent the world, while through our will we act upon the world. This at any rate is a very compelling picture. As fundamental aspects of the human condition, they have naturally occupied a central place in philosophy for as long as there has been such a thing: as we shall see, Plato was already chewing over questions about thought and will which are entirely familiar from modern discussions.

Not only are thought and will aspects of the human condition, but they are conceptually linked to a host of other phenomena, such as freedom, action, responsibility, truth, knowledge, language, mind and body . . . in fact, more or less anything of any philosophical clout. The observation that in philosophy everything is connected to everything else only partially softens the force of this remark.

It is not surprising, therefore, that the great Austrian philosopher, Ludwig Wittgenstein, should have written much, and much that is important, on the topics of thought and will. In the *Tractatus*, the young Wittgenstein mainly concerned himself with thought, his remarks on the will being both brief and as it were pessimistic, in effect denying that we do ever act upon things (see 50–51, below). The representational nature of thought he saw as a purely logical matter, i.e. as not having to do with psychological phenomena, nor for that matter with social phenomena, both kinds of phenomena being contingent and empirical in a way that put them beyond philosophical enquiry.

This principled exclusion of the psychological and the social was one of the main things which the later Wittgenstein came to reject: he saw that representation cannot be properly understood abstracted from the empirical phenomenon of human language, and in addition that a complex of psychological or part-psychological notions (understanding, intending, agreeing . . .) is associated with the representational nature of thought. Moreover, the idea that there is *one* thing we might call "representation" is a casualty of his later investigations, so that discussing intention and desire in the same breath as thought becomes (for certain purposes) entirely natural. For if my thoughts have a content, enabling them to be true or false, so do my intentions have a content, enabling them to be fulfilled or not.

x *Preface*

Thus the enquiry into the nature of thought and of the language in which thought is embodied has, in the later Wittgenstein, become extended so as to embrace what he would once have called "merely psychological" concepts. It is sometimes said that we find in the *Investigations* both philosophy of language and philosophy of mind; but it is not as if Wittgenstein just developed an interest he didn't have earlier on. The two aspects of the later book are too interconnected to be really two. The topics of thought and will are not, for Wittgenstein, topics in philosophy of mind *as opposed to* topics in philosophy of language—hence his arriving at such statements as "It is in language that an expectation and its fulfilment make contact", discussed in Chapter 2, section 2, below.

The above characterization of Wittgenstein's thought is very schematic. Flesh will be put on the bones in subsequent chapters. Now anyone who writes on Wittgenstein must be conscious of a rather glaring fact—namely, the difference between Wittgenstein's own way of presenting his ideas and the more conventional style of exposition and argument likely to be adopted by the writer. This goes for early, middle and late Wittgenstein, contrasting as those periods are; and whilst it is possible, up to a point, to explain the non-discursive style to be found in the notebooks by reminding oneself that these after all contain *notes*, it is clear that in those texts which he worked at and worked over, he was consciously adopting a mode of expression, and doing so primarily for philosophical (rather than merely stylistic) reasons. It is true that in the preface to the *Philosophical Investigations* Wittgenstein says that "I realized that . . . the best that I could write would never be more than philosophical remarks", and that "this book is really only an album" (*PI* ix). But the first statement is followed by:

> . . . my thoughts were soon crippled if I tried to force them on in any single direction against their natural inclination.—And this was, of course, connected with the very nature of the investigation. For this compels us to travel over a wide field of thought criss-cross in every direction.

Not only the album-like style, but also other features of Wittgenstein's later writing, such as the use of the imaginary interlocutor and the reflections on the nature of philosophy, are "connected with the very nature of the investigation"—so it seems to me. And it is these sorts of facts which give one pause if writing a book like the present one. But Wittgenstein's purpose, as he said, was "to stimulate someone to thoughts of his own" (*PI* x). To repeat or ape Wittgenstein's writing would run the risk of not arriving at—or anyway of not expressing—thoughts of one's own. Moreover, in what follows I do not aim merely at an exposition of Wittgenstein's views on thought and will, but also at interpretation, elaboration and comparison: comparison with philosophers who came before him, and with philosophers who have come after him. Chapter 1 deals with the first set of thinkers, Chapter 5 with

Preface xi

the second. These chapters constitute the book's frame, and the discussion of Wittgenstein himself comprises the intervening three chapters.

Still, the personal (and purposeful) mode of expression in Wittgenstein's writings which I have alluded to must not be forgotten. I hope that I have not distorted his thoughts, nor domesticated them; and—though really this goes without saying—what follows is in no way intended as a substitute for the texts themselves.

The format of this book is intended to allow the reader to "put Wittgenstein in context". It ought to become equally apparent (i) that Wittgenstein is (at least in part) tackling age-old questions and (ii) that what he has to say on those questions is radically different from much philosophy, before and after. It is radically different largely because it is radical: perhaps more than any other philosopher, Wittgenstein regarded it as essential to doing philosophy that one dig deep, going for the roots of problems. And this is how he does philosophy. For this reason, the reader of Wittgenstein does best to leave all his or her favourite theories and presuppositions behind, to the extent that this is humanly possible, and to think about such phenomena as wanting to eat an apple or believing it's going to rain with the same innocence of gaze as that with which Adam and Eve looked upon the trees and the grass. Of course, if Wittgenstein is right, the analogy is imperfect, since any *philosophizing* we do about such phenomena will be in response to confusions that have arisen in our thought: we are not, and no doubt cannot be, in a state of innocence. But we can at least try to look at the phenomena with a clear eye. Doing this while at the same time considering the relationship between Wittgenstein's thought and the thought of others requires a fair degree of concentration, but the rewards (I hope) are considerable.

Thinking (believing, judging . . .) and willing (intending, trying . . .) have both typically been treated, throughout the history of philosophy, as in some way *relational*. The relation in question may connect the subject (the "I") with reality, or elements in the subject's mind with bits of reality, or elements in the subject's mind with other such elements; and so on. Even philosophers who have argued that the subject is a fiction, or construct, have tended to espouse this picture: for them, the "elements in the mind" (perceptions, ideas, thoughts . . .) are really just "mental items"—no Mind or Self need be posited—and it is they that bear some relation to something else when there is thinking or willing. In **Chapter 1**, which outlines the historico-philosophical background to Wittgenstein, I distinguish three families of approach to the topic of thought, each characterized by what it takes those items to be which are thought of/thought about/thought/perceived/enjoyed/grasped, when thinking is going on: viz. (A) items in the world, (B) mental items or (C) abstract entities. These three approaches engender various complex problems, and my discussion of them is at times correspondingly complex, though I hope not dauntingly so. The concepts of representation, resemblance, and causation all turn out to be crucial, as does the notion of *setting up* a correlation (e.g. between idea and object).

xii *Preface*

The ways in which proponents of (A), (B) and (C) must grapple with these and other notions raise profound difficulties for all three approaches. Some of these difficulties feed into philosophical accounts of the topic of the will; but my discussion of the latter homes in especially on the relation between a willing (volition, intention . . .) and its corresponding action, and the question whether that relation is causal and/or contingent, or not.

The young Wittgenstein can be found reacting to some of these issues in his *Tractatus Logico-Philosophicus*. **Chapter 2** begins with the early Wittgenstein's revolutionary use of the idea of a logical picture, as providing the key to the representational nature of thought. This idea he came to regard as inadequate to the task; it was necessary to drop the picture of language as a sort of ideal calculus, and describe it in much richer terms, as a living, concrete phenomenon, interwoven with human life and activity. It is this conception of language that supplies the background to Wittgenstein's later account of representation, and in general of what philosophers call intentionality—an account that I introduce by means of his remark: "It is in language that an expectation and its fulfilment make contact". This account applies to both thought and will, and Chapter 2 concludes with a comparison of the early and later Wittgenstein's views on the will.

Together with an emphasis on language there is, in the later Wittgenstein, an emphasis on human behaviour. To understand what this emphasis amounts to, it is necessary to examine Wittgenstein's critique of what he called "the picture of an 'inner process'". **Chapter 3** begins with this critique, first in its general application to psychological concepts, and then in its application to thought and will. Out of this critique there emerge Wittgenstein's positive accounts of thought and of will, in which it is *context*, or the bigger picture, which above all provides the key to the solution (or dissolution) of our problems; and context includes behaviour, in a wide sense of that term. This chapter ends with a discussion of the sense in which, according to Wittgenstein, action can be seen as embodying judgement or belief. The special case of this is assertion, which is at once the paradigm expression of belief and a species of intentional action.

If it is natural to regard thinking and willing as relational, it is even more natural to assume that there is some *kind of thing* which is the possible subject of thinking and willing. At the same time, the view seems unavoidable that "I think . . ." and "I intend . . ." (etc.) have a quite different status from their second- or third-person brethren ("You think . . .", "Henry intends . . ."). These things together have tended to lead to certain views about the special status of "I", such as the Cartesian view that "I" refers to a mind with an infallible awareness of its own states. In **Chapter 4**, Wittgenstein's views relating to the use, or uses, of "I" are examined, and we see how these came to embody a radical methodological shift, away from metaphysical enquiry (as traditionally conceived) and towards what Wittgenstein termed a grammatical enquiry. This mode of enquiry among

Preface xiii

other things has the effect of utterly recasting the issue of the relation between body and soul.

Although after his death Wittgenstein's influence continued to be felt, other trends in English-speaking philosophy began more and more to dominate the scene, trends which were often at odds in various respects with Wittgenstein. In discussing his legacy, therefore, it is useful to give some picture of those trends, of their rationale and of their implications. **Chapter 5** begins with such a picture, necessarily painted with a fairly broad brush, in which one of the key issues is the relationship of philosophy to natural science. Wittgenstein regarded the two enterprises as essentially distinct, while many post-Wittgensteinian philosophers have held a contrary view, something which of course has affected what sort of philosophy they have done, particularly where this is philosophy of psychology. Other trends than scientism are mentioned which can be seen as more or less in conflict with Wittgenstein, and I look at a number of debates and contrasts arising out of these various approaches, both in philosophy and also in psychology. I then present two case studies: the contrasting philosophies of will, or more specifically of intention that have been propounded by Elizabeth Anscombe and by Donald Davidson. The former represents an approach in harmony with (though going beyond) Wittgenstein's thought, the latter an approach at odds with it. Davidson's position serves also as a good, because sophisticated, exemplar of the sort of theory that can be produced and can gain ground when Wittgenstein's ideas are ignored.

The impetus for the book came from the editors of the series to which it belongs, Severin Schroeder and Eugen Fischer. I am very grateful to both of them for their encouragement and assistance, and also for their comments and suggestions. I would also like to thank Hanoch Ben-Yami and John Hyman for comments on parts of the manuscript, and an anonymous reader for comments on the whole manuscript.

Finally, I would like to express two hopes. At the present time, students of philosophy in some parts of the English-speaking world are liable, if they develop an interest in Wittgenstein, to find themselves in the position of the naughty child who has to read his or her favourite book under the bedclothes at night. It's all right—perhaps—to treat Wittgenstein as a "historical figure", but to regard his ideas as living, and even as applicable to the sayings of local professors, carries a certain risk. My first hope is that this book may give encouragement to students who are in that position. My second hope, of course, is that I manage to shed some light in what follows on the thought of one of the greatest philosophers of our, or of any, time.

Roger Teichmann
Oxford 2014

1 The Philosophical Context

Three interrelated dualisms have characterized modern, as opposed to ancient, philosophy: dualism of mind and body, dualism of inner and outer and dualism of thought and will. The first of these is what would generally be understood by the unqualified term "dualism", and is primarily a metaphysical theory or family of theories, being concerned with the question what sorts of things exist. (Answer: mental things and material things.) The second dualism is perspectival in nature, being associated with such first-personal questions as, "What am I?", "What can I know?" and even "What can I so much as think about?" According to this second form of dualism, not only tables and chairs, but other people's minds (if such are conceivable) will be part of the outer, or external, world—from the point of view of the person or mind considering the question.

These two kinds of dualism are often associated with the philosopher René Descartes (1596–1650). A quotation from Descartes may serve to introduce the third species of dualism. In *The Principles of Philosophy*, the author lays down that "in us there are but two modes of thought, the perception of the understanding and the action of the will."[1] As stated, this is a dualism pertaining to the mind, to the "inner world"; and yet the attraction of the division surely has to do with the fact that it is the will which, as it were, connects us with the outer world, the world of bodies and of our own body. It is through the will that we act upon the world.

I have called this a dualism of thought and will, but so general is the division I am talking about that various different terms have been used for what lie on either side of the fence. For Descartes, "thought" (*cogitatio*) is "all that of which we are conscious as operating in us"[2], which is why for him the dualism is expressed as being one of understanding and will, rather than of thought and will—perceptions of the understanding and actions of the will being alike species of *cogitatio*. For Hume, the relevant distinction is between reason and passion. For Schopenhauer, it is Idea and Will. In recent times, we have become used to the "belief/desire model", a model used in accounts of human agency[3], but also used, more ambitiously, to categorize (or reduce) all mental states and processes—in much the same way that Descartes aimed to. The belief/desire model is probably best seen as an

2 The Philosophical Context

inheritance from Hume, and in moral philosophy is associated especially with the view that moral statements or judgements, being concerned with *action*, must flow above all from the will, and/or from the various alleged embodiments of the will, such as passion, desire, emotion, sentiment, etc.— rather than from anything that we think or know to be the case. In this region we find also the distinctions between the cognitive and conative, and between the factual and the evaluative.

The dualism between thought and will can be seen as embodying a picture of Man, as at once passive (acted upon by the world) and active (acting upon the world)—as a nexus of both inputs and outputs, if you like. And yet, as I remarked in connection with Descartes, it is a dualism which has typically been stated as pertaining to the mind, rather than to the whole human person. Perhaps indeed what I referred to as a picture of Man has more often been a picture of the Mind. Accounting for human agency and activity has therefore frequently resembled attempting to build a bridge while remaining on one side of the river.[4]

This makes it sound as if modern philosophy will have had greater problems accounting for action and agency than accounting for thought and judgement. But thought and judgement also involve a bridge reaching over to something else, for thought and judgement are *about* things, and they aim to achieve truth with respect to those things. The bridge between thought and reality has been just as hard to build as the bridge between will and activity, and philosophers have been engaged in attempts to build the first bridge for as long as there has been philosophizing.

1. THOUGHT AS RELATIONAL

In thinking, one thinks of something, or about something, or that something. One cannot on the face of it simply *think*. (Descartes's "I think, therefore I am" must involve a species of ellipsis.) It is extremely natural to construe "of" or "about" or "that" as indicating some kind of relation, a relation between the thinking subject and that which is thought of. "Think of" and "think about" are in fact typically followed by nouns, pronouns or noun phrases, such as "America", "him" or "ways to boil an egg". Hence, given a noun, pronoun or noun phrase as subject of the verb, the claim that thinking of/about involves a relation between a thinker and something thought of/about appears unassailable. With "think that" things are not so simple, for this phrase is typically followed by a sentence. Moreover, if truth is our topic, it is this phrase that assumes importance. If George is thinking about beer, the question of whether his thought is *true* is, as it stands, inapposite, while the same does not go for his thinking that beer is a sovereign remedy against shingles. Nevertheless, the model of thought as relational remains tempting even with "think that". Many locutions conspire to support the idea of a *something* to which the thinker is related: "What George thinks

The Philosophical Context 3

is ridiculous", "If George thinks that, he's been watching too much television", "George thinks the same on this matter as Cecilia", etc. The ordinary-language apparatus of nominalization and quantification brings "thinks that" into closer association with "thinks of" and "thinks about", with their implications of a relatum; but whether this remark constitutes a justification or a diagnosis remains to be seen.

The deepest and most ancient problem facing the idea that thought involves a relation is simple. I cannot kick a ball that isn't there, nor can I make a non-existent chair; and if "think of" behaves like "kick" and "make", I ought not to be able to think of something that doesn't exist. But I can think of all sorts of non-existent things, such as unicorns and fairies. If thinking is a relation, it must be a relation between two or more things, and a non-existent thing isn't a kind of thing. To "kick a ball that doesn't exist" could only be to fail to kick anything at all—and the same will apparently go for thinking of a beast that doesn't exist, such as a unicorn, if thinking is a relation.

In the *Theaetetus*, Socrates tackled this issue in the course of trying to establish what false belief is. ("Belief" and "judgement" are other terms for the kind of thought or thinking that can be true or false; the difference between a standing or dispositional belief and an occurrent or episodic judgement is not germane to what follows.) Parmenides had argued that false belief is impossible, since it would have to be belief of what is not, which is just believing nothing at all. Socrates agreed that believing what is not would be believing nothing at all, but concluded that false belief can't after all be belief of what is not; the objects of false beliefs must somehow exist. But why, it might be asked, did Parmenides think that false belief would have to be belief of what is not? *Some* false beliefs—if there are any—will be false because they are about fairies, or perpetual-motion machines, etc.; that is, they will be beliefs "of what is not".[5] These will face the problems just mentioned about non-existent relata, and so will be grist to Parmenides's mill. But false beliefs needn't be about non-existents. Why should there be any problem with Jack's believing that Marilyn Monroe married Charlie Chaplin, for instance?

The issue here depends on what sort of answer we give to the question, "To what is a belief related?" We could, in connection with the above example, simply say that Jack bears the, or a, believing-relation to Marilyn Monroe and Charlie Chaplin. But this relation would equally hold between the named items if Jack thought Marilyn Monroe was shorter than Charlie Chaplin, or was fonder of baseball than Charlie Chaplin, and so on. If our aim is to *explain* the nature of belief by reference to believing-relations, we may be dissatisfied unless we can posit believing-relations which apply to all beliefs and which are capable of differentiating beliefs.[6] To differentiate beliefs, we will need to mention more, or different, relata at the receiving end than just, e.g. Marilyn Monroe and Charlie Chaplin. What other items could we mention? How about the marriage between Marilyn Monroe and

4 The Philosophical Context

Charlie Chaplin? But that is a non-existent item! We might take the whole sentence after "believes that", and use it to construct the entity: *the fact that Marilyn Monroe married Charlie Chaplin*. But it *isn't* a fact that Marilyn Monroe married Charlie Chaplin—this is just another non-existent entity. Perhaps we need a special term for the item that corresponds to the sentence "Marilyn Monroe married Charlie Chaplin", a term that will apply to the item regardless of the truth-value of the sentence.

Gottlob Frege (1848–1925) introduced such a term: a Thought (*Gedanke*).[7] If Jack believes that Marilyn Monroe married Charlie Chaplin, he stands in a certain relation to a Thought, said Frege. But this raises the further question "What makes a Thought true or false?"—and Parmenides will be waiting in the wings, ready to make trouble vis-à-vis falsity. Frege's answer to the question arguably avoids Parmenidean problems, if successful, since it consists in saying that the truth or falsity of a Thought cannot be understood by reference to anything beyond the Thought: a Thought is not *made* true (false) by anything at all, at any rate if that phrase implies that the truth (falsity) of a Thought *consists in* something separately specifiable. We shall look in more detail at Frege's account presently, but it may at this point be useful to sketch the elements that are liable to enter into accounts of belief and thought as relational, in light of what has been said so far, and in anticipation of the ensuing discussion.

The *subject* of the verb "think" is most naturally taken to be a human being or other creature. But another candidate for this role has often been proposed: various philosophers, assuming the primacy of first personal psychological judgements, have taken the subject of "think", and indeed of all (or most) other psychological verbs, to be whatever it is that "I" refers to or signifies. Here we have the *philosophical* idea of the Subject, taken by many, such as Descartes, to be a mind, but taken by some others to be a fiction, or a construct, or (as in the early Wittgenstein) a limit. We will come back to the topic of the Subject later on.

What of the *objects* of thought? I shall use "object" here to mean what a thinker, or alternatively a thought, stands in some relation to—our current assumption being that thought (belief, etc.) is indeed relational. Of course, if the Subject is a fiction or whatever, thought can't consist in a relation between the Subject and something else; but many of the issues concerning objects of thought remain pressing whatever status is assigned to the Subject, so for simplicity I will simply speak of relational accounts of thought. These accounts all in effect construe "thinks" as a transitive verb, logically speaking, whether or not it takes a logical subject. Three main (species of) account may be listed, not necessarily mutually exclusive:

(A) The first sort of account identifies the objects of thought as items in the world, of the sort that can be named or in some way picked out.

(B) Another account interposes a mental intermediary between the thinker and items in the world, this intermediary being the true or immediate object of thinking; it is a private mental item, typically something like a picture or image.

(C) A third account identifies the object of thought as an abstract entity of the sort that can be true or false. This is the account adopted by Frege and some others.

2. OBJECTS OF THOUGHT AS ITEMS IN THE WORLD

With (A), we are in danger of suffering from a shortage of objects: for not only will we find no fairies or unicorns out there to do duty as objects of thought, we will also be hard pressed to find objects out there which could help to differentiate two thoughts which are about the same things, X and Y—as, "X loves Y" and "X is shorter than Y". Bertrand Russell (1872–1970) proposed ways of tackling both of these problems.

Beliefs about fairies may be particular or general. In the case of a particular belief, about the Sugar Plum Fairy, for instance, Russell would analyse "the Sugar Plum Fairy" into quantifiers, predicates and logical operators, in the manner of his well-known Theory of Descriptions[8], thus doing away with any term that either fails to refer when it should, or refers to a nonexistent thing (an absurdity). In the case of a general belief about fairies, Russell would take "fairy" as a term for a universal, or as analysable into terms for universals—which brings us to the second of the problems mentioned in the last paragraph. For to distinguish "X loves Y" from "X is shorter than Y", it is natural to posit the existence of certain *relations*, in addition to X and Y—and in the same way, "X is green" can be distinguished from "X is circular" by positing certain *properties*, i.e., entities corresponding to the adjectives "green" and "circular". All these new items will be existents, and thus will evade Parmenidean challenges. The resulting theory of thought, belief or judgement will be a multiple-relation theory, and this is the sort of theory that Russell proposed, e.g. when he wrote that "a belief has several objects; when correct, it has, in a secondary sense, the complex [consisting of those objects] as its object. Belief means a certain relation to several objects."[9]

But now we encounter another difficulty, namely that of saying how a sentence differs from a list, and thus how the mental correlates of sentence and list differ—the mental correlate of a sentence being a thought. For assume it said that when I think that X loves Y, I stand in a certain relation to three items: X, Y and (the relation of) *loving*. To be sure, this is a different trio from X, Y and *being shorter than*, so we are on our way to differentiating the two thoughts mentioned above; but what we seem to have in this trio is a mere list, and a list can't be true or false. The distinction between sentence and list was already recognized as crucial by Plato.[10]

Furthermore, if the use of the verb "loves" somehow sets up a relation between the thinker and the relation of *loving*, it is hard to avoid the

6   The Philosophical Context

conclusion that "loves" refers to this thing, i.e., refers to the same thing that "the relation of *loving*" refers to. But that seems hard to swallow, since the two quoted expressions are a verb and a noun phrase, respectively, and so cannot be intersubstituted *salva veritate* in the way such co-referential pairs as "Cicero" and "Tully" can (usually) be; indeed, they cannot even be intersubstituted *salva congruitate*.[11] Moreover, we seem committed to saying that the more perspicuous representation of my thought will be "X stands in the relation of loving to Y", which explicitly gives us the three items I am alleged to stand in the believing-relation to—and now of course an infinite regress beckons, since "stands in" is as much a verb as "loves" is, and if the latter requires further analysis, so must the former. Finally, nothing in the account enables us to distinguish the thought that X loves Y from the thought that Y loves X: if these thoughts simply concern the trio X, Y and *loving*, they are identical. (And to speak of an "ordered" trio labels the problem rather than solving it.)

What if it were simply denied that "loves" refers to something that is equally referred to by "the relation of *loving*"? Perhaps in thinking that X loves Y I stand in a believing-relation to X, Y and some third entity, different from the third entity involved when I think that X is shorter than Y; but what the third entity is cannot be stated—since to state it would require the use of a singular term, a singular term being needed to come after "I stand in the believing-relation to . . .", and *no* singular term can be substituted for "loves" *salva veritate* (or *salva congruitate*). (I am assuming that if the use of "loves" is said to *introduce* a third entity, there is no way of understanding "introduces" except as signifying the semantic relation of reference.) The entity introduced by "loves" turns out to be *ineffable*, and we have moved away from (A) as it is stated, since this object of thought (the "third entity") cannot be named or in any way picked out—unless some peculiar mode of picking out can be specified. The position we have arrived at is in fact the one Frege found himself adopting in "On Concept and Object"[12], and although Frege attempted to take some of the sting out of the phenomenon of ineffability by referring to the pinch of salt which he hoped the reader would not begrudge him, it is clear that much more needs to be said. Wittgenstein saw this, and we shall see how he dealt with the matter in the next chapter.

3.   OBJECTS OF THOUGHT AS MENTAL ITEMS

In the approach to our question which I labelled (B), we have a species of account characteristic of that strand of empiricism which may be dubbed Lockean, after John Locke (1632–1704). According to this account, to form a true belief about the world is to acquire an idea (impression, perception . . .) which accurately reflects the way things are. For empiricists, of course, the paradigm case of true belief is true perceptual belief,

The Philosophical Context 7

e.g. believing it's raining when you see that it is. A true perceptual belief may either be regarded as *derived* from a sense-impression, or be *identified* with the sense-impression (as in Hume). In either case, there is the question, "In virtue of what is the sense-impression an impression *of* something?", and the related question, "What makes a sense-impression accurate or true?" This last question need not strictly apply when the claim is that a true perceptual belief is *derived* from a sense-impression; for it is the *belief* that is after all alleged to be true, and believing and disbelieving may be two mental acts or attitudes towards an impression which in itself asserts neither P nor not-P—the acts of assent or dissent, for instance. On such a view, the second quoted question may perhaps be said to collapse into the first.

Two main notions have been made use of in responding to these questions: resemblance and causation.

For a philosopher like Locke, the sense-impression is caused by what it is of, and its truth or accuracy is (typically) conceived of as its degree of resemblance to what it is of—such resemblance, for Locke, being impossible in the case of the perception of secondary qualities, but possible in the case of the perception of primary qualities. Resemblance and causation look ill-fitted to explain the contents or truth-value of non-perceptual beliefs, such as beliefs pertaining to maths, theology or metaphysics, and it is not surprising that the history of empiricism shows various attempts to tame these and similar subjects, either by reducing their statements to perceptual ones, classifying them as analytic and hence without real content, or banishing them altogether from the scene of respectable enquiry[13]. Leaving these issues to one side, however, let us see how resemblance and causation fare when it comes to explaining the content and truth-value of perceptual beliefs.

The claim that it makes sense to say that a given sense-impression resembles the external state of affairs of which it is a sense-impression was famously attacked by George Berkeley (1685–1753), for whom it was evident that "an idea can be like nothing but an idea".[14] A sense-impression, according to the empiricist account, is private (perceived by only one Subject, at any rate in the realm of finite beings) and is not in physical space. The external objects that we are said to perceive via our sense-impressions are, if they exist, publicly accessible and in physical space, i.e. they have size, shape and location, and all the properties and relations that flow from these. Moreover, an idea must surely be an event or occurrence in the mind, and it is not really clear how an event could resemble a thing. Berkeley seems to have had a point. Could we perhaps substitute "represent" for "resemble"? The model or metaphor that is most natural here is that of the picture or image: a picture of Napoleon stands in a certain relationship to the man Napoleon, so can't we just say that a sense-impression stands in *that* relationship, the relationship of representing, to whatever it is of?

But what is that relationship? Seeing a picture of Napoleon will put you in mind of the man, especially if you have met him, or seen other pictures which you knew to be of him. Is a picture of X something the seeing of which

8 *The Philosophical Context*

puts you in mind of X? This looks fairly creaky as an account of pictures, since it is a contingent, and probably very variable, matter *what* things pictures put people in mind of. (A picture of a car may always put me in mind of the car crash I was involved in, and yet it is not a picture of a car crash.) And an analogous account of sense-impressions would have additional problems: if a sense-impression of mine is an impression of X because when I have it I am put in mind of X, what is "being put in mind of X"? Surely it is having a mental image of X. And now we must say what it is that makes a (non-perceptual) mental image of X be an image of X. Given that Berkeley was right that resemblance won't help us, we seem to be pushed towards saying that my mental image is of X if it puts me in mind of, i.e. *produces in me an image of*, X. This yields a particularly absurd form of infinite regress.—Mental images in general, by the way, will be necessary in an empiricist account of thought, since not even the most hardcore empiricist ever restricted the contents of the mind to sense-impressions; room has to be made also for memories, imagining, and so on.

Returning to physical pictures, a more promising account of pictorial representation invokes the *intention* of the maker of the picture. If I write underneath my drawing of Napoleon, "Napoleon on the eve of the Battle of Austerlitz", then it seems that this is enough for my picture to be a picture *of* Napoleon on the eve of the Battle of Austerlitz, even if the man in the picture looks more like Johnny Rotten. Could this idea be used in connection with sense-impressions and mental images? The first question to present itself would be, "What is an intention to take an image a certain way?" If an intention is just another mental image, we will again face a regress, on account of having to say why a given intention has the content it has. But maybe we need not regard intentions as images or image-like; after all, if we adhere to that dualism between thought and will which is so characteristic of modern philosophy, we may well want to give an account of intention along quite different lines from our account of thought.

An interesting example of an attempt to use intention or decision as the source of the differentiable contents of private mental items can be found in Berkeley's theory of general ideas. It was one of Berkeley's main themes that what Locke had called abstract general ideas were an impossibility, and that a thought that was about all triangles, for instance, was not what it was in virtue of the Subject's having an idea of *triangles in general*, a single idea abstracted from several ideas of particular triangles, but rather was a thought about all triangles in virtue of the Subject's deciding to take a certain idea *as* general. He wrote that "an idea, which considered in itself is particular, becomes general by being made to represent or stand for all other particular ideas of the same sort"[15]. For analogy, he mentioned geometrical proofs: thus, a particular line drawn in demonstration of how to bisect lines "represents all particular lines whatsoever, so that what is demonstrated of it is demonstrated of all lines or, in other words, of a line in general".

The Philosophical Context 9

That a particular drawn line represents all lines is clearly down to somebody's stipulating that it does. It makes no sense to ask of a line one finds drawn on a piece of paper, "Does that represent all lines?", unless one means, "Did the person who drew this intend it to represent all lines?", or possibly, "Has the person who is using it [perhaps he found it] decided that it shall represent all lines?" And Berkeley appears to be arguing that the same goes for a particular idea in the mind: "Is this idea of a dog a general idea?" can only mean, "Is this idea being used to represent all dogs?" He speaks of an idea's being "made" to represent all the members of some class, which sufficiently expresses the notion of intentional stipulation; and I think we must read him as invoking intention rather than, say, the negative phenomenon of merely *not* attending to certain features of an idea[16], since among other things it would be extremely obscure (and unBerkeleian) to distinguish *attending to this line as having length* from *attending to this line as having such-and-such a length*. (How could one explain the first without bringing in the very notion to be explained, that of generality?)

In fact, Berkeley says that a general idea represents "all other particular *ideas* of the same sort" (my italics), but of course tables and chairs were, for Berkeley, nothing but collections of ideas. The thought of a particular chair is simply a certain complex idea, while a thought about chairs in general involves such an idea, intended to represent all similar ideas. The relationship between the Subject and any given idea Berkeley expresses by means of the verb "perceive" (*percipere*): a mind or spirit *perceives* its ideas. So thought about particulars is relational, while general thought is doubly relational, involving as it does both the relation of perception (of an idea) and the relation of representation (by that idea of several other ideas). Hence we may have to say that Berkeley's account of particular thought belongs to category (A) (above, p. 4), while his account of general thought belongs in a sense to category (B); though of course the "private mental item" referred to in (B), alias the empiricist's "idea", is in fact the building-block of both thought and world, for Berkeley. It's just that it doesn't function as an intermediary in the case of particular thought or perception, and indeed is only an "intermediary", in the case of general thought, by dint of representing something; the *something*, or *things*, can themselves be directly accessed, unlike the things represented by Locke's ideas.

The analogy drawn by Berkeley between a general idea and a line drawn in the course of giving a geometrical proof is very interesting. But Berkeley did not go on to address the questions: (i) what is it for a line (symbol, image, etc.) to represent, or stand for, something?; (ii) how can an individual's decision or act of will bring it about that something represents something else? It seems likely that his answer to (i) would involve the idea of resemblance, since evidently the capacity which my idea of a particular dog has to represent other ideas is explained by its similarity to those ideas: it is "made to represent or stand for all other particular ideas of the same sort". So my decision to take the idea as a general one is not *pure* stipulation; it is

10   *The Philosophical Context*

not arbitrary in the way in which stipulating a meaning for a new sign may be arbitrary. This constrains possible answers to (ii).

In fact, the conception of thought as involving (something akin to) pictures or images very naturally goes with a view of thoughts as somehow *resembling* what they are about. This is in contrast to the conception of thought as like speech or writing—e.g. the conception of it as "inner speech". For, as just mentioned, the signs that go to make up speech are arbitrary—they represent things without having to resemble what they represent. Philosophers have very often regarded language as having the function of *expressing* thought, so that meaning and truth apply primarily to thought and only derivatively to language; the arbitrariness of linguistic signs is then explained as a matter of the arbitrariness of what noise or shape to attach to, or associate with, an already meaningful mental item—thus leaving resemblance as the key to meaning and truth, if our model of such mental items is imagistic. But it has always been a bit of a poser how to "get at" thoughts except via the sentences that express them, particularly if the thoughts are abstract or in some other way non-sensory, so that the model of thought as inner speech has a tendency to reassert itself.

One reason why pictorial representation can appear to be a superior model to that of linguistic representation in a philosophical account of thought is this: the problem of how to distinguish a sentence from a list, touched on above, has no analogue when it comes to pictures. A picture can be called accurate, hence "true", without its involving us with "super-items", such as properties and relations. These were the items which bedevilled our account (A): if referred to, they turned sentences into lists, and if not referred to, they landed us with the Ineffable. But in a picture of a man on a horse, though we find a bit of paint depicting the man, and a bit of paint depicting the horse, we find no extra bit of paint depicting *being on top of*. It is this feature of pictures which enabled Wittgenstein to develop such a powerful pictorial account of truth and meaning in the *Tractatus*, as we shall see—though it ought to be said that the early Wittgenstein had nothing against the Ineffable. The idea of a *resemblance* between picture and fact, of the sort at the heart of empiricist accounts, has in the *Tractatus* been replaced by the much more linguistic notion of shared logical form— a revolutionary use of the notion of a picture.

Berkeley's account of general thought, I have argued, involves both the notion of representation and that of intention or decision. It is interesting to note that these two notions also appear, employed rather differently, in Plato's account of false opinion in the *Theaetetus*. As I've said, Socrates meets Parmenides's challenge by insisting that the objects of false thoughts must somehow exist. He likens memory to a block of wax which takes imprints of the things we perceive, and says:

> Then the possibility of forming false opinion remains in the following case: when, for example, knowing you [Theaetetus] and Theodorus, and having on that block of wax the imprint of both of you, as if you

were signet-rings, but seeing you both at a distance and indistinctly, I hasten to assign the proper imprint of each of you to the proper vision, and to make it fit, as it were, its own footprint, with the purpose of causing recognition; but I may fail in this by interchanging them, and put the vision of one upon the imprint of the other, as people put a shoe on the wrong foot.[17]

Theaetetus and Theodorus both exist all right, and Socrates's ideas of them are thus ideas "of what is"; and these ideas represent their objects in the way in which an imprint in wax represents the object that produced it. But it is possible for Socrates to *misassign* an idea of memory, matching it with the wrong vision. His aim is to assign a given idea to the correct vision, and such assigning is evidently an intentional act of the mind, just as putting on a shoe is. And like putting on a shoe, the mental act of matching idea to vision can fail of its purpose, its purpose being "to cause recognition".

In fact, Socrates's (or Plato's) account of thought cannot be classified as imagistic *as opposed to* linguistic, since he also employs the metaphor of speech, defining thought "as the talk which the soul has with itself"[18]. Whether the metaphor of wax imprints can be successfully yoked to the metaphor of talking to oneself perhaps doesn't matter: the richness of a dialogue which throws out so many ideas is what must impress us. Another idea present in the passage quoted above is that of causation, since a certain memory is *of* a certain person on account, at least in part, of that person's having produced the "memory-imprint" in the soul. In other words, the object of a memory-idea is the causal origin of that idea.

This brings us to the second of the two notions typically employed by proponents of (B). The first of these was resemblance—the second is causation. (See p. 7, above.) Our questions are, first, "In virtue of what is an idea an idea *of* a certain thing?", and second, "What makes an idea accurate or true?" (The second question may collapse into the first.) "Idea" is being used as a term for the "private mental item" referred to in (B). If Berkeley was right, resemblance can't help us. He himself, and Plato in the *Theaetetus*, invoked intention or decision when giving (partial) answers to our two questions, but in both cases the suggestion was really just that—a suggestion, in need of further development. The view according to which the object of an idea (i.e. the thing it is *of*) bears a causal relationship to that idea has, by contrast, been developed in various ways and directions over the centuries.

This view has generally taken the form of claiming that the object of an idea is a, or the, cause of the idea. But there are also accounts according to which it is the *effects* of an idea that go to determine its object. These effects may be behavioural or psychological. Russell, for instance, wrote in *The Analysis of Mind* that

> what is called an image "of" some definite object, say St. Paul's, has some of the effects which the object would have. This applies especially to the effects that depend upon association. . . . To arrive at the

12   *The Philosophical Context*

> meaning of an image. . . . we observe that there are certain respects, notably associations, in which the effects of images resemble those of their prototypes.[19]

On this view, my image of St. Paul's produces similar effects in me to those produced by St. Paul's itself—effects such as associated images, i.e. images which regularly occur together with the sensation or image in question. Presumably in talking of the effects of St. Paul's itself Russell meant the effects of my perceptions of that building, i.e. of certain of my sensations; indeed, being phenomenalistically inclined, Russell was no doubt thinking of St. Paul's as itself constructed out of sense-data (or "sensibilia"). But that he took the causal efficacy of images to have a determining role also shows the influence on him of the scientific outlook associated with behaviourism. This influence is yet more apparent in what he had to say about desire, as we shall see when examining his views on that topic in sec. 6 of this chapter. What may be noted here is that the main problems with causal accounts of (the contents of) thoughts, ideas, images, and so on—certainly the main ones that Wittgenstein was to highlight—are problems faced both by accounts which look to the effects of an idea (etc.) and by accounts which look to its cause(s). Since, as I have said, the latter have been more predominant in the history of philosophy, I will briefly discuss what is arguably the central such problem, as it surfaces in accounts which look to the cause(s) of an idea.

The problem is this: there can be doubt as to what caused some known effect, but there seems to be no room for doubt as to what one is thinking of, what one's idea is an idea of. Just as I cannot doubt that I am thinking, so I cannot doubt that it is cheese I am thinking of, if indeed it *is* cheese I am thinking of. This fact has traditionally been explained by reference to the first-personal authority attaching to psychological states; but whether or not this explanation is along the right lines, a fact it is, at any rate in normal or everyday situations.[20] But how am I to know what the *cause* of my present idea is (or was)? That X is a cause of Y is, at least typically, something that experience teaches me[21]: I cannot infer X as the cause from my knowledge of Y alone, nor indeed from my knowledge, if I have it, that X preceded Y. But when I have an idea of cheese, all I have is the idea, and that is clearly all I need to have in order to say that it is an idea of cheese. The cause, if cause there be, is not in view; and for Lockean empiricists, it is something I could never have in view, since for such philosophers, all that could be meant by "experiencing a lump of cheese" is "having an idea (sense-impression) of a lump of cheese". I can't pretend to have found the external cause of an idea by virtue of having (or having had) another idea.

Latter-day post-empiricist philosophers have used causal origin as the determinant of the contents of ideas and thoughts, and for these philosophers the problem of the inaccessibility of external objects doesn't arise: no "veil of perception" stands between the Subject and the objects around him/her/it. But the problem of the dubitability of causes does still afflict

The Philosophical Context   13

post-empiricist accounts of this sort. I will be looking at such accounts later on, especially in Chapter 5.

4.   OBJECTS OF THOUGHT AS ABSTRACT ENTITIES

We have looked so far at two kinds of philosophical account of thought, conceived of as relational, the kinds of account I labelled (A) and (B). Each has been seen to face various problems or lacunae. Let us now turn to the third kind of account, (C), according to which the object of thought is an abstract entity of the sort that can be true or false—what Frege called a Thought, and later philosophers a proposition. I said when introducing them that the three characterizations, (A), (B), and (C), were not to be regarded as excluding one another, and in fact (A) and (C) are compatible given a certain reading of "in the world". This can be seen when we consider the position adopted by Frege in "The Thought".

For Frege, a Thought is in the world just as much as is a chair, in the sense that it does not belong to the *inner* world of someone's mind. It is not, as he puts it, an idea. In arguing for the distinctness of Thoughts and ideas, Frege puts especial emphasis on the issue of truth. If the object of a thought were an idea, in what (he asks) would the truth of that idea consist, in the case where I think something true? Evidently, in the correspondence between the idea and what it is of. But what *is* the idea of? Frege considers the possibility, discussed above, that the content of an idea is like the subject-matter of a picture. If a proposition (the object of thinking) is an idea, and an idea is like a picture, then truth might seem to consist in resemblance. This would mean either perfect resemblance, or less-than-perfect resemblance. As to the first, "a correspondence . . . can only be perfect if the corresponding things coincide and are, therefore, not distinct things at all. . . . It would only be possible to compare an idea with a thing if the thing were an idea too." This last remark is reminiscent of Berkeley, but Frege's point is not just the Berkeleian one that an idea and a thing are very different items. It is rather that perfect resemblance would mean *identity*—which is hopeless, given that the notion of "correspondence" could only help us (in our definition of truth) if it were a two-place relation.[22] "It is absolutely essential that the reality be distinct from the idea", Frege writes. Imperfect resemblance, on the other hand, comes in degrees, and truth does not: "Truth cannot tolerate a more or less."

What if the specific respects in which an idea was meant to resemble its object were laid down in advance? Wouldn't that exclude degrees of truth? And couldn't we then also test for truth, ascertain it in a given case?—Such a view, note, invokes intention or decision, in much the same way as was done by Berkeley in his account of general ideas: a decision by the Subject would determine which features of an idea were to correspond to something in the object. (The decision would have to be the Subject's, since only the Subject

14 *The Philosophical Context*

is acquainted with this particular idea.) Frege no more goes into the question of what such a decision would consist in than does Berkeley, and after all he has less reason to at this point, since he is attacking a view, not defending it. But it is perhaps of some interest that when he later gives an account of the term "idea", he does not include under that heading *all* the contents of the Subject's "inner world", but specifically, though without explanation, excludes decisions[23]. He thus seems to adhere to some version of that general dualism of thought and will (as I characterized it) which was discussed at the start of this chapter. Whether Frege can afford to say as little as he does about subjective decision is a question we shall return to presently.

The argument Frege gives against the account of truth now on offer, which elucidates correspondence by reference to stipulated "respects of resemblance", turns out, famously, to be an argument against *any* attempt to explain or define truth. Frege appears to assume that a definition of truth will be an analysis of that notion, an analysis into notions that are in some sense more primitive. Let us take such a definition of truth to be of the form: P is true if and only if P is A, B, C. (An instance of this being: P is true if and only if P corresponds in respects *a, b, c* to X). To ascertain, for some given P, whether P is true, we must therefore first ascertain whether it is true that P is A, B, C (since *A, B, C* are more primitive notions than *true*). But our analysis tells us that *P is A, B, C* is true if and only if *P is A, B, C* is A', B', C'. So we must first ascertain whether this last is true, i.e. whether it is true that *P is A, B, C* is A', B', C'.[24] And so on. In the face of this infinite regress, Frege concludes that "it is probable that the word 'true' is unique and indefinable."

At this point, a proponent of (B) might say: "If the word 'true' is indefinable, why can't it be alleged to apply to ideas, with as much justice as you allege it to apply to Thoughts?" Frege's reply is that if truth were a property of ideas, then since ideas are private, there could be no communication, no collaborative enquiry, no science. That way lies solipsism. Frege's discussion here becomes very interesting, as when he argues that idealism and realism collapse into one another[25]—but to examine such themes would take us too far afield.

What, then, is a Thought if it is not an idea? And what goes on when a person actually thinks something, acquires a belief, etc.?

Frege's explanation of what a Thought is explicitly relies on the model of the declarative sentence; his account of thought and thinking is linguistic as opposed to imagistic or pictorial.[26] Different Thoughts are expressed by sentences with different senses, even if the sentences have the same truth-value. Thoughts thus belong to the "realm of sense", whereas the True and the False are what sentences *refer* to. (This last claim is perhaps best understood *via* the thought that two expressions count as co-referring if and only if they are intersubstitutable in "normal" contexts *salva veritate*: propositions having the same truth-value are in this way intersubstitutable, for Frege, and hence are co-referential.) The complexity to be found in a Thought mirrors that to be found in the corresponding sentence. A proper name or singular term refers to an object, a predicate refers to a concept, and the *sense* of each expression determines its referent. These senses are thus components of the Thought corresponding to the sentence in which occur the name and the predicate.

A Thought is the sense of a sentence. And the Thought *Danny is a horse* is constituted by the sense of "Danny" plus the sense of "is a horse". "The sense of 'Danny is a horse'" (being a singular term) must, it seems, refer to an object, an object we might also refer to by the complex singular term: "The sense of 'Danny' conjoined with the sense of 'is a horse'". And passing over the question what "conjoining" might amount to, we are faced with the problematic conclusion that a Thought, i.e. the sense of a sentence, must be a species of complex object. After all, if Thoughts are objects, then truth is a property of some, but not all, objects, and we might wonder why we are so certain that it is *not* a property of, say, Danny himself. This issue is analogous to the issue whether Julius Caesar might have been a number, which Frege realised was an issue which his theory of numbers as objects required him to take seriously.[27] But these "issues" are on the face of it forms of nonsense. Certainly a theory of truth which simply characterizes truth as "an indefinable property found to inhere in some but not all objects" appears to be at the very least worryingly laconic. (It won't look much better to say that the True is an indefinable object, referred to by some but not all proper names.)

So there seem to be grave difficulties surrounding the Fregean notion that the object of thought is a Thought or proposition. But even if these difficulties could be overcome, there remains the second of our two questions: What goes on when a person actually thinks something, acquires a belief, etc.?

Frege writes:

> Although the thought does not belong to the contents of the thinker's consciousness yet something in his consciousness must be aimed at the thought. . . . How does a thought act? By being apprehended and taken to be true. This is a process in the inner world of a thinker which can have further consequences in this inner world and which, encroaching on the sphere of the will, can also make itself noticeable in the outer world.[28]

Thus something in the inner world, some idea, must occur (be experienced) in order for a Subject to apprehend a Thought. This idea "aims at" that particular Thought, rather than another. How does it do that? Frege is silent on this point. But the alleged relationship between an idea and a Thought will face similar problems to those which beset the alleged relationship between an idea and what it is of, problems which were discussed in connection with (B). The relationship, Frege would agree, cannot be one of resemblance; nor apparently can it be some species of causal relationship—indeed,

16   The Philosophical Context

for Frege a Thought is timeless and unchangeable.[29] If the idea has a complexity that mirrors that of the Thought, and of course that of the sentence that expresses it, it would seem natural to take sentential meaning for our model and invoke decision or stipulation. Just as the correlation of a noise or shape, "Danny", with a certain horse is a matter of human decision, so we might say that the correlation of an idea with a Thought, and of a given feature of the idea with a given element of the Thought, are matters of subjective decision. We are back with Berkeley. And like Berkeley, Frege gives us few hints as to what a "correlation" (or "representation") could amount to, nor how a subjective decision could bring it into being.

The idea that subjective decision *could* bring it about that (a feature of) an idea corresponded to (an element of) a Thought in any case involves us in a vicious circle. For even if the dichotomy between thought and will is real enough, I cannot decide, "Let the idea α be correlated with the Thought β", unless I can already entertain the Thought β, which is a component of my decision.[30] But our hypothesis requires that for me to entertain the Thought β I must already have set up a correlation between some idea and it—which is only possible if I can already entertain the thought β, etc. Similar remarks apply, *mutatis mutandis*, to alleged correlations between features of an idea and elements of a Thought.

I have devoted as much space as I have to Frege, not only because he is a classic exponent of the account I labelled (C), but also because he had a crucial influence on the development of Wittgenstein's views. Frege can, indeed, be seen as in some ways the forerunner of Wittgenstein, e.g. in his "anti-psychologism" with regard to logic, an anti-psychologism we see at work in his account of Thoughts as objective entities, to be distinguished from ideas. But in hanging on to a conception of ideas as items within an inner world of consciousness, items which still seem to be required if anyone is to think or judge, Frege was unable fully to expunge from his account of thought and judgement the taint of subjectivity. The thinker's relation to what is thought remains baffling, and the world of Thoughts, like Plato's world of forms, seems to be too far above and beyond the natural world to be capable of supplying those explanations of natural phenomena which ultimately it is one of the aims of the philosopher to give us.

5.   WILL AND ITS RELATION TO ACTION

At the start of this chapter I spoke of two bridges that philosophers have struggled to build—one bridge linking thought and reality, and another linking will and activity. Two related questions faced would-be builders of the first bridge: "In virtue of what is a thought a thought *of* (or *about* or *that*) such-and-such?", and "What is the relationship between a thought and that in virtue of which it is accurate or true?" An analogous pair of questions faces would-be builders of the second bridge: "In virtue of what is a willing

The Philosophical Context   17

(or decision or intention or desire . . .) a willing *to do* such-and-such?", and "What is the relationship between a willing and that which fulfils or manifests it (i.e. an action)?"

Parmenides's problem of false opinion has its analogue for the will. Wanting and desiring are often taken to be on the "conative" side of the fence; and just as thinking about fairies seems impossible if there are no fairies, so wanting a flying horse appears to be impossible, if wanting is a relation. Thinking that Marilyn Monroe married Charlie Chaplin was likewise puzzling, since no fact or state of affairs exists corresponding to the sentence "Marilyn Monroe married Charlie Chaplin"; and in the same way, the marksman who intends to hit the bullseye but fails seems to have intended a non-existent outcome or action. It is natural, in order to maintain a relational model of willing, to posit some kind of existents as the relata of unfulfilled wants or intentions—and just as with thought and judgement, this could mean either positing "special" entities in the world, or positing items in the Subject's inner world as the objects of wanting or intending (i.e. as the logical or genuine objects of the verbs "want" and "intend").

The dualism between thought and will characteristic of modern philosophy is motivated, I suggested, by an association with the latter of acting in the world. Why then does wanting a flying horse typically count as sitting on the "conative" side of the fence? For if there are no flying horses there can be no actions involving flying horses, such as buying them. Nevertheless, you can *try* to buy a flying horse (maybe from the person who persuaded you they exist), and such trying would be some sort of acting—writing out a cheque, say. The action-description "trying to buy a flying horse" itself manifests Parmenidean peculiarity, given a relational reading of "try to buy". But this doesn't affect the claim that wanting involves (a disposition to) action. *Wishing* is different, for one can wish for things one knows it is impossible to do anything about: I can wish I had passed my driving test, having just failed it, for example. There is no such thing as trying to have passed your driving test, given the knowledge that one cannot affect the past.

This last sort of case may encourage the idea that what characterizes the will and its various forms or subcategories is not so much action as a certain *feeling*, or feelings—of dissatisfaction, unease, longing, or whatever. Such was the view held by Schopenhauer, for whom the answer to the problem of living lay in a hoped-for deliverance from the tyranny of the will and the suffering which is essential to it. But there are many forms of what might be called negative emotions with objects: you can fear that p, or be disgusted at X, or be nervous about having to do such-and-such. Those who adhere to the dualism of thought and will, while they might analyse such cases so as to bring out a "conative" aspect in them, would surely not regard them all as simply manifestations of the will, on account of their negative affect. The deep motive underlying the dualism must relate somehow to action, and on that account wishing looks more like one of Descartes's "perceptions

18   *The Philosophical Context*

of the understanding" (accompanied, perhaps, by certain sensations) than it does one of his "actions of the will"—at any rate when it is wishing for something one knows one cannot have.

Returning to the relational model of the will, and to the parallels with the relational model of thought, we can see that in the case of unfulfilled wants or intentions only the first of our two questions has application, namely the question that asks what it is that determines that a want or intention is a want or intention *for*, or *to do*, such-and-such. One way of answering this question simply makes use of the answer, whatever it is, that is given to the parallel question about thought: thus in intending to hit the bullseye, the marksman must have a thought, or an idea, of his hitting the bullseye, and the question what makes that thought or idea have the content it does can be dealt with along the lines of (A), (B) or (C), from the last section—ignoring for the moment the difficulties faced by these views. That *intention* is involved could then be put down to the fact that this thought or idea results in certain actions, these being taken to be states or motions of the person's body or mind. This causal conception of intention (desire, etc.) would of course apply even more clearly to the case of fulfilled intentions (desires, etc.), thus supplying an answer to the second of our two questions, above. The difference between fulfilled and unfulfilled intentions would then naturally be taken as residing in some relationship, other than that of cause and effect, between the intention and the action(s) it produces. The relationship could be one of (non-)resemblance, for example.[31]

This sketch of a theory of intention both acknowledges the shared content of an intention and a corresponding thought, and characterizes intention by reference to its effects "in the world". But in many traditional accounts of the will, it is only the first feature that we find, not the second. (Building a bridge while remaining on one side of the river is the metaphor that comes to mind.) An example is the account to be found in Descartes's *Meditations*, in which Descartes equates *believing that p* with *inwardly affirming the idea that p*, where "affirming" is an exercise of one's will. This affirming-an-idea need have no effects, external or internal. The alternative use of the faculty of the will, in intentional or voluntary action, is something about which Descartes says little, but if an intention to do X involves the idea of one's doing X, it seems that some inner act other than affirming must be postulated in order to distinguish *intending that I do X* both from *believing I am doing X (or: will do X)* and from simply *entertaining (having) the idea that I am doing X (or: will do X)*. Such an inner act Descartes does indeed postulate, writing that

> . . . the faculty of will consists alone in our having the power of choosing to do a thing or choosing not to do it (that is, to affirm or deny, to pursue or to shun [*prosequi vel fugere*] it), or rather it consists alone in the fact that in order to affirm or deny, pursue or shun those things

The Philosophical Context   19

placed before us by the understanding, we act so that we are unconscious that any outside force constrains us in doing so.[32]

Assuming that "those things placed before us by the understanding [*intellectus*]" are of a single kind, they must be ideas or perceptions, so that Descartes's view is this: not only can you affirm an idea, you can also "pursue" it. Of course, in ordinary English, one pursues whatever an idea is of, not the idea itself, and the same goes for the Latin "prosequi"—so the verb, "prosequi" or "pursue", must in this context have a special philosophical sense. (Descartes is not claiming that one can *try to get hold of* an idea, an activity that would be rendered futile by the fact that one already has it.)[33] That you have "pursued" a given idea will be something you know with infallible authority for Descartes, and although bodily movements no doubt frequently occur as a result of such acts of pursuing, the identity of an act of will *as* an act of will is quite independent of any effects that might ensue.

In drawing a parallel between affirming things and pursuing things, Descartes was following a tradition going back at least to Aristotle, according to which the Good and the True are the respective, and parallel, goals of action and of judgement. But Descartes's mentalistic version of this parallelism leaves him with the question: how do I know that I have pursued, rather than affirmed, a given idea of mine? There must be an intrinsic qualitative difference between pursuing and affirming, a difference available to introspection. And the view that acts of will, or volitions, are known by their intrinsic character has been endorsed by many philosophers, along with the view just mentioned, its natural concomitant: that the identity of an act of will *as* an act of will is independent of any effects that might ensue.

One philosopher to have employed the thought that a volition's nature is something available to introspection is David Hume (1711–1776). Hume makes a characteristically negative use of this idea when he attacks the notion that we derive the idea of causal efficacy from the exercise of our own wills, something he does by denying that any "power" or "energy" will be found, on introspection, to inhere in an act of the will. Any effects that follow upon acts of the will can only be known to do so on the basis of experience, and this even goes for such acts of the will as a decision to "raise up a new idea, fix the mind to the contemplation of it, turn it on all sides, and at last dismiss it for some other idea".[34]

> Volition is surely an act of the mind, with which we are sufficiently acquainted. Reflect upon it. Consider it on all sides. Do you find anything in it like this creative power, by which it raises from nothing a new idea, and with a kind of *Fiat*, imitates the omnipotence of its Maker, if I may be allowed so to speak, who called forth into existence all the various scenes of nature? So far from being conscious of this energy in the will, it requires as certain experience as that of which we are

20   The Philosophical Context

possessed, to convince us that such extraordinary effects do ever result from a simple act of volition.[35]

For Hume, cause and effect are always distinct existences, and one can never "read off" from some event what effects it will have, however intimately one is acquainted with that event. This teaching of Hume's has been enormously influential; and combined with the view that intentions (volitions, etc.) are mental events, it almost inevitably leads to Hume's conclusion, that my knowledge, e.g. that a given intention of mine is liable to lead to my boiling a kettle must be knowledge derived from experience—that is, from an experience of a constant conjunction in the past of intentions like this one with kettle-boilings (or attempted kettle-boilings). How else could I know that a current state of my mind will probably be followed by various movements of my body?

This account of intention faces the same kind of problem as do accounts of (the contents of) thoughts, ideas, images, and so on, that invoke either the causes or the effects of those thoughts, etc.—namely, the problem of the dubitability of causes and effects (see pp. 12–13 above). If my knowledge that my present intention will (probably) lead to my boiling a kettle is based on past experience, in the same way that my knowledge the kettle will boil if put over a flame is, then my predictions of what I will do must be as liable to uncertainty or error as are my inductive predictions generally. This will be particularly noticeable when I form an intention I have never formed before, or which is sufficiently unlike any intention I have formed before. But it seems crazy to say that when I intend to boil a kettle I have much stronger grounds for believing that I *will* boil a kettle than the grounds I have for thinking that I will shave all my hair off, when I have decided to do so to raise money for charity and have just picked up the electric shaver.

Even worse would be the prospect of my being uncertain what intention it was that I had; and this prospect is raised by those forms of causal account which specify the *content* of an intention by reference to its effects, or more generally by reference to future or possible causes and effects. Hume's theory does not do this, so for him it is simply the uncertainty in my predictions of what I will do, not in my assertions of what it is my present intention to do, that renders what he says hard to swallow. For a theory which attaches first-personal uncertainty *both* to the issue of what actions I will perform *and* to the issue of what I now intend or desire to do, we may turn to a philosopher who was in many ways Hume's intellectual descendant, Bertrand Russell.

6.   A BEHAVIOURIST THEORY

In the account of desire which he gives in *The Analysis of Mind*, Russell begins by outlining what he takes to be "ordinary unreflecting opinion", or at any rate "a view against which common sense would not rebel", according to which

> when we say: "I hope it will rain," or "I expect it will rain," we express, in the first case, a desire, and in the second, a belief, with an identical content, namely, the image of rain. It would be easy to say that, just as belief is one kind of feeling in relation to this content, so desire is another kind. According to this view, what comes first in desire is something imagined, with a specific feeling related to it, namely, that specific feeling which we call "desiring" it.[36]

The view thus outlined is at least structurally the same as that which we encountered in Descartes's *Meditation IV*, with "believing" for Descartes's "affirming" and "desiring" for his "pursuing", and with a more empiricist reliance on such terms as "image" and "feeling". That part of the view which is concerned with desire Russell takes to be mistaken, but as far as belief goes, the view Russell describes is in fact the view he himself endorses, in Lecture XII ("Belief"); and the continuing tug of empiricist (as opposed to behaviourist) notions leads him to lapse more than once from his official account of desire, towards something like the one sketched in the above quotation. But it is the official account which will be our main focus.

Russell had been influenced both by the writings of William James (1842–1910), especially his monumental *Principles of Psychology* of 1890, and by more recent work, of a behaviourist tendency, such as that of Edward L. Thorndike (1874–1949). The latter was a pioneer in the use of animals for psychological research, and Russell was clearly impressed by the comparisons to be made between animals and human beings, as also by the methodology characteristic of research into animals. Indeed, his view of the methodology seems to have determined how he regarded the available comparisons. Animals, he writes,

> *may* have minds in which all sorts of things take place, but we can know nothing about their minds except by inferences from their actions; and the more such inferences are examined, the more dubious they appear. It would seem, therefore, that actions alone must be the test of the desires of animals. From this it is an easy step to the conclusion that an animal's desire is nothing but a characteristic of a certain series of actions . . . And when it has been shown that this view affords a satisfactory account of animal desires, it is not difficult to see that the same explanation is applicable to the desires of human beings.[37]

Perhaps the most notable feature of this passage is the drawing of what might appear to be a substantive conclusion ("an animal's desire is nothing but a characteristic of a certain series of actions") from considerations about what tests can or cannot be used to yield sufficiently certain results.

22 The Philosophical Context

The only way of reading Russell here is as proposing a meaning for "animal desire" which enables us to apply the expression and its cognates with relative certainty, so that his "conclusion" is not after all a substantive one, but is rather a statement that we will accept *if* we accept his semantic proposal. The presumed alternative is the view that animal desires are inner states inaccessible to observers, inferences to the occurrence of which must be "dubious". This would lead to a form of scepticism or agnosticism, and would seem to rule out the possibility of a science of desire—an unpalatable result. The motivation behind the form of behaviourism Russell here advocates is similar to that which had been expressed by J. B. Watson (1878–1958), who like Russell allowed the reality of "inner states", but declared that scientific procedures could *ex hypothesi* never discover anything about such states, and so should concern themselves only with behaviour.[38]

One might ask *why* inferences from animal behaviour to inner states should be dubious. If it is because of the inaccessibility to observers of such states, then for consistency's sake Russell would have to accept either behaviourist or sceptical accounts of the similarly inaccessible images, sensations, etc. of other people, something he does not show himself willing to do in *The Analysis of Mind*. But if it is because of the fact that animals are unlike human beings (e.g. insofar as they lack language), then Russell has insufficient reason to state that "it is not difficult to see that the same explanation is applicable to the desires of human beings".[39] A third possibility would be that the inferences in question are only dubious if alleged to be the sort of inferences that can play a role in scientific theory; but on this interpretation we would have a Watsonian proposal about how most fruitfully to pursue empirical psychology that seems to stop well short of the claim with which Russell begins his lecture, that "Desire is a subject upon which, if I am not mistaken, true views can only be arrived at by an almost complete reversal of the ordinary unreflecting opinion."

Like many other philosophers and psychologists, Russell faced what seemed to him to be an inevitable dichotomy: either the mind (desire, belief, etc.) is an inner realm of self-intimating items of consciousness, or it is somehow reducible to behaviour describable from a scientific point of view. A passage between the mentalist Scylla and behaviourist Charybdis was eventually to be charted by Wittgenstein, and the impetus for him to do so was in part Russell's inadequate theory of desire. To the details of that theory we may now turn.

Russell's account is embodied in the following "definitions":

> A "behaviour-cycle" is a series of voluntary or reflex movements of an animal, tending to cause a certain result, and continuing until that result is caused, unless they are interrupted by death, accident, or some new behaviour-cycle. (Here "accident" may be defined as the intervention of purely physical laws causing mechanical movements.)

The "purpose" of a behaviour-cycle is the result which brings it to an end, normally by a condition of temporary quiescence—provided there is no interruption.

An animal is said to "desire" the purpose of a behaviour-cycle while the behaviour-cycle is in progress.

According to this account, if one says that one's purpose in walking to the shop is to buy a pint of milk, one is predicting that one's present behaviour-cycle will (unless interrupted) result in something, one's buying some milk, which itself will result in the cessation of the behaviour-cycle. The status of this prediction will be like that of causal predictions generally, inductive in nature; the prediction will be rather like the prediction that if I fall asleep I will cease to sit upright in my chair. Since it is this feature of Russell's account that was to be especially criticized by Wittgenstein, I will not discuss it further here, but will instead note the reference to the "voluntary or reflex movements" constitutive of a behaviour-cycle.

What, it might be asked, is a voluntary movement? Whatever it is will clearly be something an account of which lies on that side of the fence we have called "conative", like desire itself. And Russell answers the question later on in *The Analysis of Mind*, writing that "movements which are accompanied by kinaesthetic sensations tend to be caused by the images of those sensations, and when so caused are called *voluntary*." When I reach for a book, I feel certain sensations in my arm, etc., and when on later occasions images of these sensations occur in me, they rather often make my arm move towards a book, which reaching then counts as a voluntary movement. Russell had acquired this strange view from William James (Ch. 26 of the *Principles*), and he repeats, apparently approvingly, James's remark that on such an account "no movement can be made voluntarily unless it has previously occurred involuntarily". Possibly James and Russell were thinking only of simple movements, described in simple terms, such as *lifting my left arm*, for it would be a hard thing if I were prevented from voluntarily shaving the hair off my head by the obstacle of never having done so by accident. This points towards the need for an examination of the different species of action-description, since a single "movement" can typically be described by means of various descriptions, under some but not all of which it may be voluntary (or intentional), and what *counts* as a single movement will in most cases depend on what descriptions we have in mind.[40] But Russell appears unaware of the need for such an enquiry.

What earlier empiricists would have called acts of the will, or volitions, have in Russell's theory been replaced by images and sensations, especially memory-images and kinaesthetic sensations; and he tells us that by "volition" he means only "decision after deliberation", something which involves a little more than just voluntary movement, namely

24   *The Philosophical Context*

...a judgment: "This is what I shall do" [the judgment itself presumably being an image or sensation]; there is also a sensation of tension during doubt, followed by a different sensation at the moment of deciding. I see no reason whatever to suppose that there is any specifically new ingredient; sensations and images, with their relations and causal laws, yield all that seems to be wanted for the analysis of the will, together with the fact that kinaesthetic sensations tend to cause the movements with which they are connected."

We see Russell here reverting to that mentalism which one feels was always his more natural home than the new-fangled behaviourism embodied in his official theory of desire. We also see the heavy reliance made on the idea of causation and of causal laws, a reliance which in Russell's case seems ironic, given the attempted demolition of the notion of cause to be found in his earlier essay "On the Notion of Cause".[41] We may perhaps take it that the arguments of that essay no longer weighed with their author; and indeed very few philosophers have been persuaded by them. It is worth asking, however, whether the notion of cause can bear the sort of burden which not only Russell, but many other philosophers, have subjected it to in their accounts of will and action.

7.   CAUSE AND EFFECT

An interest in causes and effects is of course connected with an interest in *explaining* phenomena. And of the many phenomena which human beings are in the habit of explaining or purporting to explain, that of human and animal behaviour is a very central one. Hence it may look unsurprising that philosophical accounts of such behaviour so often make use of the notion of cause. But the idea that empirical explanation must be in terms of causes and effects is a modern, as opposed to ancient, one, and in fact can be associated with those dualisms of thought which I have alleged to be so characteristic of modern philosophy. Aristotle had famously distinguished four causes (to adopt the traditional translation): efficient cause, final cause, formal cause and material cause. It has been aptly said that his theory really has to do with four "becauses", and hence with four senses of the question "Why?" to which "because"-answers can be given. It is in fact a theory about different species of explanation. The important distinction for our purposes is that between efficient cause and final cause: for when we consider voluntary or intentional action, there is a strong prima facie case for the Aristotelian claim that explanations of such action typically invoke final, rather than efficient, causes. But in modern times, the very idea of final causes has been thrown into doubt as something akin to superstition, with efficient causes and effects (and the explanations that embody these) being alleged to suffice for all respectable empirical explanation.

The Philosophical Context   25

An example may illustrate these remarks, as well as helping to convey the meanings of the technical terms. Jones is seen sharpening an axe in his garden, and is asked, "Why are you sharpening that axe?", to which he replies, "Because I'm going to cut down this apple tree". His answer mentions a final cause, that is, it mentions a goal or purpose or end, relative to which his present action of sharpening makes sense. It does not on the face of it mention an efficient cause, that is, some event, state or process prior to (or perhaps simultaneous with) the act of sharpening the axe, relative to which that sharpening makes sense—as the lighting of a fire under a kettle helps make sense of the kettle's subsequently coming to the boil. Now the final cause, *cutting down the apple tree*, may never come about, e.g. if Jones changes his mind, or is dissuaded, or dies suddenly. But it will still have been the final cause of Jones's axe-sharpening, even if it doesn't come about. So this "cause" exhibits just that Parmenidean peculiarity which has so puzzled philosophers over the centuries when discussing thought, intention and related topics: for it seems that in some cases we are attempting to explain an event by reference to a second event that is non-existent! Of course, if Parmenides was wrong, and false thought, etc., are not impossible, then final cause-explanation will very likely be safe on this count; but until an actual solution of Parmenides's problem is forthcoming, philosophers may feel happier with efficient cause-explanations, e.g. as (apparently) exemplified by "Jones is sharpening his axe *because he wants to* (or: *has decided to*) cut down the apple tree".

More than this last-mentioned motivation lies behind the modern turning away from final causes, a turning away we find already in Descartes, for whom mechanical forces appeared to suffice for all explanation of natural phenomena, at any rate in the material realm. But it would go beyond the remit of my discussion to examine the various impulses at work in that historical development. Whatever those impulses were, many of the difficulties faced by traditional accounts of the will and of action can surely be diagnosed as arising, at least in part, from the idea that there must be just one species of proper empirical explanation. The philosopher who perhaps more than any other was able to resist the pull of all such monisms, and to do justice to the conceptual pluralism actually to be found in our thought and talk, was Ludwig Wittgenstein, especially in his later work. And it is to Wittgenstein's ideas concerning thought and will that we now turn.

NOTES

1. Part I, Principle XXXII (Descartes 1967: 232).
2. Part I, Principle IX (Descartes 1967: 222).
3. See e.g., Davidson 1980.
4. This simile is not intended to rule out the possibility that the river, the banks, and the bridge are all illusory.

26   *The Philosophical Context*

5. Such beliefs have been regarded by some philosophers as not false, but rather lacking a truth-value; if these philosophers are right, Parmenides' assertion of impossibility will apply to such truth-valueless beliefs, as well as (if Parmenides is right) to false ones.

6. Part of the later Wittgenstein's philosophical approach was to ask such questions as, "*Why* should we make this our aim?", and "What sort of 'dissatisfaction' results from the lack of an account of the sort mentioned?"

7. See Frege 1967.

8. This states that "The F is G" can be analysed as "There is exactly one F, and it is G". Russell argued that ordinary proper names, like "Marilyn Monroe" or "Santa Claus", were disguised definite descriptions; e.g., the first could be taken to mean something like "The blonde American actress who famously appeared in a film standing above an air vent in a white skirt". Whether "The Sugar Plum Fairy" is a definite description or proper name thus does not matter for Russell, since it would receive the same logical treatment in either case.

9. Russell 1907, 5.

10. See Plato's *Sophist*, 262.

11. A and B are intersubstitutable *salva veritate* if substituting one for the other in the context of a sentence has no effect on the sentence's truth-value (true or false); while A and B are intersubstitutable *salva congruitate* if substituting one for the other in the context of a sentence has no effect on the meaningfulness (not the *meaning*) of the sentence. "Meaningful" here means roughly "well-formed".

12. Frege 1952, 42–55.

13. For the first tendency, see Locke's inclusion of *number* among the primary qualities of things, qualities being "powers to produce various sensations in us" (*Essay*, II.viii.10); for the second and third, see Ayer 1936.

14. Berkeley *Principles of Human Knowledge*, sec. 8.

15. Berkeley, *Principles of Human Knowledge*, sec. 12.

16. Cf. *Principles of Human Knowledge*, sec. 16: "And here it must be acknowledged that a man may consider a figure merely as triangular, without attending to the particular qualities of the angles and relations of the sides."

17. Plato *Theaetetus* 193B-C.

18. Plato *Theaetetus* 189E.

19. Russell 1921, "Lecture X".

20. Somebody might talk nonsense on some topic, or when e.g., doing philosophy, and so might sincerely reply to "What are you thinking about?" with a statement that is not true, because it is meaningless. "I'm thinking about what would be the case if time were cylindrical, rather than linear", say. But this is not a case of one's having an idea and there being room for doubt what it's an idea of; either we should say, with the early Wittgenstein, that no idea at all is expressed by a nonsensical form of words, or we should after all allow the person's say-so: he *is* thinking about cylindrical time, or whatever.

21. I say "at least typically" because of the phenomenon, discussed by Elizabeth Anscombe, of what she called "mental causation" (Anscombe 1963, 16). An example: I can know straight off, and not on the basis of experience, that the cause of my jumping was a loud bang in my vicinity. But it would seem absurd to liken the object of an idea to such a mental cause. If someone says, "This idea is *of* whatever caused it", and we then ask, "So what did cause it?", the person may reply, "A lump of cheese." But his reason for judging this is evidently that the idea *is an idea of a lump of cheese*. By contrast, jumping may be caused by many different things, and the fact that loud bangs can cause it is quite contingent; hence "I jumped because of that loud bang" is an informative statement. (And note that not *any* answer to "Why did you jump?" will be

The Philosophical Context   27

accepted as intelligible). Nothing like that could be said of ideas, if their objects were whatever caused them.

22. I have phrased the argument in terms of resemblance, not merely (as Frege does) in terms of correspondence, since the claim that perfect correspondence amounts to identity seems to require that correspondence = resemblance. If correspondence were isomorphic mapping of some sort, then two distinct entities could correspond perfectly; and this indeed seems to be the sort of account of correspondence Frege goes on to consider, and to attack by means of his reductio ad absurdum.

23. Frege 1967, 26.

24. In this informal exposition, I have ignored such distinctions as that between "P is true" and "It is true that P", and have left undetermined what "P" stands for (an idea, a proposition, a sentence . . .). None of this matters for the purposes of Frege's reductio.

25. Frege 1967, 31–2. Something similar is to be found in the early Wittgenstein: "Here we see that solipsism strictly carried out coincides with pure realism." (*TLP* 5.64)

26. Frege's contemporary, Edmund Husserl (1859–1938), also used linguistic categories as the basis of his explanation of thought and thinking, distinguishing "nominal meaning" (i.e. name-meaning) from "propositional meaning" (i.e. sentence-meaning), such "meanings" being constituents of subjective consciousness. See Husserl, *Logical Investigations* vi 1.

27. See Frege, *The Foundations of Arithmetic*, sec. 66.

28. Frege 1967, 35, 38.

29. Ibid, 37.

30. It won't help to say that I do not entertain Thought T, but merely (in making my decision) *refer* to it, since I would have had to *set up a correlation* between the referring term and Thought T. If in the course of these various decisions I at no point entertain Thought T, then how else to do I involve it in my life?

31. Very often the alleged mismatch between an unfulfilled intention and the resultant action would be down to the possibility of an action's having "wide descriptions", i.e. descriptions that involve facts about the world beyond the agent's body. The unsuccessful archer does something that fails to match his intention: the content of the latter is *shooting and hitting a target*, while what he does is *shoot and miss a target*.

32. Descartes, *Meditation I*, AT VII 57 (Descartes 1967, 175).

33. Descartes elsewhere uses "prosequi" and "fugere" as applying to things out there, rather than to ideas; e.g. "I am also taught by nature that various other bodies exist in the vicinity of my body, and that some of these are to be pursued and others avoided" (*Med. VI*, AT VII 81). But if the will consists in our power to pursue things in *this* sense of "pursue", then evidently we can pursue things that aren't there, and Descartes' own view of the will as infinite suggests that such failure is in his view impossible. Indeed, if external objects are what are pursued, then failure won't be restricted to the will, for it will be possible for me to believe that my intellect has placed something before me when it hasn't: in which case my consciousness of the activities of my own intellect will be fallible—a very unCartesian result. And since pursuing an external object typically involves moving my body, my consciousness of which is derived from the senses, it will even be dubitable for me whether I have done any pursuing at all! Hence it seems to me that, in connection with Descartes's account of the will, we must (if only for charity's sake) take the objects of "pursuit" to be, like the objects of "affirmation", ideas or perceptions.

34. Hume, *An Enquiry Concerning Human Understanding*, sec. VII, Part I; Hume 1975, 67.

28   *The Philosophical Context*

35. Hume 1975, 69.
36. Russell 1921, Lecture III.
37. Ibid.
38. See Watson 1913.
39. The waters are further muddied when Russell suggests that the existence of behaviour-cycles in animals "leads us to attribute desires to animals, since it makes their behaviour resemble what we do when (as we say) we are acting from desire".
40. As Anscombe stresses in her 1963 work.
41. See Russell 1918.

2 Thought, Will and World

1. THE THOUGHT AS LOGICAL PICTURE

In the last chapter I characterized the accounts of thought and will that have prevailed in modern times as being ones that typically conceive of thought and will as relational. Our discussion focused on the *objects* of thought and will, and it was conceded (p. 4) that for a philosopher who regards the Subject as in some sense a fiction there could of course be no relations of any kind between a Subject and anything else; but even for such a philosopher it seems that there will be *something*, e.g. something mental, whose relationship to something else goes to determine the meaning and the truth-value of such a statement as "I am thinking of cheese", or "Mary is trying to swat that fly". Hume in his *Treatise* presents a view according to which the Subject or self is best regarded as either a complete fiction or, alternatively, as a mere bundle of ideas and impressions.[1] But for Hume the question must remain what makes a given idea be an idea *of cheese*, or a given volition be a volition *to swat a fly*. If cheese and flies are independently existing things, our answers to such questions will surely at least *involve* some sort of relation between the idea or volition, on the one hand, and cheese or a fly, on the other. Idealists and phenomenalists have denied that cheese and flies are independently existing things, arguing them to be either collections of, or logical constructions out of, ideas (sense-data, etc.)—but it should be recognised that this manoeuvre cannot do away with questions of the form, "In virtue of what is idea X an idea *of* Y?", X and Y being distinct. This is guaranteed by the form of the philosophical theories themselves, since they ask us to consider, think about, such things as an idea of a fly, and when we do this we are evidently not ceasing to do philosophy and instead doing entomology: we must in fact have the idea of *an idea of a fly*. Idealists and empiricists have tended to look askance at the distinction between an idea and the idea of that idea, but it appears to be crucial; and when we turn to general ideas, there is simply no avoiding the issue of how these are related to what they are of.[2] Locke's abstract general idea of a fly must somehow relate to other, particular ideas (of particular flies); and even Berkeley's non-abstract general idea of a fly must "represent" all sufficiently similar ideas.[3]

30   *Thought, Will and World*

All this is just to say that the kind of account of thought labelled (B) in Chapter 1, even though it takes the immediate objects of thought to be ideas, nevertheless faces the further question what these ideas are related to. Recall that in delineating (A), (B) and (C)[4], I used "object of thought" so as to indicate how these accounts all in effect construe "thinks" as a transitive verb, logically speaking. "Object of thought" is also, perhaps usually, used to mean whatever a thought is of—alias the intentional object of the thought—something that "may or may not exist". If only in the case where the intentional object of a thought, or for that matter of a volition, *does* exist, we face the issue I have just mentioned, that of how an idea (etc.) is related to what it is of.

These remarks have a relevance for the account of thought to which I now turn, that of Wittgenstein in his *Tractatus Logico-Philosophicus*. The remarks in the *Tractatus* that concern the Subject deny that there is any thing, or object, referred to by "I", so that it is nonsense to talk of any relations holding between the Subject and anything else; but Wittgenstein does not regard the Subject as a *fiction* in the way that Hume did or may have done—unless indeed by "Subject" we mean *the (purported) referent of "I"*. Rather, he speaks of the Subject as "a limit of the world" (5.632). But despite the fact there is no *thing* that thinks, judges, wills, etc., Wittgenstein still—on the face of it—characterizes thought in terms of a relation: a relation between a thought conceived of as a "logical picture", on the one hand, and on the other, elements of reality corresponding to elements of the thought. This *seems* to be the sort of relation I referred to in the last paragraph, between something mental and what it is of (at least when it is of something real).

For Wittgenstein, however, a relation can only be meaningfully said to hold between objects, i.e. things which can be referred to by proper names; and, unlike Frege, he denies that expressions of the form "the thought that p" are construable as proper names. And this is because "thought" (or "proposition") expresses what he calls a *formal concept*. Now this term is liable to mislead, on account of the fact that in it the adjective "formal" is what the mediaevals would call an *alienans* adjective, like the adjective "forged". Just as a forged £10 note is not a £10 note, so a formal concept is not a concept. A concept, as Frege said, is what is expressed by a logical predicate, such as "x is a horse" ("x" here functioning as a gap for a proper name), and there is no logical predicate "x is a proposition"; "Karen is a proposition" (assuming "Karen" to be a proper name) is not false but meaningless. In fact, the term "concept" is itself a formal concept word[5], which is to say that meaningful propositions containing it can be paraphrased as propositions containing either a certain predicate or a predicate-variable, and would appear as such in a logically pure language or conceptual notation. Examples: "Danny falls under the concept *horse*" is more perspicuously rendered "Danny is a horse", and "There is a concept which both Danny and Misty fall under" is more perspicuously rendered "For some F, Fd and Fm", where

Thought, Will and World   31

the quantifier binds predicate-variables—the proposition being a mere existential generalization from (and no more "ontologically committed" than[6]) a proposition such as "Danny is a horse and Misty is a horse". Among other things, this account, if true, means that we must be careful not to construe as relation-words what are in fact expressions of a different kind, for instance "expresses", in "The predicate 'horse' expresses a concept".

Now the *Tractatus* is full of sentences containing formal concept words. And one might therefore presume that Wittgenstein regarded these sentences as in principle paraphrasable, especially by means of various categories of bound variable. But this would be to reckon without Wittgenstein's famous distinction between saying and showing, as enunciated in particular at 4.1212: "What *can* be shown, *cannot* be said." Formal concepts are not only expressed (signified, represented) by variables occurring in meaningful propositions, they are also *shown* in language: "A name shows that it signifies an object, a sign for a number that it signifies a number, etc." (*TLP* 4.126) (*Object* and *number* are both formal concepts.) If I understand "Danny is a horse", I grasp that "Danny" is a name, and not, e.g. a predicate—and I also grasp that the sentence shares its logical form with "Napoleon is a man", "Sarah is a doctor", etc.[7] It is really this grasping-of-a-form that Wittgenstein thinks cannot be put into words: what one grasps is something manifest or shown in language, not something sayable by means of language. Thus one cannot *refer* to what is shared by "Danny is a horse", "Napoleon is a man", etc., if only because reference must be to objects, and to posit an abstract object, *Subject-predicate form*, would be simply to add another (putative) object to the list of objects, not to say something that in the relevant sense encompasses the propositions "Danny is a horse", etc. Attempts to say what can only be shown result in nonsense, and the propositions of the *Tractatus* (or many of them?) themselves count as attempts of this sort, and hence as nonsensical. (*TLP* 6.54)

It is thus quite likely that its author regarded "A picture is a fact" (*TLP* 2.141) as a species of nonsense, employing as it does the formal concepts *picture* and *fact*; but even so, the nonsensical propositions referred to in 6.54 are also called "elucidatory", thus distinguishing them from "Ying tong iddle ay po", "Dog quickly the if", *et al.*, and "A picture is a fact" does in fact serve to convey what is special about Wittgenstein's account of thought, and why it cannot be called a relational account—and this regardless of whether we follow Wittgenstein in calling it nonsense.

In the last chapter, we encountered the problem of how to distinguish a sentence from a list; I mentioned this problem in particular in connection with the account of thought labelled (A). When discussing Frege, the proponent of the type of account labelled (C), there was a different, but related, problem: that of our having to swallow the idea that the sense and the reference of a sentence (a Thought and a Truth-value, respectively) might be species of objects. Wittgenstein avoids both of these problems, in the following way. Names refer to objects, and these latter are as a matter of fact

32   *Thought, Will and World*

arranged in certain ways. In saying something about a given set of objects, we produce a proposition (a picture) in which occur their names, and these names are also, logically speaking, arranged in a certain way: "The fact that the elements of a picture [the names] are related to one another in a determinate way represents that things are related to one another in the same way." (*TLP* 2.15) *That* "A" and "B" and "C" are related in such-and-such a way means *that* A and B and C are related in such-and-such a way.[8] The italicized occurrences of "that" indicate that we have two facts, not two things, nor yet a thing and a fact. But "We have two facts", employing as it does the formal concept word "fact", does not mean "We have two objects falling under the concept *fact*". The temptation to assimilate a sentence with a name, or a proposition or fact with an object, must be always resisted—as, for instance, when we encounter the expression "assimilate a fact with an object".

Hence a picture of A and B standing in a certain relation to one another contains only elements (names, bits of paint, whatever) corresponding to A and B—it does not contain an element corresponding to the relationship between A and B. If we say that the picture or proposition represents the relationship between A and B, we are not using "represents" as a genuine relation-word, and are using "the relationship between A and B" as a formal concept phrase—at any rate, if what we say is to be called meaningful.

This sort of account had already been hinted at by Russell, e.g. when he wrote:

> It is obvious . . . that when all the constituents of a complex have been enumerated, there remains something which may be called the form of the complex, which is the way the constituents are combined in the complex. It is such pure forms that occur in logic.[9]

The way the constituents are combined is not itself a constituent. But a little later we find Russell saying that to understand the term "relation" means *being acquainted* with the pure form xRy, and other such forms[10]. And given his notions as to the nature of acquaintance, this seems to reinstate "forms" as a species of things, available as objects of the logically transitive verb "be acquainted with". Some such doctrine as Wittgenstein's doctrine of formal concepts does appear to be needed if we are to manage to resist that temptation referred to a couple of paragraphs back.

But we have been talking only of sentences, propositions, pictures. What about someone, some person, thinking that p? Isn't this a psychological, and not a merely logical, question?

Quite early on in the *Tractatus*, Wittgenstein says that "We picture facts to ourselves". (*TLP* 2.1) But who or what "we" are, and how we do this picturing-to-ourselves, is something he postpones discussion of. It is at 5.541 that he brings up the question whether in "A believes that p is the case" and similar propositions we find a relation asserted between an object (e.g. a person), A, and something else—something like a proposition. From

Thought, Will and World   33

what we have already seen, we can predict that "believes that" will not be regarded by him as a relation-word, since *proposition* is a formal concept; but couldn't "A" still be a name of an object, with "believes that" functioning as a predicate at one end and a sentential connective at the other, to use Arthur Prior's phrase?[11] Wittgenstein thinks not:

> 5.542 It is clear, however, that 'A believes that p', 'A has the thought p', and 'A says p' are of the form '"p" says p': and this does not involve a correlation of a fact with an object, but rather the correlation of facts by means of the correlation of their objects.
> 5.5421 This shows that there is no such thing as the soul—the subject, etc.—as it is conceived in the superficial psychology of the present day.
> Indeed a composite soul would no longer be a soul.

In '"p" says [that] p' it might seem that the subject term is the name of an object—perhaps the name of a sentence (type or token) in some language. But it is not. We are evidently talking not of an object, but of a logical picture, i.e. of a fact. (And in "We talk of a logical picture", "talk of" does not function as a relational expression.) If believing and thinking are mental phenomena, then we are talking of a mental picture, in Wittgenstein's sense of "picture", and this mental picture is something that belongs to a different *logical* category from that of an idea—either the British empiricists' idea or Frege's idea, to mention the two species that were discussed in the last chapter. That there is no Subject is really a further point.

A mental picture, like a proposition of language, will be an arrangement of (mental) elements which are correlated with certain objects; and *that* the elements are related to one another in a determinate way represents *that* the objects are related to one another in a certain way, to use the phraseology of 2.15. But now we must face the question: *What sets up the correlations between mental elements and objects?* We encountered analogous questions in the last chapter, addressed in particular to Berkeley (*How does one idea get to represent other ideas?*) and Frege (*How does an idea come to "aim at" a particular Thought?*). The answer which seemed to force itself upon both Berkeley and Frege was, "Through a subjective decision", an answer which raised further, and as yet unanswered, questions. Would the same answer be appropriate in response to the question just addressed to Wittgenstein?

There are various considerations that might incline one to say "No". For one thing, public linguistic meaning is a matter of use and of convention, rather than of subjective decision. Having explained that a symbol is what is logically common to a variety of different signs (these being perceptible sounds or marks on paper, etc.), so that talk of symbols is talk of signs-insofar-as-they-signify-in-the-same-way, Wittgenstein writes: 'In order to recognize a symbol by [or: in] its sign we must observe how it is used with a sense' (*TLP* 3.326). At 4.002, he writes that "Language disguises thought"; but it is clear that in this context "thought" is for Wittgenstein,

34 *Thought, Will and World*

as it was for Frege, a logical, not a psychological, notion. ("A thought is a proposition[12] with a sense." *TLP* 4) What is the reason for this capacity of language to disguise the very senses, inferential relations, and so on, that are embodied in it? The answer comes at the end of 4.002: "The tacit conventions on which the understanding of everyday language depends are enormously complicated." An accurate overview of this complicated set of conventions is extremely hard to achieve. (We find this thought playing an important role in the later philosophy.)

Continuing down this avenue, it might be suggested that when Wittgenstein says that "A believes that p" is of the form "'p' says p", this latter proposition, rather than being a form of nonsense, for example, is itself intended to express a fact, namely that such-and-such perceptible signs (expressed symbolically as "p") are by convention used by these and those human beings to say that p. This reading would not as it stands distinguish "A believes that p" from "B believes that p". To allow for such a distinction, we would have to re-insert A into our analysis, perhaps positing that A be one of "these and those human beings", and be disposed to produce some of the signs in certain circumstances. But it would be truer to Wittgenstein's meaning to take the subject of "'p' says p" to be a mental (logical) picture *correlated with* the public proposition "p", rather than that public proposition itself; this mental picture would belong to, or in some sense help constitute, the Subject vulgarly referred to as "A".

Someone might wonder whether the imputation to the early Wittgenstein of an account of "meaning as use" squares with those remarks in the *Tractatus* where he talks of our "giving meaning" to a sign, e.g. ". . . the reason why 'Socrates is identical' says nothing is that we have not given *any adjectival* meaning to the word 'identical'." (*TLP* 5.4733) Doesn't such a phrase imply some initial stipulation, some initial act of meaning-giving, of a kind which (in some sense) determines what shall subsequently count as a correct use of a sign? If this were a correct interpretation, the question would arise whether this act of meaning-giving need be public: couldn't I make a subjective decision to mean something by a word, a decision that then bound my subsequent use of the word? And yet it doesn't seem as if the phrase "giving meaning" can signify any *act*, when we consider its occurrence in 6.53:

> The correct method in philosophy would really be the following: to say nothing except what can be said, i.e. propositions of natural science . . . and then, whenever someone else wanted to say something metaphysical, to demonstrate to him that he had failed to give a meaning to certain signs in his propositions.

To *demonstrate* to someone that he has failed to give a meaning to certain signs must mean to show how his current or recent use of those signs in propositions fails to constitute the expression of determinate sense; we are

Thought, Will and World   35

not being recommended to demonstrate to someone that a certain biographical event (an act of meaning-giving) never took place in his past!

It looks, then, as if in the *Tractatus* we can discern an account of meaning as use, or at any rate as connected with use in the sort of way that makes it possible to demonstrate to someone that some of his signs lack a meaning. Where does this leave believing and thinking, if these are construed as "private" mental phenomena? On the one hand, meaning and truth get explained in the *Tractatus* in terms of symbols, which, if they are signs-insofar-as-they-signify-in-the-same-way and if signs are "perceptible", might seem to be necessarily public—since one does not "perceive" one's inner mental goings-on.[13] On the other hand, what is essential to the identity of a symbol is not its perceptible features, but its sense, as embodied or reflected in its use, and there is nothing in the *Tractatus* that suggests a distrust of the notion of "private use"; the remarks about "convention" occur only in connection with everyday language, and just as a description of the workings of conventions would, for the early Wittgenstein, belong not to philosophy but to social science, so the phenomena determinative of "inner" or "private" meaning and truth, if there are such, would belong to psychology.[14] We should also note how *broad* Wittgenstein's conception of depiction and representation is, e.g. at 4.014, where he says: "A gramophone record, the musical idea, the written notes, and the sound-waves, all stand to one another in the same internal relation of depicting that holds between language and the world". The isomorphism between the grooves of a record and certain sound-waves is clearly not mediated by either convention or use. And when in the next paragraph, Wittgenstein explains what he has said in 4.014 by reference to "rules", we must again note how broadly he is using his terms—thus he speaks of "the rule for translating this language [musical notation] into the language of gramophone records", i.e. into certain patterns of grooves! Evidently what Wittgenstein regards as essential—shared logical form—is something that is neither public nor private. (It is in fact ineffable.)

Moreover, and perhaps most significantly, we have the evidence of those solipsist-leaning paragraphs from 5.6 onwards, including such first-personal statements as "*The limits of my language* mean the limits of my world" (5.6), "The world is *my* world" (5.62), and "I am my world" (5.63)—all of which seem to point to a first-personal, even if not private, realm of meaning and truth. (The "truth in solipsism" presumably undermines any private/public distinction.)

But what is of most interest for our purposes is not the dichotomy *public vs. private*, so much as the dichotomy *internal relation vs. external relation*. An external relation between X and Y is one that holds contingently, one whose holding is not guaranteed by the very identities of X and Y. And it is central to Wittgenstein's thought that the relations between symbol and what is symbolized, between proposition and fact, and between thought and reality, are all of them internal relations, relations whose holding is somehow guaranteed by the identities of the relata. Once again, we have to

36   *Thought, Will and World*

allow for the fact that such terms as "symbol", "proposition", "fact", and "reality" are formal concept words, so that strictly speaking there can be no relations of any kind between objects falling under the concepts *symbol, proposition,* etc.—since there are no such objects (because no such concepts). Our interpretation of what Wittgenstein is saying here must then either be couched within the terms of the saying/showing distinction, and so embrace the nonsensicality of his utterances, or involve some kind of "higher-order" notion of (internal and external) relations.

What seems clear is Wittgenstein's opposition to any account of the relationship between thought and the objects of thought which characterizes that relationship as consisting entirely of external, e.g. causal, relations. It is true that the proposition which does duty for "A believes that p", namely "'p' says that p", will, if it is to express something contingent, have to be about an external relation—namely, the relation between an arrangement of certain (e.g. mental) *signs* and an arrangement of objects. But those signs will also be symbols, and the relation between the arrangement of these symbols and the arrangement of objects will be an internal relation: that of depicting. And it is this internal relation which is of philosophical interest, being directly connected with issues of truth, meaning, and so on.

In fact, it is only ever *under certain descriptions* that a given group of objects will stand in an internal relation to another group; the same objects, under different descriptions, may stand in external relations. *Qua* sound or visible shape, a word bears an external relation to a chair, say, while *qua* symbol it can bear an internal relation, or relations, to it. Wittgenstein writes: "The existence of an internal relation between possible situations expresses itself in language by means of an internal relation between the propositions representing them." (*TLP* 4.125) Different propositions can represent (what may be called) the same situation, and in this sense of "situation" the question, "Is the relation between situation X and situation Y internal or external?" poses a false dichotomy. This thought will play a crucial role in Wittgenstein's later treatment of the topic of intentionality, as we shall see.

2.   "IT IS IN LANGUAGE THAT AN EXPECTATION AND ITS FULFILMENT MAKE CONTACT."

In the decade following the production of the *Tractatus*, Wittgenstein's ideas underwent a radical evolution. But certain ideas persisted, though in an evolved or evolving form. At the end of that decade we find him writing:

> If you exclude the element of intention from language, its whole function then collapses.
>
>   What is essential to intention is the picture: the picture of what is intended.

It may look as if, in introducing intention, we were introducing an uncheckable, a so-to-speak metaphysical element into our discussion. But the essential difference between the picture conception and the conception of Russell, Ogden and Richards, is that it regards recognition as seeing an internal relation, whereas in their view this is an external relation.

That is to say, for me, there are only two things involved in the fact that a thought is true, i.e. the thought and the fact; whereas for Russell, there are three, i.e. thought, fact and a third event which, if it occurs, is just recognition. This third event, a sort of satisfaction of hunger (the other two being hunger and eating a particular kind of food), could, for example, be a feeling of pleasure. (*PR*, III, 20–21; p. 63)

The last sentence will bring to mind Russell's theory of desire, which was examined in Chapter 1, according to which the object of desire is whatever it is that would bring a certain behaviour-cycle to an end. Such a cessation-of-activity counts as an instance of the "third event" referred to above by Wittgenstein, just as much as does any hypothetical feeling of pleasure; as he goes on to say, "It's a matter of complete indifference here how we describe this third event; that is irrelevant to the essence of the theory"—the essence of the theory being that it tries to explain matters by positing a causal (external) relation between desire (intention, thought . . .) and the object of desire (intention, thought . . .). Russell's behaviourist theory is more directly alluded to a moment later when Wittgenstein ascribes to Russell the thought that "If I wanted to eat an apple, and someone punched me in the stomach, taking away my appetite, then it was this punch that I originally wanted."[15] The absurdity Wittgenstein is pointing to has to do especially with that *dubitability of causes and effects* which I alleged in the last chapter to be a problem faced by various empiricist accounts of the mind, including Russell's (see above, e.g. 12–13, 20). According to Russell, my statement that I want an apple can be simply mistaken, since it is in effect a conditional prediction, akin to "I will stop having this headache if I take some aspirin". And this absurdity, naturally enough, generates the further absurdity of desire-ascriptions that are clearly wrong (e.g. "He wanted a punch in the stomach").

"Well", someone might say, "if the relation between a mental state and its object is internal, not external, how is it that, e.g. desiring that p looks like an entirely distinct and different phenomenon from the fact that p?" No doubt it was this distinctness of phenomena which so easily led Russell to posit an external relation: a "behaviour-cycle" such as climbing up a ladder, is obviously quite *different* from the event that "satisfies" it, such as reading a book taken off a high shelf, so it is hard to see how any species of a priori interdependency could hold between the two phenomena. But perhaps this just means that behaviourism is no good; what of the view that desire is some kind of inner experience, such as the having of certain

38 *Thought, Will and World*

images? Couldn't we take the representational nature of a mental image as consisting in some internal relation between image and object? We earlier on encountered some of the difficulties that attend an explication of representation in terms of *resemblance*—but couldn't the notion of *logical isomorphism* to be found in the *Tractatus* help us?

One of the ways in which Wittgenstein's philosophical method developed after the period of the *Tractatus* was in his aiming to make use of a broader diet of examples. And a very effective way with the question just asked is to turn to cases involving instructions or orders. If I understand an order, do I then have a mental image, or the like, bearing an internal relation of logical isomorphism to whatever action of mine is meant to satisfy the order? If such an image is to be of any use to me, I must in some sense translate it into action[16]. There are two problems worth mentioning in connection with this. The first is that one can be asked or ordered to form a mental picture or image; and the second is that the ways of taking or interpreting a picture, even a "logical picture", are infinite. I will consider each of these problems in turn.

In the *Blue Book*, dating from 1933–4, Wittgenstein considers a person being given the order, "Fetch me a red flower from that meadow".[17] If the person understands this order, we may think, then surely he must have some sort of mental picture which corresponds to the action that will satisfy the order, and corresponds to it in such a way as to *justify* that action and no other. The mental picture will in some "logical" sense guarantee the action—picture and action will be internally related. (Of course the picture won't empirically guarantee the action, since the person might be prevented from carrying out the order.) A natural version of this account involves saying that the mental picture includes an image of *red*: perhaps the person "went to look for a red flower carrying a red image in his mind, and comparing it with the flowers to see which of them had the colour of the image."

Wittgenstein remarks that as a matter of fact things aren't like that: ordinarily, "we go, look about us, walk up to a flower and pick it, without comparing it to anything". His technique at this point is simply to remind us of what we actually find when we consider some phenomenon, a technique characteristic of his later philosophy and expressed famously in the *Investigations* by the exclamation, "Don't think, but look!"[18] But of course, as Wittgenstein was well aware, the response in philosophy to not finding something which your theory says must be there is often to say something like, "Well, since it must be there, it's presumably happening subconsciously (if it's a mental process), or we weren't looking properly, or . . ." Given Wittgenstein's aim of trying to say or write what will persuade actual human beings, he therefore does not rest content with the remark about what actually happens, but asks us to

> consider the order "*imagine* a red patch". You are not tempted in this case to think that *before* obeying you must have imagined a red patch to serve you as a pattern for the red patch which you were ordered to imagine.

Thought, Will and World   39

The question "*How* do I obey the order to imagine a red patch?" seems to have something wrong with it. I just *do*, one feels inclined to say; and indeed the alternative on offer threatens a vicious regress. "I just do" means that when given the order my first, my immediate, response is simply to imagine a red patch. This also means that the question, "How did I know what sort of patch to imagine?" is empty, unless it is a question about my linguistic competence.[19] And if when obeying the order "Imagine a red patch" *I just do*, what's to stop me obeying other orders in the same manner, orders like "Fetch a red flower" or "Tell me your name"?—But now it may look as if we have depicted my obedience to an order as robotic, as completely unintelligent—a mere response to a stimulus. It is one of Wittgenstein's main themes in the later philosophy that this appearance is deceptive, and that an automatic response, with no prior or accompanying justificatory thought, very often counts as intelligent, as a sign of understanding. The reason for this has to do with what he would call the grammar of "understand": to understand something is to be able to *do* certain things. Which things? The things that count as "getting it right", "responding appropriately", etc. And terms like "right" and "appropriately" point to standards that are typically set by background practices, institutions, and the like—rather than by the occurrence of some mental state that somehow "justifies" what one does.

The otiose nature of such an occurrence is brought out by the above considerations relating to being ordered or asked to produce in oneself the mental state; it is also brought out by the consideration that the ways of taking or interpreting a picture are infinite (as I put it above). In the *Investigations* Wittgenstein writes:

> What really comes before our mind when we *understand* a word?—Isn't it something like a picture? Can't it *be* a picture?
>
> Well, suppose that a picture does come before your mind when you hear the word "cube", say the drawing of a cube. In what sense can a picture fit or fail to fit a use of the word "cube"?—Perhaps you say: "It's quite simple;—if that picture occurs to me and I point to a triangular prism for instance, and say it is a cube, then this use of the word doesn't fit the picture."—But doesn't it fit? I have purposely so chosen the example that it is quite easy to imagine a *method of projection* according to which the picture does fit after all.
>
> The picture of the cube did indeed *suggest* a certain use to us, but it was possible for me to use it differently. (*PI*, 139)

It is tempting to respond to such a case by saying that the person who understands "cube" will have, in addition to a mental picture of a cube, a mental picture of the method of projection itself: "say a picture of two cubes connected by lines of projection." (*PI*, 141) Anyone with a nose for vicious regresses will start to worry at this point, and of course Wittgenstein

40 *Thought, Will and World*

immediately asks, "Can't I now imagine different applications of this schema too?" Here, "different applications" means "different, self-consistent, ways of interpreting the signs [e.g. the connecting lines and the second picture-cube]". Different interpretations come out in different applications, manifest for example in pointing gestures—e.g. to triangular prisms, or colour-schemes, or lists of numbers. And the list of possible such interpretations is infinite.[20] If the solitary mental picture of a cube couldn't rule out multiple applications, how after all can two such mental pictures, with some additional mental lines, do so?

In our discussion of the *Tractatus* we encountered the question, in connection with mental pictures: *What sets up the correlations between mental elements and objects?* The early Wittgenstein seems to have regarded this question as one for psychology, not philosophy, to answer[21]; but his later self saw that there is at any rate a purely philosophical difficulty with any answer to the question that relies on a subjective decision or stipulation, in particular if the content of that decision or stipulation is itself regarded as a "logical picture". Not only does an infinite regress beckon if we thus rely on the idea of a logical picture, but the infinity of different ways of taking (interpreting) a picture shows how some quite different species of notion is needed if we are to make headway in our enquiry. One may perhaps see the early Wittgenstein invoking such a notion when he writes of the *use* of terms as showing their meaning (*TLP* 3.326), and in those passages where he seems to rely on facts about use as determinative (e.g. 6.53, discussed above, 34–5); hence it is not wholly clear whether the later remarks of Wittgenstein concerning the interpretation of pictures can be taken as an outright rejection of the Picture Theory of meaning and truth to be found in the *Tractatus*. It is undeniable, however, that he came to see a philosophical reliance on the notion of a picture as typically leading to confusion.

But let us return to the view which he certainly did not give up, that the relation between thought (desire, expectation . . .) and the objects of thought (desire, expectation . . .) is an internal one. Given a rejection of Russellian behaviourism with its causal relations, and a rejection of putative internal relations between mental pictures and reality, what is left? Specifically, what kind of internal relation can he mean?

It was the *distinctness of phenomena* that led Russell to posit his causal relations, and this distinctness is real enough. In the *Philosophical Grammar*, dating from around the same time as the *Blue Book*, Wittgenstein puts it thus:

> But it might now be asked: what's it like for him to come?—The door opens, someone walks in, and so on.—What's it like for me to expect him to come?—I walk up and down the room, look at the clock now and then, and so on. But the one set of events has not the smallest similarity to the other! So how can one use the same words ["he", "come"] in describing them? (*PG* VII 91; p. 139)

Thought, Will and World   41

This last question and the tackling of it will be what supply the clue. Back with the imaginary red patch we get:

> "The red which you imagine is surely not the same (the same thing) as the red which you see in front of you; so how can you say that it is what you imagined?"—But haven't we an analogous case with the propositions "Here is a red patch" and "Here there isn't a red patch"? The word "red" occurs in both; so this word cannot indicate the presence of something red. The word "red" does its job only in the propositional context. (*PG* VII 88; p. 135)

Both these passages (with the exception of the last sentence of the second passage) were kept by Wittgenstein for inclusion in the *Investigations*, where they appear in sections 444 and 443 respectively. But before we as it were reach the punchline, it is useful to expand a little on the message of the passage just quoted.

A tempting view of the meaning of a word is that it is some sort of *thing* with which the word is correlated, so that the sameness of meaning of different occurrences of the word is explained by the sameness of the thing signified by the word in each of those occurrences.[22] Thus, many philosophers have posited a universal, redness, as what is signified by "red"; Frege posited the concept *red*; and so on. But what is meant by saying, "The same thing is signified by 'red' in the sentences 'This is red' and 'That is not red'"? It could of course just mean, "In these two sentences, the word 'red' means the same"; but then we obviously haven't explained sameness of meaning by sameness of thing-signified. On the view of meaning we are considering, it is natural to explain the *truth* of an utterance of "This is red" by reference (i) to a given situation or state of affairs, and (ii) to the identity of the thing signified by "red"; and in fact to make out that the thing signified is somehow present in the situation, since evidently there must be some sort of *connection* between (i) and (ii). But what about a true utterance of "That is not red?" *Ex hypothesi*, redness is not present in the situation in question. There is nothing in common to the situations of a thing's being red and another thing's not being red. So what justifies our using the same word in both situations? Wittgenstein's answer is, in effect, "Nothing justifies it—just as nothing justifies our employing the sound 'red' instead of the sound 'quork'". There is a *fact*—the fact that we, the members of a linguistic community (as it is often put), do use "red" in a wide variety of interconnected situations, in various interconnected "propositional contexts".

Similar examples of interconnectedness include: that the use of "LW is expecting him to come" and the use of "He has come" are connected in certain ways. For there is a familiar and recurrent complex phenomenon of human life, involving behaviours, events, human needs, etc., which *makes sense* of our having developed a certain language-game, i.e. a rule-governed practice typically involving both actions and words (words such

42   *Thought, Will and World*

as "expect"). "NN is expecting him to come" couldn't have the function it does have if "He has come" were not a possible statement, or if those words were used in a way quite unrelated to the way in which "NN is expecting him to come" were used. And where a language-game manifests a certain unity (which is why we pick it out as one language-game), the various uses of a given word within that language-game will very often count as "meaning the same", in virtue of the interconnections between the uses.[23]

The question appearing in *PG* VII 91 and *PI* 444 was: "So how can one use the same words in describing them?" But we can now see that we should not at any rate be looking for some situational feature shared by a person's expecting some event and that event, a feature that will justify our using e.g. "Jack" and "come" in connection with both phenomena; our question can in fact be replaced by such questions as, "What is the nature of the language-game which involves these different but connected uses of 'Jack' and 'come'? How do we come to go in for it? etc."

In the light of these thoughts, we see that there *is* after all a species of possible similarity between a person's expecting some event and that event:

> But perhaps I say as I walk up and down: "I expect he'll come in"—
> Now there is a similarity somewhere. But of what kind?!
>   It is in language that an expectation and its fulfilment make contact.
> (*PI* 444, 445)

The "similarity" between the two phenomena resides in the applicability to both of them of such words as "he" and "come", the applications of these words being embedded within a single (i.e. unified) language-game. Wittgenstein has in effect reversed the order of explanation—though he would advise us to be careful with the term "explanation"—by saying that it is the fact that the same words play a role in both situations which explains our regarding the situations as "similar", or at any rate as connected, rather than the situations' being similar that explains the words' playing the same role. And the connection between the two phenomena, expecting an event and the event itself, turns out to be an internal connection or relation. For the *descriptions* of the two phenomena are conceptually linked, that is to say they employ shared expressions[24]; and this fact yields such further facts as that if I expect Jack to come, then if Jack comes my expectation is fulfilled—a tautology. This is what is meant by "It is in language that an expectation and its fulfilment make contact."

On the interpretation I have been offering, it is the unity of the language-game which accounts for the fact that two occurrences of e.g. "come" count as meaning the same. Moreover, the unity of the language-game itself has to do with the empirical fact that there exists a complex phenomenon involving human behaviour, "on the back of" which we may assume the language-game to have come into existence. Certainly, mastery of linguistic expressions such as "I expect . . ." requires an ability to use those expressions in sync

Thought, Will and World   43

with the appropriate behaviours and in the right sort of circumstances. My interpretation of what Wittgenstein is up to consequently differs from that of certain other commentators, if only in saying more than they. (But this "more" I suggest is needed if we are fully to dissolve our puzzles.) Peter Hacker has presented a detailed exegesis of Wittgenstein's remarks concerning intentionality, and in connection with "I expect that he is coming" and "He is coming" he writes: "That the words 'he is coming' mean the same in both sentences is evident from the fact that the same ostensive explanations would do service for the words in both sentences".[25]

It is true that the phrase used here is only "is evident from"; but it is clear from Hacker's account that he doesn't think there is any *other* fact, beyond such facts as that we would give similar explanations of what we meant, relevant to the synonymy of "he is coming" in the two contexts. Hacker's main purpose is to bring out the senselessness of a question like "How can the later occurrence be *the very thing* that you had expected?", and related questions. Given this purpose, it is understandable that he should regard the key to an understanding of intentionality as being "an intra-grammatical elucidation of the internal relations (e.g. between 'I expect that p' and 'p')".[26] But on the face of it the term "intra-grammatical" excludes context and behaviour. The end result is that we seem to be left with certain brute facts. Let me explain what I mean.

Imagine that there were a linguistic form "N peebles that p", such that a person's peeblement counts trivially as fulfilled (i.e. is *described* as "fulfilled") if and only if (a) not-p and (b) N's aunt once asked whether p. If George peebles that Lincoln wasn't assassinated, and his peeblement is fulfilled, then it would be futile to ask, "How can he peeble the very thing that his aunt asked about?" Still, we might want to be told what peebling *is*. If the answer came, "It is what is done by one who has learnt to say 'I peeble that . . .'", we would be unlikely to be satisfied. Would our dissatisfaction disappear once we were told that a person normally says "I peeble that . . ." without the need for self-observation, spontaneously, etc.? I do not think so. Of course, we might begin to wonder whether peebling that p involves, or is constituted by, thinking that p, or guessing that p, or finding it amusing that p (etc.); but let us assume that we are told that peebling is no more susceptible of such conceptual analysis than is thinking or imagining.

Two questions that we would surely want to ask, in order to clear up the mystery, would be: (i) In what circumstances do people say "I peeble . . ."?— and (ii) What are the consequences of their making such statements? This second question does not ask after any old effects, such as people's eardrums being affected in certain ways; it asks after those consequences that make sense of the activity, including those consequences which arise as part of the language-game—in the way in which it is a consequence of a footballer's being shown the red card that he is to leave the pitch, and also a consequence (very often) that he does leave the pitch. If we were told that one typically says "I peeble that p" when one has just spotted a rainbow,

44   *Thought, Will and World*

and that a normal consequence of one's saying "I peeble that p" is that others are in a position to predict that one will sleep badly that night, then we would look on the verb "to peeble" as an element in an arbitrary and pointless game. There would be no temptation to think of peebling as a psychological phenomenon, or indeed as a genuine feature of human life. (And of course actual human beings would find the game an extremely laborious and brain-teasing one to master.)

Expectation looks quite different from peebling in these respects. Now Hacker might agree, saying that, after all, his main exegetical point had to do only with the internal relation, e.g. between "I expect that p" and "p". But we must in that case return to the question, "In virtue of what do the two occurrences of 'p' mean the same?" Hacker replies that you would give the same sort of explanation if asked "What do you mean by 'p'?" in connection with both statements. Behind this fact is another: that a person must first know the meaning of "p" (at least in the sense that he has learnt what the constituent words mean, etc.), if he is to be able intelligently to utter "I expect that p".

But let us now imagine another strange language-game: in this one, a person will say "I greeble that . . .", this phrase being followed by a form of words derived from an English sentence by retaining the first word and adding the mirror image of the rest of the sentence, ignoring gaps between words. Emma might thus say or write, "I greeble that Lincoln detanissassatonsaw", something she can only do because she has already learnt the words "Lincoln", "was", "not" and "assassinated". If asked what or whom she meant by "Lincoln", she would give the same sort of explanation as the one she would give if asked the same question about the statement "Lincoln was assassinated". The fulfilment-conditions for greebling are like those for peebling, with the scrambled sentence appearing in the fulfilment-conditions in unscrambled form. NB we cannot assume that a person is meant to aim to say things whose fulfilment-conditions are or will be met. After all, the fulfilment-condition of "I fear lest p" is "p", in our sense of "fulfilment-condition": a person's fear that it will snow is fulfilled if and only if it snows, but their expression of fear is not faulted in the event of the fear's not being fulfilled. Similarly, the fulfilment-conditions for Emma's "greeble"-utterance simply record what Hacker would call intra-grammatical internal relations.

Does "Lincoln" mean the same in "I greeble that Lincoln detanissassatonsaw" as in "Lincoln was assassinated"? Surely not. One might try to explain this by alleging that "I greeble that Lincoln detanissassatonsaw" could not be a meaningful English sentence, since "Lincoln detanissassatonsaw" is gobbledygook, even on the hypothesis of there being a practice of greebling. However, this verdict would change if what we stipulated about the fulfilment-conditions for "I greeble that X" did after all involve some norm, e.g. that the speaker know that p, "p" being the unscrambled form of "X". The greebling-game would in that case just be a coded form of the language-game with "knows", and Emma's utterance could be faulted as

Thought, Will and World   45

involving a false assertion, one in which the name "Lincoln" did indeed appear—not to mention the word "assassinated". Thus whether a word can be said to appear with the same meaning in two contexts, contexts bearing the sort of syntactical relation to one another we have been considering, would appear to depend on more than just whether a person would give the same explanation of the word as it appeared in each context. To this Hacker might reply that in our original hypothesis about "greeble", Emma was not in fact in a position to explain what she meant by "Lincoln", since what she said was nonsense. But why call it nonsense? Haven't we described a game that *could* be played? If we say "nonsense", it is because the game in question is pointless, its moves have no humanly significant consequences, and so on. If we reimagine the game as having a genuine point or purpose, we no longer say "nonsense".

Without some account of why we go in for the language-game of "expecting", of how it fits into human life, connects with human behaviour, etc., the internal relation between "I expect that p" and "p" appears as a sort of brute fact: we just do talk this way; we just do say that the expectation was fulfilled if and only if p. But we need not leave it at that. And indeed we cannot justify the claim that "p" means the same in the two sorts of context without going further, and describing the human background to the language-game in the sort of way I have alleged. The unity of the language-game underlies the unity of meaning of "p"; and the unity of the language-game rests, as I have said, on its human and empirical background.

There is a question whether my account should be called an interpretation of Wittgenstein, or rather an elaboration of him. Perhaps it is the second, and Hacker's exegesis stays closer to what Wittgenstein wrote, retaining the gaps (if gaps they are) in the original. But nothing in my account, I think, is at odds with Wittgenstein's overall approach to these topics. And as I have argued, philosophical puzzlement about intentionality can only be fully dispelled if we do *not* limit ourselves to intra-grammatical elucidation.

At the beginning of the last chapter, I referred to the attempts that have been made over the centuries to build two bridges, the bridge connecting thought and reality, and the bridge connecting will and action. This was a metaphor, of course; perhaps a better one would have depicted philosophers trying to describe already existing bridges. But the *picture* of a bridge, of something connecting two distinct realms, is evidently embodied again and again in philosophical theorizing about thought and will—and by "picture" I mean here what Wittgenstein meant when for example he wrote, "A *picture* held us captive. And we could not get outside it, for it lay in our language and language seemed to repeat it to us inexorably." (*PI* 115) The picture of a metaphysical bridge lies in our language; we find it in such simple assertions as "John thinks something, and what he thinks is true" and "Sally intended to do something, and she did it". There are two realms, the mental (whatever that means) and what it corresponds to, and these realms are not disconnected: the whole *point* of thinking, intending, and

46 *Thought, Will and World*

the rest is that they should not be. And yet this connection, this bridge, is somehow paradoxical. For a thought and what it is of, or an intention and what would fulfil it, appear to be *different and yet the same*. How can I answer "*What* do you think?" except by saying something like "It will rain", or "That it will rain"? But this sentence and that phrase surely describe reality, not my mental life?[27] Are the realms of the mental and of reality after all not two, but one? But then what is the difference between being right and being wrong, or between carrying out an intention and failing to?

What Wittgenstein does is show us how there *is* a sense in which a thought and what it is of, or an intention and what would fulfil it, are different and yet the same. The seeming paradox[28] dissolves along with the picture of the bridge somehow connecting two realms. The picture lay in our language in two senses—for as well as our being misled by the forms of our own assertions ("John thought something" being akin to "John broke something", etc.), there is the sort of fact which Wittgenstein expressed by saying, "It is in language that an expectation and its fulfilment make contact." He could have added, "It is in language that a thought and what renders it true make contact". For if I think it is raining, and it *is* raining, then my thought is true; and this can be generalized and represented by a schema in which occurs a repeated variable that can be replaced by any sentence which can meaningfully come after "think(s) that": If N thinks that p, and p, then N's thought is true. Our grasp of the notion of truth is connected with our grasp of this schema, which in turn rests upon our ability to discern (produce, manipulate . . .) indicative sentences, the possible substituends for "p". Specifically, it rests on our ability to use the same sentence in two different but interconnected ways: on its own, and after "N thinks that . . ." (also "N says that . . .", etc.).

"But this is all too linguistic!" the metaphysically-minded philosopher will splutter. "After all, animals can believe things, desire things, and so on, and they don't speak a language." Such an objection would show a misunderstanding. For of course Wittgenstein has not analysed "think" and "desire" in terms, e.g. of a creature's disposition to say "I think/desire . . .", nor done anything like that. Indeed, he has not proposed any *analyses* of concepts, say into necessary and sufficient conditions. The idea that only such analyses can supply full and complete philosophical accounts shows a view of concepts as both precise and determinate (predetermined in their extension) which Wittgenstein undermined several times over, so to speak. But in any case, the bearing that language has in Wittgenstein's account upon the nature of thought, of desire, and of intentional states generally, is clearly more to do with the linguistic capacities of those who ascribe such states to others than with the linguistic capacities of those who enjoy such states. (NB This way of talking, in terms of the ascription or enjoyment of intentional states, will come under some scrutiny in Chapter 4, as a source of possible confusion.)

Thought, Will and World 47

Not that there are *no* implications arising from Wittgenstein's account for what may be said about non-human animals.

> One can imagine an animal angry, frightened, unhappy, happy, startled. But hopeful? And why not?
>
> A dog believes his master is at the door. But can he also believe his master will come the day after tomorrow?—And *what* can he not do here?—How do I do it?—How am I supposed to answer this?
>
> Can only those hope who can talk? Only those who have mastered the use of a language. That is to say, the phenomena of hope are modes of this complicated form of life. (*PI*, ii, p. 174)

The use of concepts like *angry* and *frightened* is bound up with what Wittgenstein calls their natural expressions: thus certain behaviour, such as trembling, cowering, whining, fleeing, may constitute fearful behaviour, given appropriate settings, and the teaching, learning and use of "fear", "frightened", and so on, rely on the shared human capacity to perceive such behaviour (in its setting) as salient, to be struck by it. This natural capacity is essentially prelinguistic, though its manifestations will no doubt be influenced by the learning of language; its prelinguistic manifestations are such multifarious responses *to* behaviour as are absent or defective, e.g. in severely autistic persons, such as fear in the presence of another's anger, or affection in return for another's affection. Our natural reactions to various behaviours are as a matter of fact "triggered" when a non-human animal manifests similar behaviours, so that we find it natural to apply such terms as "angry" and "frightened"—we as it were find ourselves wanting to apply such terms. The phrase "similar behaviours" in the last sentence includes the sorts of similarities a biologist or zoologist might record; the *explanation* for the fact that we are readier to apply psychological vocabulary to the higher mammals than to birds or snakes is in the end an empirical explanation. The importance of the *explanandum* for our enquiry is this: our agreement in our responses to animal behaviour underpins that agreement in the use of words which makes for meaning and objectivity. (cf. *PI*, 241–2)

The above is a sketch of what I take Wittgenstein to be saying concerning psychological concepts and "natural expressions". For some psychological concepts the notion of a natural expression is either inapplicable, or at least cannot serve as a conceptual backbone in the way it does for *angry, frightened*, etc. Examples of such concepts are *hope, believe, intend*. Although we can speak of behavioural manifestations in connection with these concepts, they would not be the concepts they are without the possibility of linguistic expression. A human being, unlike a dog, can believe or expect that something will happen the day after tomorrow, and this is because a human being can say or otherwise produce various sentences,

48   *Thought, Will and World*

notably "I expect X to happen the day after tomorrow" (or an equivalent sentence), in the context of the relevant complex language-game. The speaker will manifest her understanding of what she had said e.g. by admitting she had been wrong when later on it turns out to be appropriate to say, "Two days ago I said X would happen today, but it hasn't happened", which involves her being able to do such things as count days; if she were simply to look puzzled, scratch her head, and the like, we should need a reason to say, "She's puzzled because her expectation that X would happen has been foiled".

What if I regularly rang a bell within Fido's hearing, and two days later fed him on a juicy steak, with the result that over time he developed the Pavlovian trait of salivating, etc., two days after a bell-ringing? The "etc." could include sniffing expectantly around the place where I always present him with his steak, and/or similar voluntary actions. Would we have any reason to call any of this behaviour, voluntary or involuntary, an expression of puzzlement that his earlier expectation that he'd be fed in two days' time had not been fulfilled? We would surely do better simply to say that we had inculcated in Fido the disposition to start expecting a steak two days after a bell is rung. The expectation comes on at around that time, we should say. Right after a bell-ringing, it would be crazy to claim, "And now Fido expects to get a steak the day after tomorrow".

One could put it this way: in the case of a non-human animal, considered independently of human life and thought, the phenomena that we (in fact) pick out as *expecting (desiring, etc.) that p* and the phenomena we pick out as *subsequently perceiving that p* are phenomena that are externally related. "The one set of events has not the smallest similarity to the other"—and one might well go about hunting for causal connections between the two in the manner of Russell. But the behaviour of animals can strike us, affect us, in the same sort of way as behaviour in human beings, the latter being embedded in a social and linguistic context in a way that justifies our saying that between, e.g. an expectation and its fulfilment, there exists an internal relation. So if we find it natural to say of a dog that it expects to go for a walk, we thereby bring certain internal relations into being; but it doesn't, as we saw, follow from our being able to do this in some cases that we can meaningfully do it in any case.[29]

"Fido expects to get a steak the day after tomorrow" is rather like "The cooking-pot can hear what we're saying".

> "But in a fairy tale the pot too can see and hear!" (Certainly; but it *can* also talk.)
>
> "But the fairy tale only invents what is not the case: it does not talk *nonsense*."—It is not as simple as that. Is it false or nonsensical to say that a pot talks? Have we a clear picture of the circumstances in which we should say of a pot that it talked? (Even a nonsense-poem is not nonsense in the same way as the babbling of a child.) (*PI* 282)

Many a philosopher would insist that "Fido expects to get a steak the day after tomorrow", or "The cooking-pot can hear what we're saying", although they may well be false, nevertheless must make sense. This insistence surely stems from a view of words as carrying their meaning around with them, as a snail carries its shell, so that you have only to put words together in a grammatical order and you will have a meaningful statement. But it is not as if we can just say that a sentence is either meaningful or it isn't—"it is not as simple as that". For there are various notions of meaningfulness. "Consisting of real words put together according to the rules of grammar" may be one such notion; this would be a notion we could employ, for example, in connection with translating from English into French, so that there really might be a piece of French nonsense that was a good translation of "A half-empty square root of ducklings recurred with avuncular butter". (Presumably the result would sound a bit like Rimbaud.) But there is a more stringent notion of meaningfulness that has to do with (i) whether one could ever use a given (indicative) sentence with the intention of saying something true, and (ii) whether there would be ways of deciding what it *was* that one had said to be true. The importance and usefulness of this notion of meaningfulness might be apparent from a dialogue like the following: "Did the defendant lie in court?"—"Well, he wasn't making a great deal of sense, so that question can't really be answered." And it is this notion of meaningfulness, or one like it, which is relevant if we are faced with a philosopher who says that Fido's incapacity to expect something to happen the day after tomorrow must be down to the size of Fido's cortex, if anything. The impulse to look for a scientific or a metaphysical explanation for an impossibility often arises when the source of that impossibility—e.g. in the relationships between our language, our form of life, and the form of life of a dog—is hard to discern. And often it *will* be hard to discern. Staring hard at the sentence itself ("Fido expects to get a steak the day after tomorrow") is unlikely to get you very far, and nor is concentrating on the images and experiences that you have when you say or read the sentence. You may indeed have a vague feeling that there is something about the sentence that is odd, or funny—a feeling that can after all provoke an enquiry into what exactly is wrong with the sentence; but that enquiry will not be furthered by more summoning up of such feelings, even if it is decided to honour some of them with the title of "intuitions".

3. WILL AND WORLD

In discussing those accounts of the relation between thought and fact, desire and fulfilment, etc., which take the relation to be causal in nature (e.g. Russell's account), I characterized a, or the, main problem with such accounts as stemming from the dubitability of causes and effects. In the

50   *Thought, Will and World*

light of this species of dubitability it is interesting to contrast what the early Wittgenstein has to say with what the later Wittgenstein has to say, on the topic of the will and voluntary agency.

When he wrote the *Tractatus*, Wittgenstein regarded internal relations as logical in nature (in perhaps rather a wide sense of "logical"). And it is hard to see how the relation between intention and action could be a *logical* one, especially given the obvious empirical fact that our intentions can be thwarted in all sorts of ways. A logical relation ought to be a necessitating relation, it might be said. But if I can't necessitate any happenings in the world, it seems as if all I can do is *hope* that they occur, much as I can hope that Arsenal will win the cup. For I can never say, "I *know* that such-and-such will occur". This is at any rate so if knowledge requires genuine grounds for a belief, rather than just a strong psychological disposition to hold the belief; and it does seem that the early Wittgenstein, like Hume, was wont to regard our beliefs about the future as groundless in this sense. Proper grounds for such beliefs would have to invoke some sort of necessity or indubitability—which is impossible.[30]

These thoughts led Wittgenstein to write:

> 6.373 The world is independent of my will.
> 6.374 Even if all that we wish for were to happen, still this would only be a favour granted by fate, so to speak: for there is no *logical* connection between the will and the world, which would guarantee it, and the supposed physical connection is surely not something that we could will.

But how can the world be independent of my will? Surely I can raise my own arm?—Wittgenstein would reply that all you strictly *do* is: will that your arm go up. Whether it then goes up is up to fate, which is just to say that it will or it won't. You do not "affect the probabilities", for probabilities are not in the world: statements of probability do not describe reality.

> 5.153 In itself, a proposition is neither probable nor improbable. Either an event occurs or it does not: there is no middle way.
> . . .
> 5.155 The minimal unit for a probability proposition is this: The circumstances—of which I have no further knowledge—give such and such a degree of probability to the occurrence of a particular event.

You do not affect probabilities; rather, you assign them. You assign them on the basis of incomplete knowledge. In the actual complete history of the world, in which no probabilities figure, your willing something might be followed by a certain event; but how could that event be ascribed to *you*? It would be something quite separate and distinct, whatever it was. If we wanted to evaluate you, by evaluating your will, we would have to consider what was internal to your will. Of course we could use the word "will" to describe some psychological phenomenon, standing in purely external relations to other phenomena; but that would clearly be something incapable of being *evaluated* (unless "evaluation" is in turn used merely to describe some psychological reaction, i.e. event). Insofar as the will is relevant to ethical evaluation it must have nothing to do with the empirical world, the world of externally related phenomena—the world of facts. And so "It is impossible to speak about the will in so far as it is the subject of ethical attributes . . . If the good or bad exercise of the will does alter the world, it can only alter the limits of the world, not the facts—not what can be expressed by means of language." (*TLP* 6.423, 6.43)

Wittgenstein's position can be criticised even from the standpoint of the *Tractatus* itself. A moment ago I characterized his view of internal relations as logical, and hence (according to him) as involving the sort of necessity that simply *could* not obtain between an exercise of the will and "the facts". But we might wonder why what he had said earlier concerning "A believes that p" could not be suitably tailored to apply to "A wills that p", or "A intends that p". Recall that at 5.542 "A believes that p" was rendered "'p' says that p", which is a proposition that involves "the correlation of facts by means of the correlation of their objects". The facts that are thus correlated stand in an external relation, specifically the relation between an arrangement of signs and an arrangement of objects; but insofar as these signs are also symbols (signs with meaning), the relation between the two arrangements is internal. There are two relations involved, internal and external.[31] For the Wittgenstein of the *Tractatus*, believing something appears to mean having a mental picture of a state of affairs, the picture standing in an internal relation to the state of affairs; why shouldn't intending something involve this also? Where an intention was carried out, there would be an internal relation between the mental picture and a deed, i.e. a fact: for not only are elements of the picture correlated with objects, but *that* the elements are arranged in such-and-such a way means *that* the objects are arranged in such-and-such a way—which they would be in the case of the intention's being carried out. We would of course be left with the question, "What distinguishes a thought from an intention, if both are mental pictures of reality?" Any answer that mentioned different psychological attitudes to a picture, such as *affirming* and *pursuing*[32], would no doubt have struck Wittgenstein as bringing in empirical psychological phenomena in a way that was illicit; for the distinction between thought and intention is shown to be logical (not psychological) in nature by the logical, non-contingent nature of such correlative distinctions as true/false vs fulfilled/unfulfilled.

There are probably a number of reasons why he did not develop (or hint at) a view of intention and will analogous to his view of thought, of which this problem of distinguishing thought from intention may have been one; but the point of the foregoing paragraph is independent of such

52 *Thought, Will and World*

questions, being to do with Wittgenstein's apparently unjustified inference from "The will could only be related to the world [sc. my deeds] by an internal relation" to "The world is independent of my will, since no such internal relation is possible".

It could be objected that Wittgenstein does not explicitly affirm this last proposition, saying rather that "there is no *logical* connection between the will and the world, which would guarantee it". Perhaps he did allow for the possibility of non-necessitating internal relations, but was hamstrung by the thought that *knowledge* would require the sort of certainty only vouchsafed by strictly logical necessity, which evidently does fail to connect will and deed. Well, if he did think this, he would apparently have to say the same about thought and belief: that I have such-and-such a thought does not logically guarantee that it corresponds to a fact—if it does so, that will "only be a favour granted by fate". So I can never *know* that my beliefs are true, and the world is independent of my thought. And this is neither a very impressive philosophical claim nor one to be found in any form in the *Tractatus*.

There could hardly be better evidence of how far Wittgenstein had moved away from his early views by the time of the *Investigations* than the following statement: "When people talk about the possibility of fore-knowledge of the future they always forget the fact of the prediction of one's own voluntary movements." (*PI* 629) For the later Wittgenstein, foreknowledge of the future does not require a connection of a logically guaranteeing kind between prediction and fact, and this goes for pre-dicting one's own voluntary movements as much as for predicting other events. In both cases, knowledge is compatible with contingency (dubita-bility) of outcome. What then distinguishes these two forms of prediction? The relation between a prediction of either sort and what fulfils it is an internal relation. We have discussed Wittgenstein's account of this kind of internal relation above, e.g. in connection with expectation, whose expres-sion of course paradigmatically takes the form of a prediction, i.e. a (non-necessary) future-tensed assertion. But we can see what distinguishes the two sorts of prediction when we consider what *grounds* might be given for them:

> "I am going to take two powders now, and in half-an-hour I shall be sick."—It explains nothing to say that in the first case I am the agent, in the second merely the observer. Or that in the first case I see the causal connexion from the inside, in the second from outside. And much else to the same effect . . .
>
> It was not on the ground of observations of my behaviour that I said I was going to take two powders. The antecedents of this proposition were different. I mean the thoughts, actions and so on which led up to it. And it can only mislead you to say: "The only essential presupposi-tion of your utterance was just your decision." (*PI* 631)

Thought, Will and World 53

My grounds for saying "In half-an-hour I shall be sick" are such things as: I have in the past been sick after taking the powders; I have observed other people being sick after doing so; I have read about the biochemical effects of the powders; and so on. These grounds concern things experienced or observed, and they supply, or purport to supply, justification for a belief. When given in answer to the question "Why do you think so?", they will, if accepted by the enquirer, give *him* reason for his belief that I will be sick: and his reason will be identical to mine, e.g. "In the past, ingestion of those two powders has always made RT sick".

What sort of grounds, if any, do I have for saying "I am going to take two powders now"? Wittgenstein speaks only of grounds that I do *not* have, in the above passage. And his remarks concerning expressions of intention are in fact generally negative: such statements are not equivalent to statements of wishing or trying, they are not reports of inner processes, they are not made on the basis of observation, etc. But we can in fact give an answer of sorts to the question at the start of this paragraph, insofar as a statement of intention may be *justified*, and in that sense "given grounds". For a statement of intention, like a statement of belief, is a move in a language-game—it is itself a sort of act. A move in a language-game may be said to have a purpose, or point, internal to that language-game (or a number of such purposes/points). In that sense, the assertion that p is "meant to" be true (typically); and so justifying the making of an assertion, by giving reasons, has the character that it does have. What is the point of expressing an intention? I mean, what sort of point internal to the language-game of expressing intentions? (For of course one can express an intention with any number of ulterior motives.) Part of its point, as we shall see in a moment, is to allow others to predict what one will do. But this would not on its own distinguish it from first-personal predictions like "In half-an-hour I shall be sick", or "At some point in the coming year, I shall use the word 'only'"—the latter being particularly relevant, since the predicted action is a voluntary one, as it is in an expression of intention. What further point or purpose characterizes expressions of intention?

The language-game of expressing intentions is one in which a person declares a plan, as it were—a plan being something with a goal, aim, or rationale. Thus the statement "I am going to take two powders now" may indeed be backed up or given grounds, as: I've just eaten a poisonous mushroom and so need to vomit. The justification here is not a justification of a belief, so much as an explanation of why it would be a good idea for me to make myself sick. It is justification by reference to an aim or goal. (It can in turn be asked of the goal "Why aim for that?", although this series of "Why?" questions cannot go on forever; see Anscombe 1963, sec. 37, on "desirability characterizations".) Reference to a goal serves both to justify what I am going to do and to justify my present expression of intention. The latter form of justification relates to the role of the expression of intention within a language-game, a language-game that has a certain point (or points).

54 Thought, Will and World

The foregoing remarks are not meant as straight exposition of Wittgenstein. The connection between expressions of intention and reason-giving is something the importance of which he does not particularly stress. It took other philosophers, notably Elizabeth Anscombe, to bring out the significance of that connection. Anscombe in fact takes issue with the extent to which Wittgenstein appears to portray expressions of intention as akin to expressions of pain, fear, and the like—and to that extent as independent of language mastery—when he writes: "What is the natural expression of an intention?—Look at a cat when it stalks a bird; or a beast when it wants to escape." (*PI* 647) Anscombe remarks that "one might as well call a cat's stalling the *expression* of its being about to stop".[33] In her own account, Anscombe draws our attention to the kinship between an expression of intention and the giving of an order, both of which bear an internal relation to subsequent actions, that sort of internal relation of which Wittgenstein had given such an illuminating account; but it is clear that giving an order is not the *natural* expression of anything (such as a peremptory desire), being "purely conventional"—the epithet which Anscombe likewise applies to expressions of intention. Whether Wittgenstein's use in *PI* 647 of "natural expression" helps to explain his relative silence on the subject of reason-giving is an interesting question. But I do not think that his overall account of intention resists the addition of those considerations to do with reason-giving which I introduced in the last paragraph. Indeed Wittgenstein alludes, as we have seen, to "the antecedents of this proposition [sc. 'I am going to take two powders']", by which he means "the thoughts, actions and so on which led up to it"; and important among such antecedents will presumably be ones that express or embody *reasons* for taking the powders.[34]

Let us return to the two predictions conjoined in "I am going to take two powders now, and in half-an-hour I shall be sick." We have looked at the different sorts of grounds that I might give for each prediction. Consider now the position of an observer, or rather listener. If Smith hears me saying "I am going to take two powders now", there are two questions to ask concerning Smith: (i) on what grounds does he believe I will take the two powders (if he does believe this)?—(ii) what does he think my reasons are for taking the two powders?

The second will be fairly easily answered if I have actually *said*, "I have eaten a poisonous mushroom, etc." But in lieu of my having said this, Smith may still be able to posit a reason for action, based on his particular knowledge of what "led up to" my statement of intention, but also on his general knowledge of what is normal or natural for human beings. The facts thus known by him will enable him, ideally, to see why it would be a good idea for me to take the powders. The answer to (i) will be similarly straightforward given that I actually *say* "I am going to take two powders"; in my mouth, this statement does not express a belief susceptible of justification[35], but my saying it can of course supply justification of *Smith's* belief that I will take the powders. It is an empirical fact that human beings are able to learn and use a language-game in which "I will do X" is meant to be followed up by one's doing X—since for that "meant to be" to have application, human beings must as a matter of fact be able to follow up that statement with that deed without prompting. (Thus they must have certain powers of memory, etc.) Hence it is an empirical fact that Smith can use my having said "I am going to take two powders" as a reason for his belief that I am going to take two powders. This does not mean that my statement (or some mental state accompanying it) stands to my subsequent deed as cause to effect; for what we have is a learnt procedure or chain of actions, like that of making tea. If Smith is acquainted with the procedure of making tea, Smith can predict from my opening a box of teabags and filling a kettle with water that I will later pour the hot water onto some teabags; but my opening a box of teabags is not properly thought of on that account as a *cause* of my pouring the hot water. That's to say, to call it a cause is liable to mislead if our reason for so calling it relates to Smith's ability to make the prediction.

> I do not want to say that in the case of the expression of intention "I am going to take two powders" the prediction is a cause—and its fulfilment the effect. (Perhaps a physiological investigation could determine this.) So much, however, is true: we can often predict a man's actions from his expression of a decision. An important language-game. (*PI* 632)

That we can often predict a man's actions from his expression of a decision is part of the *point* of the language-game of expressing decisions or intentions, part of its usefulness for us, in a fairly obvious sense of that phrase.

But now an objection may come: "Certainly other people can predict what I'll do on the basis of my expression of an intention, but can my expression of intention itself be regarded as a prediction, i.e. as a statement about the future?" The objector may have either of two alternative claims in mind: (i) an expression of intention is really about a present ("occurrent") state of the speaker; (ii) an expression of intention is not the sort of statement of which truth or falsity may properly be predicated, being instead a performative utterance, or akin to a performative utterance.

Roughly speaking, a performative verb V is one such that if NN says (in the right sort of circumstances) "I hereby V . . .", then NN in making that utterance makes it true that she did V.[36] Examples of such verbs are "name", "give", "promise", "marry". And it is true that a successful statement using a performative, such as "I hereby name this ship *The Bounty*", can hardly be called true; "She's quite right, she did name it *The Bounty*!" would be a sort of joke. Could expressions of intention be thought of as

56   *Thought, Will and World*

(akin to) performative utterances? This is not a question that Wittgenstein would have addressed, since the notion of a performative utterance was dreamt up after he died. But we can surely adduce the following important difference: an expression of intention can be deceitful, its aim being to lead another to falsely believe that the agent will do X, where doing X was precisely what was mentioned in the expression of intention; whereas the closest we get to deceit in the case of a performative utterance is where the speaker knows that the right background conditions do not obtain—e.g. where he is not an ordained minister, but pretends to be one and says "I pronounce you husband and wife". What the poor couple were led falsely to believe, what the deceit consisted in, was not so much that the impostor had pronounced them husband and wife as that he was in a position to do so. Indeed, given the non-truth-aptness of the performative utterance, we cannot say that *it* was false and hence a lie. Whereas even if it is only later on that an expression of intention can be deemed false and hence possibly deceitful, falsity and deceit are applicable notions; and this connects with what Wittgenstein says at *PI* 632, to the effect that part of the point of the language-game of expressing intentions has to do with enabling others to predict our actions—the very actions that we mention in expressing our intentions.

This last point can be brought to bear also in arguing against (i) the view that a statement of intention is really about a present (esp. mental) state of the speaker, being most perspicuously expressed in the form "I (now) intend/desire/want . . .". But (i), unlike (ii), is a view that Wittgenstein did address, and his critique of it is sufficiently important for his overall enterprise for us to postpone discussion of it until the next chapter.

NOTES

1. Hume, *A Treatise of Human Nature*, Book I, Part 4, sec. 6.
2. Even if this is a pseudo-issue, it cannot simply be avoided: we will at any rate need to *show* that it is a pseudo-issue.
3. See Ch. 1, 9.
4. See Ch. 1, 4–5.
5. In Fregean mode, Wittgenstein refers to the word "function", rather than "concept": "The same applies to the words 'complex', 'fact', 'function', 'number', etc. They all signify formal concepts, and are represented in conceptual notation by variables, not by functions or classes (as Frege and Russell believed)." (*TLP* 4.1272.) We can fill out Wittgenstein's "etc." with such further instances as "proposition" and "picture": the former is represented in conceptual notation by sentential variables, as is the latter (in Wittgenstein's sense), since a picture is a (kind of) fact. Thus different formal concepts can be represented by the same category of variable. Consider: "Every proposition materially implies a proposition" and "Every fact materially implies a proposition"; translated into conceptual notation these become "For all p, for some q, if p then q", and "For all p: if p, then for some q, if p then q".

Thought, Will and World   57

6. i.e. the existential generalization is about the same sorts of entities as the unquantified proposition—e.g. Danny and Misty—and not additionally about concepts, conceived of as possible referents (à la Frege). cf. Chapter 5, 129.

7. Here and elsewhere I assume for the sake of exposition that such ordinary names as "Danny" are logically proper names; but it is clear that the Wittgenstein of the *Tractatus* would not regard them as such, any more than did Russell.

8. The two occurrences here of "in such-and-such a way" need not, in fact, indicate the *same* way, despite what Wittgenstein writes in 2.15, since it must be a matter of convention *what* way of arranging the names will say that the corresponding objects are arranged thus and so. A convention could exist of writing "A" above "B" in order to say that B was above A. We may adduce such a consideration also when applying what Wittgenstein says to propositions about a single object (of the form Fa). Despite Wittgenstein's only mentioning arrangements or concatenations of objects, such propositions cannot all plausibly be regarded as stating e.g. that something stands in a certain relation to itself. Nevertheless it seems that we could have a convention whereby, for example, *that* "A" is written in green ink says *that* A is circular, and that this would be in line with Wittgenstein's overall account.

9. Russell 1984, 97–8.

10. Ibid., 99.

11. Prior 1971, 135.

12. Or "sentence": the German is *Satz*.

13. cf. "In a proposition a thought finds an expression that can be perceived *by the senses*" (*TLP* 3.1)(my italics).

14. In a letter to Russell written in 1919 from the prison camp at Monte Cassino Wittgenstein says, "I don't know *what* the constituents of a thought are but I know *that* it must have constituents which correspond to the words of language. Again the kind of relation of the constituents of the thought and of the pictured fact is irrelevant. It would be a matter of psychology to find out" (quoted in Anscombe 1959, 27–8).

15. *PR*, III, 22, p. 64.

16. cf. *PR*, III, 27; p. 67: "I should like to say, assuming the surrogate process [an inner surrogate for an outer act of execution] to be a picture doesn't get me anywhere, since even that does not do away with the transition from the picture to what is depicted."

17. *BB*, p. 3.

18. *PI*, 66.

19. cf. "How do I know that this colour is red?—It would be an answer to say: 'I have learnt English'." (*PI*, 381.)

20. It might be thought that it would have to be *shown* that such a list is infinite, as opposed to merely open-ended, say. Wittgenstein's famous discussion of understanding how to continue a series of numbers (*PI* 143 onwards) does in fact have this looked-for feature, i.e. it is mathematically demonstrable that a given finite series of numbers can be continued according to some formula in infinitely many different ways. The possibility of such a demonstration has of course to do with the nature of mathematics, so if by "shown to be infinite" we mean "demonstrated to be infinite", the desire alluded to in the first sentence of this footnote will probably be unsatisfiable.

21. See n. 14, above.

22. It is this view with which Wittgenstein begins the *Investigations* by describing, in order to undermine and eventually replace it; see *PI* 1.

23. This point will crop up again in Ch. 4, in connection with first *vs*. third person uses of psychological verbs.

58 *Thought, Will and World*

24. Part of Wittgenstein's point, of course, is that we are liable to be misled by phrases like "descriptions of the phenomena", "applicability of these words to the same situations", etc., even though these phrases have an innocent enough use. For such phrases can encourage the thought that the words under discussion (e.g. "he", "come") have, joined together with other words, a single basic function: that of *describing situations*. This thought goes with the tendency to look for a feature shared by different situations and justifying the use in them of the same words.—It should be noted that to say there is an internal relation arising from descriptions of the two phenomena is not to say there are no other descriptions of those phenomena. What fulfils LW's expectation could be re-described e.g. as "the arrival of a man wearing red socks"; but this description can only be *arrived at* via the description invoked in the expression of expectation ("He will come"). Tim Crane is surely mistaken in stating that "Wittgenstein's point . . . is that you can only describe the object of the expectation in the way it is specified in the description of the expectation itself", and his criticism of Wittgenstein is consequently off-target. See Crane 2010, 99.
25. Hacker 1996, 109.
26. Ibid., 99. The use being made here of "grammatical" comes from Wittgenstein, and corresponds very roughly to "conceptual". Thus a "grammatical proposition" is *roughly* the same as what other philosophers would mean by "conceptual truth"; say, "A proposition is true in virtue of some fact's holding" or "Socks can't be blind". Wittgenstein's choice of the term "grammar" has puzzled many. For a persuasive defence of that choice, see the last few pages of Anscombe 2011.
27. This thought is what feeds our puzzlement that there should be anything wrong with such a statement as "It's raining and I don't believe it's raining" (Moore's Paradox): if the first conjunct concerns the weather and the second concerns my mental life, why can't the conjunction simply express a possible truth, depict a possible state of affairs? And yet the statement *is* somehow contradictory. See Ch. 4, 115–16.
28. Not the only one of this form to figure in the history of philosophy. Consider "Socrates is wise; Plato is wise; so Socrates and Plato are different and yet the same."
29. That there is room in philosophy for this sort of resistance to "All or nothing" is very important. A number of philosophers, such as Davidson, have argued that non-human animals can have *no* beliefs, and indeed *no* propositional attitudes. Like Wittgenstein, Davidson stresses the importance of language; like Wittgenstein, Davidson evinces a kind of "holism"; but in Davidson the result is a theory which achieves an abstract generality at the cost of our common-sense thought and talk about animals. William Child seems to be viewing Wittgenstein through Davidsonic spectacles when he writes that "the crucial point about intention is that having states with intentional content depends, for Wittgenstein, on mastery of, or participation in, practices." (Child 2016, forthcoming)—For an incisive discussion of the difference between Wittgenstein's and Davidson's holisms, and the relevance of this to animal minds, see Finkelstein 2007.
30. See, e.g. *TLP* 6.36311, 6.37.
31. See 36, above.
32. See the discussion of Descartes in Ch. 1, 18–19.
33. Anscombe 1963, 5.
34. And Wittgenstein does distinguish the two senses of "grounds" I have alluded to, e.g. when he writes in *Remarks on the Philosophy of Psychology*: "Asked: 'Are you going to do such-and-such?' I consider *grounds for* and *against*

[*Gründe* und *Gegengründe*]." (*RPP* vol. I, 815) And in the *Blue Book* he refers to "the double use of the word 'why', asking for the cause and asking for the motive," and to the similarity in this context of the grammars of "motive" and of "reason"; see *BB* 15.

35. And for that reason one can question the appropriateness of saying that the statement expresses a belief at all; certainly, Wittgenstein would look askance at such a saying.

36. See J. L. Austin 1962, 5.

3   The Inner and the Outer

1.   THE PICTURE OF AN "INNER PROCESS"

In the last chapter, I presented Wittgenstein as holding that the relation between thought and fact, and that between will (or intention) and deed, are internal relations. Only as regards the relation between thought and fact can this view be ascribed to the *early* Wittgenstein, and even there the view needs to be qualified, given that strictly speaking a relation can only hold between objects, and "the thought that p" is not the name of an object. As for the relation between will and world, the early Wittgenstein adopted an extreme, and so to speak quietist, position, as we have seen—a position whose distance from his position concerning belief seemed worth questioning.

That distance is purposely reduced in his later philosophy[1]. In the *Philosophical Remarks*, the discussion in Part III centring on expectation explicitly treats that "cognitive" phenomenon as comparable to such "conative" phenomena as desire and intention (also wishing, if that is conative). We find Wittgenstein writing:

> I only use the terms the expectation, thought, wish, etc., that *p* will be the case, for processes having the multiplicity that finds expression in *p*, and thus only if they are *articulated*. But in that case they are what I call the interpretation of signs.
>
> I only call an *articulated* process a thought: you could therefore say 'only what has an articulated expression'.
>
> (Salivation—no matter how precisely measured—is *not* what I call expecting.) (*PR* III, 32; 69–70)

He had not yet abandoned the idea that expectation (e.g.) must be a process that mirrors a proposition: since "I expect that p" has an articulated form involving the proposition p, so must the psychological phenomenon of expecting that p, and this sufficiently accounts for the internal relation between proposition and process. But as we saw in the last chapter, Wittgenstein moved to a point where he was happy to speak of walking up and down, looking at one's watch, etc. as constituting expectation on a given occasion

The Inner and the Outer 61

(if we are to speak of something's *constituting* expectation, that is); and if such processes are to be called "articulated", that will only mean that one who has learnt the language-game of expressing expectation will, or would, be warranted in uttering "I expect that p" in the context of such processes (activities)—the use of this sentence being *connected* in various ways with the use of "p", and both these uses being possible moves in that language-game. Evidently the expectation that p need not itself involve any "interpretation of signs", and the nature of the internal relation between proposition and process is explained, not by reference to any multiplicity in the process, but by reference (if you like) to the multiplicity in the language-game.

But if Wittgenstein thinks that walking up and down, looking at one's watch, etc. can constitute expectation, doesn't that mean that he is some sort of behaviourist? This is a well-worn question, provoked by Wittgenstein's later treatment of psychological concepts generally. Since the term "behaviourist" does not have a single, clear sense, a possible answer to it is: he may indeed be a behaviourist, on certain interpretations of "behaviourist"— and not on others. The interesting question must be, not whether some label shall be applied to him, but what *sort* of employment of the notion of behaviour he does in fact make. But it is best to approach this question *via* an examination of what Wittgenstein has to say about "inner processes", since it is especially on account of his critique of this notion that people are wont to regard him as a behaviourist, or as overly interested in behaviour.

To regard thinking, expecting, remembering, etc. as inner processes is extremely natural. Philosophers have also frequently seen the "conative" phenomena of intending, willing, etc. as inner processes. Where inner processes are taken to be mental *acts*, problems of a quite peculiar kind arise, especially in connection with the conative concepts: if in order to raise my arm intentionally I must use my faculty of will, e.g. by "pursuing" the idea of my arm's going up[2], it seems that the inner act of willing (or pursuing) must itself be intentional, rather than "just happening"—and an infinite regress threatens. Problems also beset attempts to see thinking, judging, etc. as mental acts, such as acts of inwardly assenting to, or asserting, some idea or proposition. An outward assertion can be insincere, in jest, or uncomprehending, which is to say that it can be made in the absence of belief in what is asserted. Surely then the same will be true of an internal assertion—that is, if inward assertion is the same as outward assertion, but just "inner". And after all, I can in fact inwardly say to myself something I know to be absurd. But this seems to show that believing or judging that p cannot be equated with inwardly asserting that p, unless "assert" is being used differently from how it is used when applied to ordinary public assertions— in which case we are owed an explanation of how it *is* being used.

Wittgenstein does touch on the problems of regarding willing as an internal act[3]. But an adherent of inner processes need not see them as acts at all; and it will be most instructive if we look at Wittgenstein's remarks on inner

62   The Inner and the Outer

processes in general, since these remarks cast the net wider—or in other words, go deeper. And to begin with, it is important to see what he is *not* denying.

> "But you surely cannot deny that, for example, in remembering, an inner process takes place." . . . The impression that we wanted to deny something arises from our setting our faces against the picture of the 'inner process'. What we deny is that the picture of the inner process gives us the correct idea of the use of the word "to remember". We say that this picture with its ramifications stands in the way of our seeing the use of the word as it is. (*PI* 305)

What is the difference between denying that Fs exist and "setting your face against the picture of the F"? *The picture of the "inner process" is not the same as the statement that there exist inner processes*—so much is clear. In fact, this notion of a picture is of considerable importance in the later Wittgenstein. In thinking about certain topics, we often find it natural to express ourselves using particular metaphors or turns of phrase, which expressions we take to represent something essential to the phenomenon in question, but which can hardly be deemed to do so in any ordinary or literal way. These metaphors or turns of phrase embody pictures, in Wittgenstein's sense. Examples include the picture of the self as a little person or homunculus; the picture of time as a river (or as a line, or . . .); the picture of a mathematical series as already there, waiting to be discovered; the picture of a property of something as an ingredient of that thing; and of course, the picture of the mind as a private, inner, theatre. Wittgenstein is not *against* pictures; thus he writes:

> What am I believing in when I believe that men have souls? What am I believing in, when I believe that this substance contains two carbon rings? In both cases there is a picture in the foreground, but the sense lies far in the background; that is, the application of the picture is not easy to survey.
>
> *Certainly* all these things happen in you.—And now all I ask is to understand the expressions we use.—The picture is there. And I am not disputing its validity in any particular case.—Only I also want to understand the application of the picture. (*PI* 422, 423)

Wittgenstein here speaks of the possible "validity" (*Gültigkeit*) of a picture, i.e. its strength or effectiveness. What would such validity amount to in a given case? It would reside in the "applications" that the person who presents or subscribes to the picture makes of it. Such applications would not be translations of sentences invoking the picture, but would in some sense, taken together, give the "cash value" of the picture. The effectiveness of a picture would be akin to that of a metaphor or simile—indeed, the picture

The Inner and the Outer   63

could *be* a metaphor or simile—having to do with the comparison of phenomena, the making of connections, the pointing to certain lines of enquiry
or thought, and so on.

A picture makes trouble when the person who presents or subscribes to
it is led to deny obvious truths, or to misuse language, or to give one-sided
and unbalanced accounts of things. It may lead to the person's taking a form
of words or signs as meaning something when they (as yet) mean nothing.
Thus the representation of the temporal order of events by means of a line
can lead philosophers to talk of time as linear, and then go on to ask such
questions as, "What would be the case if time were circular?—or if time
bifurcated?" For you *can* draw a circular line, and you *can* draw a line
that bifurcates. The symbolism takes on a life of its own: if the straight
line represented time as it is, surely the circular line must represent time as
other than it is, but nevertheless as *something*? Such a case may well lead us
to agree with Wittgenstein that "philosophers are often like little children,
who first scribble random lines on a piece of paper with their pencils, and
now ask an adult 'What is that?'" (*PO* 193)

Into what sort of error or confusion is the picture of inner processes
liable to lead us? One kind of error arises through associating "process"
with those processes the investigation of which consists in homing in on a
process, observing it in detail, and describing its nature by describing what
is observed. Our activities here partly determine the sense, in such contexts,
of the term "nature", a term which in other contexts has a patently different sense. This conception of a process is tied up with the aims and methods
of natural science. When it is applied, e.g. to remembering, expecting, or
intending, it can result in a kind of obscurity against which behaviourism is
but a natural reaction—and by "behaviourism" I mean the sort of science-
inspired trend of thought we found in Russell's account of desire.

> How does the philosophical problem about mental processes and states
> and about behaviourism arise?—The first step is the one that altogether
> escapes notice. We talk of processes and states and leave their nature
> undecided. Sometime perhaps we shall know more about them—we
> think. But that is just what commits us to a particular way of looking
> at the matter. For we have a definite concept of what it means to learn
> to know a process better. (The decisive movement in the conjuring
> trick has been made, and it was the very one that we thought quite
> innocent.)—And now the analogy which was to make us understand
> our thoughts falls to pieces. So we have to deny the yet uncompre-
> hended process in the yet unexplored medium. And now it looks as
> if we had denied mental processes. And naturally we don't want to
> deny them. (*PI* 308)

We don't want to deny them because (for instance) "to deny the mental process [of remembering] would mean to deny the remembering; to deny that

64　*The Inner and the Outer*

anyone ever remembers anything" (*PI* 306). It might be asked: "But aren't you denying that remembering is a *process*?" To which Wittgenstein would respond that although "Remembering is a process" *can* quite possibly have an innocent use, it very often *does* go with a conception of a process that doesn't fit the concept of remembering. "For we have a definite concept of what it means to learn to know a process better": homing in on it, observing it in detail, and describing its nature by describing what is observed. Wittgenstein is not so much saying that "Remembering is a process" is a false statement as noting how it tends to mark a step in a philosopher's movement towards a certain kind of obscurity and confusion.

An example of the sort of confusion into which we can be led is that which may surround the issue of a mental state's intentionality: its being about something, or having an object. This was the issue that especially received attention in the last chapter. If thinking (remembering, desiring . . .) is taken to be an inner process, a "process" being something whose nature is discovered or shed light on by observing or attending to it, then it is natural to regard the content or object of thinking (remembering, desiring . . .) as itself an observable or introspectable feature of the process, since it is evidently an essential feature of it—part of its nature. That I am thinking *of cheese*, or planning *to swat a fly*, ought to be facts concerning the intrinsic nature of my thought or plan. The metaphor that now suggests itself to us is that of the image or picture, for it can also seem as if what a picture is of is something intrinsic to the picture. The feeling that this is so, however, would seem to arise more than anything else from the immediacy and spontaneity of the experience of seeing a picture as this or as that. For if we try to say what it *is* in a picture that determines that it is of this or of that, we quickly face philosophical difficulties of the sort that were outlined in Chapter 1, e.g. surrounding the idea of resemblance, and in addition face the deep challenge presented by Wittgenstein's observations concerning methods of projection and the multiple ways of interpreting a picture (see 39–40, above).

Another instance of the confusion into which the picture of the inner process may lead us is this: I know that I am thinking, and what it is I am thinking of, by inner observation or introspection. A process can be going on, but for someone to know about it, they must evidently observe or attend to it, e.g. by looking at it. Do I or don't I know that I am thinking of cheese, if I am? Faced with this choice, one will most likely opt for "I do know". And after all, surely what I say goes in such a matter, except perhaps in pathological cases?—Now it *is* a fact that on the topic of my thoughts etc., what I say goes (typically), a fact which very naturally leads us to posit first-person authority, authority based on the "transparency of the mind" (another picture, in Wittgenstein's sense); but as we shall see, the fact in question is one susceptible of a quite different account. And the model of knowing by looking (feeling, etc.) falls down when applied analogically to one's thinking. One reason for this is that *getting it wrong, being mistaken,* are in this context inapplicable concepts.

The Inner and the Outer   65

It seems impossible that someone should sincerely assert "I think it's going to rain", "I plan to finish this book by the end of the month", "I am trying to solve this puzzle", etc. and be simply *mistaken* (as to whether they think, plan, try). This fact has traditionally been accounted for by ascribing a sort of infallibility to people, infallibility concerning their current mental states.[4] If we have adopted as our model for such first-personal knowledge that of knowing by looking (feeling, etc.), we are committed to the idea that the faculty whereby one forms beliefs about one's current mental states is an infallible faculty—unlike looking, feeling, etc. But there seems to be no *logical* connection between the fact that I think that p and the fact that my introspective faculty is in a particular state, namely that of reporting "I think that p"; the two facts are logically independent, and the claim that one fact is a necessary concomitant of the other thus cries out for justification. After all, this claim is not itself being presented as a mere surmise, along the lines of "I bet that every time someone thinks that p, her introspective faculty reports 'I think that p' if it reports anything"—the claim is alleged to be something known. But what grounds could be given for saying "Whenever P, Q", P and Q being logically independent? One could answer, "I just do know this", thus rejecting the question "How do you know?" But why not give the same answer to "How do you know you think that p?"? If assertion of the philosophical necessity-claim need not be justified by reference to a special faculty, why should assertion that one thinks that p be so justified? (And of course in real life, if you ask someone, "How do you *know* that you think it's going to rain?", they will not—unless a philosopher—respond, "By means of my introspective faculty", but will rather regard you as talking nonsense.) Alternatively, a special infallible faculty may be posited to explain how one knows the philosophical necessity-claim to be true, in which case the same problem will arise one level up: in the absence of a logical connection between the philosophical necessity-claim and the special faculty's being in such-and-such a state, what grounds are there for saying that the special faculty gets things right?

Of course the idea of first-person infallibility may be denied by philosophers who regard introspection as just as fallible as seeing, and for essentially the same reasons. For these philosophers, we can quite easily be mistaken in our first-person psychological statements, and "I am trying to solve this puzzle" and "I believe that I am trying to solve this puzzle" are indeed as logically independent as are "Jim is in Paris" and "I believe that Jim is in Paris". After all, is not self-deception a real phenomenon?—Self-deception, however, does not involve being simply *mistaken*, in the way that, e.g. sensory judgements can be mistaken; and the range of cases where self-deception may be imputed is quite severely restricted by considerations to do with the overall intelligibility of a person's (linguistic and non-linguistic) behaviour. (Could someone in ordinary circumstances who is tying his shoe-laces be *deceived* when he says that he intends his shoes to be firmly on

66   *The Inner and the Outer*

his feet?) Moreover, the sort of causal account of first-personal knowledge which we are liable to be landed with here faces just those problems relating to the dubitability of causes and effects that were discussed in the two previous chapters. So we may after all say that, except in really pathological cases, sincere assertions of the sort listed above cannot be mistaken. But an explanation of this fact by reference to an infallible faculty can be undermined by the argument of the previous paragraph.

That argument is not derived from Wittgenstein, however much it is in the spirit of Wittgenstein, and it is perhaps doubtful whether he would have bothered to spell out in such detail the consequences and commitments of philosophical infallibilism. It is the responses of a soul less corrupted by philosophy that interest him more, as are to be found expressed in the following:

> Compare the two cases: 1. "How do you know that *he* has pains?"— "Because I hear him moan". 2. "How do you know that you have pains?"—"Because I *feel* them". But "I feel them" means the same as "I have them". Therefore this was no explanation at all. (*BB* 68)

This imaginary dialogue concerns the sensation of pain, Wittgenstein's standard example when discussing "infallible" first-personal present-tense statements. But a similar dialogue concerning, e.g. thought or intention would surely yield a similar conclusion. Indeed, the intermediary "I *feel* it" would probably be absent, and the answer to "How do you know?" would simply be "Because I *have* the thought/intention". And "I have the thought that p" just means "I think that p": this is no explanation at all.

Someone might respond that it is really the other way around: "I think that p" just means "I have the thought that p". It is the latter statement that shows us what is really going on, and it is this statement that supplies us with the right sort of answer to "How do you know?" The picture involved here is that of a relation of some sort subsisting between thinker and thought, a relation that may be expressed by various terms, as "has", "perceives", "is acquainted with". If the thinker is taken to be the philosophical Subject, we face all the difficulties attached to that notion, some of which will be examined in the next chapter. But the thinker might be regarded just as a human being or person; we can for the moment pass over this question. It is the idea of a transitive verb taking for its object such things as *the thought that p* and *the intention to do* X that needs to be examined.[5] One model for such a verb is a verb like "sees". But whereas the faculty of sight is fallible, that of "inner seeing" appears to be infallible, in a way that raises the sorts of problems mentioned a couple of paragraphs back; and whereas the concept of a faculty such as sight is connected with that of an organ, or embodiment, of that faculty (the eyes), the very idea of an organ of introspection seems dubious.

2. PRIVACY AND UNSHARABILITY

But why should we even *want* to posit a transitive verb with its attendant inner objects? Part of the answer to this surely has to do with a certain conception of knowledge: the conception of knowledge as acquaintance.

The verb "knows" can be followed by a proposition, as in "Jack knows that it's raining", but also by a noun or noun phrase, as in "Jack knows the alphabet" or "Jack knows a woman who can knit while standing on her head". A bias in favour of nouns and nominalization is a well-documented feature of natural languages, and the very form of "What does Jack know?" invites a nominal answer; and this is no doubt *one* reason why philosophers have found it natural to take "N knows X", with "X" a noun or noun phrase, as embodying a paradigm. A prime example is Russell, who in outlining what he took to be the foundations of knowledge, distinguished knowledge by acquaintance from knowledge by description[6], both kinds of knowledge being knowledge *of things*, and knowledge by acquaintance being the more fundamental of the two. For Russell, the things with which we are acquainted are such inner items as we have been discussing, in particular sense-data. Now it is very natural to think something like the following: only I can know that I am thinking/intending/in pain (etc.)—and this is to be explained by the fact that that only I can *have* my (this) thought/intention/ pain (etc.). Unique (unsharable) propositional knowledge is to be explained by reference to unique access to, or acquaintance with, a thing or process. These facts are what are conveyed by the term "inner", in "inner process".

Wittgenstein subjects both "Only I can know . . ." and "Only I can have . . ." to critical interrogation. Again, his discussion typically concerns sensations such as pain, since the picture of the private, inner process is especially tempting in the case of sensations; but his remarks can be applied also to the view of thoughts, intentions, etc. as private, inner processes.

> In what sense are my sensations *private*?—Well, only I can know whether I am really in pain; another person can only surmise it.—In one way this is wrong, and in another nonsense. If we are using the word "to know" as it is normally used (and how else are we to use it?), then other people very often know when I am in pain.—Yes, but all the same not with the certainty with which I know it myself!—It can't be said of me at all (except perhaps as a joke) that I *know* I am in pain. What is it supposed to mean—except perhaps that I *am* in pain? (*PI* 246)

And a little later we get:

> "Another person can't have *my* pains."—Which are my pains? What counts as a criterion of identity here? . . . In so far as it makes *sense* to say that my pain is the same as his, it is also possible for us both to have the

68 *The Inner and the Outer*

same pain . . . I have seen a person in a discussion on this subject strike himself on the breast and say: "But surely another person can't have THIS pain!"—The answer to this is that one does not define a criterion of identity by emphatic stressing of the word "this". (*PI* 253)

In both passages Wittgenstein invokes a standard of meaningfulness, namely that of how words are in fact used. In the second passage, he regards "My pain is the same as his" as only meaning anything at all if you might actually use it, i.e. assert it truly—which indeed you might.[7] You could say it truly if you had a headache and your friend also had a headache. In the first passage, he points out that if we are using the word "to know" as it is normally used, then other people very often know when I am in pain; and asks rhetorically "and how else are we to use it?" Like many rhetorical questions in philosophy, this one is not *merely* rhetorical; philosophers have after all wanted to distinguish between the "loose and popular" meaning of a word and its "strict and philosophical" meaning.[8] Wittgenstein's account of linguistic meaning as in some sense determined by actual use will, if accepted, lead us to cease imagining a quasi-Platonic *Meaning* as that with which actual usage should struggle to be in keeping. It would take me too far afield to examine that account in detail. Nevertheless it is worth considering the sort of challenge, so characteristic of Wittgenstein, embodied in such a question as, "What is ['I know I am in pain'] supposed to mean—except perhaps that I *am* in pain?"

The question "What is X supposed to mean?" asks for explanation, for if a statement in a shared language means something, its meaning can be explained. The notion of explanation here is very liberal, indeed open-ended; it is not just a demand for a "semantic equivalent". But it is a *realistic* demand: an intelligent person, hearing a good or adequate such explanation, will know where the speaker is going with his statement, what consequences making it has or could have, how it connects with other statements, and so on. And one sort of explanation which will often *not* work is the sort produced by the person who says, "I am using that word in such a way that it has the same meaning as it does in this other context (where you will admit it makes perfect sense)". For one thing, a decision or intention to use a word meaningfully, or to use it with the meaning which it has elsewhere, is no guarantee of anything; meaning something is not a state or process about which a speaker has infallible knowledge, as is evident, apart from anything else, from the ease with which people can utter nonsense in the sincere belief that what they say makes sense. For another, such a purported explanation will only be any good if as a matter of fact it enables an intelligent person who hears it to see where the speaker is going with his statement, what consequences making it has or could have, how it connects with other statements, and so on; and if the use of a word in one context appeared unintelligible or hard to understand, the fact that a use of it in another context is quite intelligible may well be of no help at all.

The Inner and the Outer   69

These remarks have a bearing on the statement "My pain is the same as his", when it is coupled with the claim that one intends "same" here to mean "one and the same", or "numerically the same". It is *this* interpretation of the statement which the devotee of the private, inner process wishes us to take on board and understand to be impossible. Saying that in such-and-such a statement "same" means "numerically the same" is really a way of saying that in such-and-such a statement "same" means what it means, e.g. in "This is the same chair as the one I saw here yesterday". But we understand the latter statement only to the extent that we already have and can operate with criteria of identity (through time) for physical objects like chairs, criteria which will of course not help us in understanding "My pain is the same as his". So the question that is forced on us is: Do we have such criteria of identity for pains? And if so, what are they? Only when we have an answer to this question will we be able to assess "My pain is the same as his". And one thing that is surely clear is that "one does not define a criterion of identity by emphatic stressing of the word 'this'".

Maybe location supplies a criterion? But, as Wittgenstein says, two Siamese twins might be said to have a pain in the same shoulder (*PI* 253): would this then refute "Only I can have my pains"? The devotee of the private, inner process would say "No". And in fact his denial may be seen as deriving from the recognition of an alternative criterion of identity, namely that whereby the identity of the pain depends on the identity of the person, the person being that which can express pain, behaviourally or linguistically. By this criterion, if there are two Siamese twins, and each separately evinces shoulder pain, then there are two pains. One might state this criterion of identity by saying, "Sameness of pain entails sameness of person", or indeed by saying, "Only I can have my pains". Wittgenstein's attitude to statements that give criteria of identity in this way is that they lay down linguistic rules, or in other words are "grammatical propositions", and it is a theme that runs through his philosophy that we are tempted to misconstrue such statements as reports, true or false, of the "metaphysical facts" (e.g. when we succumb to the picture of the inner process). And he would not, I think, reject "Only I can have my pains", understood not as a metaphysical proposition but as a statement about the grammar of "pain". For it is true that *one* way of identifying (counting, etc.) pains is just by identifying the bearers of pains.

Some commentators have taken Wittgenstein as altogether ruling out "Another person can't have my pains". Peter Hacker in his exegesis of *PI* 253 seems to do so, referring to the quoted sentence as "this misbegotten proposition".[9] But in 253, as so often, Wittgenstein is imagining somebody *producing* the quoted sentence, somebody in the grip of a particular (metaphysical) picture. In general, Wittgenstein rarely outlaws a *sentence*, asking rather "But what do/could you mean by that?" And very often, he allows a possible use, but not the one the interlocutor (or whoever) had in mind; cf. 246 ("... except perhaps that I *am* in pain?"), 247, 458, etc. We might

70 *The Inner and the Outer*

usefully compare "Another person can't have my pains" with "Another person can't have my shadow", or indeed with "Another person can't have my possessions". The latter is true in one sense, false in another.

Moreover, at *PI* 248 Wittgenstein writes: "The proposition 'Sensations are private' is comparable to: 'One plays patience by oneself'." The notion of the private is here the same as that which appeared in 246, i.e. a notion having to do with unique knowledge of one's sensations; but the comparison with patience surely indicates that he (also) has in mind the notion of unique ownership (unsharability) of sensations. And the point of the comparison is that here we have a grammatical, not a metaphysical, proposition. "One plays patience by oneself" is a perfectly correct statement, of the sort that might be used in teaching someone how to play patience, or just in explaining what sort of thing patience is. (Or: explaining what the word "patience" means; cf. 247.)[10]

One who utters the sentence "Only I can have my pains" will be a human being, or at any rate will be sufficiently like a human being for us to take the utterance *as* an utterance, and not just as a noise; and this fact bears on what "I" is doing in the sentence. The sentence can in effect be generalized as "A given human being's pains can only be had by that human being". And it is in the pre-linguistic interactions between fellow human beings that the roots of the concept of pain are to be found. Wittgenstein alludes to these roots when discussing why it is a person, not a body or bit of a body that we ascribe pain to:

> What sort of issue is: Is it the *body* that feels pain?—How is it to be decided? What makes it plausible to say that it is *not* the body?—Well, something like this: if someone has a pain in his hand, then the hand does not say so (unless it writes it) and one does not comfort the hand, but the sufferer: one looks into his face. (*PI* 286)

The bearer of pain is that which one might comfort, or indeed that at which one might laugh sadistically. You do not pity hands, nor do you laugh sadistically at them. These attitudes and reactions are directed at people. People, i.e. human beings, are the units of psychology, so that it makes sense for us to count sensations in parallel with our counting of people, i.e. to employ such a criterion of identity for sensations.[11] The same is true of thoughts and intentions, something which we need to be reminded of when we are tempted to talk of the brain, or a bit of the brain, as thinking or intending. You do not agree with or obey frontal lobes—you agree with or obey people.

I said above that *one* way of identifying (counting, etc.) pains is by identifying the bearers of pains. There is of course another, namely by their bodily location. Wittgenstein denies that one's capacity to point to where it hurts is based on or derived from an already existing knowledge of where the pain is—saying rather that "the act of pointing *determines* a place of pain"

The Inner and the Outer 71

(*BB* 50). He could have added to pointing such things as rubbing or nursing the place, wincing when it is pressed, etc., some of those natural criteria of pain which are at the heart of the concept. The case he makes here is philosophically important as well as persuasive, but is not sufficiently relevant to my topic to merit close examination. But it does seem to have the following consequences: that the two criteria of identity for pains, as (i) person-dependent and (ii) location-dependent, may in principle give different answers to the question "How many pains?" (as in the Siamese twins case, where one *could* say they share a single pain)—and also that the second criterion allows of "an innumerable variety of cases . . . in which we should say that someone has pains in another person's body; or, say, in a piece of furniture, or in an empty spot" (*BB* 50). It is possible that the confidence of this latter assertion is more characteristic of the *Blue Book* than of the *Investigations*, and that the author of the later work might have said, "If someone regularly pointed to his desk when asked where it hurt we might just regard him as mad or as linguistically defective—and if many people started doing this sort of thing, we might or might not adjust the conduct of our language-game so as to include 'out-of-body' pains; it would depend on all sorts of factors".

When it comes to thought, intention, etc., criterion (ii) has no application. "Only I can think my thoughts" faces no subversion or derailment from odd phenomena of pointing and the like, and for thoughts and intentions there is a case for saying that we identify or count these things simply by identifying or counting people. As: "Whose idea was it to have the dog put down?"—"It was Sam's, but I had come to the same conclusion." Sam's idea (thought, plan . . .) is distinguished from Bill's, partly as having been responsible in some sense for the dog's actually getting put down, but prior to that as being *Sam's* idea. The distinction between token and type will be of help to us here, since we can *either* count two ideas, with identical content, hatched by Bill and Sam, *or* count the single idea that they both hatch. "Their thoughts were in complete harmony" and "A single idea united them" are both possible ways of speaking. It is the former case, the case of token-identity, which we have been discussing.

I have argued that "Only I can have my pains" can be regarded as a grammatical proposition laying down one, if not the only, criterion of identity for pains. And something similar can be said of "Only I can think my thoughts/intentions/ etc." Taking "Only I can have my pains" as representative of these various statements, we might well think that, understood as a grammatical proposition, it surely makes sense. And if "Only I can have my pains" makes sense, the same would appear to go for its negation, "Another can have the same pains as me", where "same" must mean "numerically the same" (for "Only I can have my pains" rules out the *sharing* of pains—it doesn't rule out our both having a headache). This will be necessarily false, if intended as the negation of the grammatical proposition—or so it is natural to argue.[12] But we found Wittgenstein saying that "in so far as it makes

72   *The Inner and the Outer*

sense to say that my pain is the same as his, it is also possible for us both to have the same pain", i.e. that any meaningful assertion of "My pain is the same as his" will be a statement of type-identity, not one of token-identity. What is going on here?

Just before the discussion of "Another person can't have my pains" we find:

> "This body has extension."—To this we might reply: "Nonsense!"—but are inclined to reply "Of course!"—Why is this? (*PI* 252)

Wittgenstein does not answer his own question. But the answer is surely something like this: a grammatical proposition, like the statement of a rule in chess, does have a possible use—it can be used when teaching language, or indeed when clearing up linguistic confusions (when it will probably have the function of a "reminder"). The negation of a grammatical proposition has no such use or usefulness. While there is *a* sense in which "Only I can have my pains", "This body has extension", *et al.*, are meaningless ("Nonsense!")—for they appear to impart information about their subject-matter when they do no such thing—there is also a sense in which they are meaningful, namely when intended as grammatical propositions ("Of course!")[13]; though "A body . . ." would more usually be employed in the latter role than "This body . . .". But "His pain and mine are numerically the same" lays down no rule and serves as no reminder of how words are used; and its main interest for Wittgenstein lies in its being a sentence which it is tempting, but wrong, to regard as describing a particular situation, a situation which is "metaphysically impossible". If taken as necessarily false, it describes no situation at all, any more than does "Three is the same number as four", or "A half-empty square root of ducklings recurred with avuncular butter". If taken as describing a situation, e.g. that of Siamese twins with a pain in the same shoulder, it is not necessarily false; but in this case of course it employs a different criterion of identity from that embodied in "Only I can have my pains".

If "Only I can have my pains" has at best the status of a grammatical proposition, it will be difficult to press it into service as a statement capable of justifying or explaining the truth of "Only I can know I'm in pain". One can bring out the problems inherent in the idea of such justification in various ways. If having a pain (thought, etc.) is conceived of as standing in some relation to a thing or item—the pain (thought, etc.)—then this relation will need to be something like Russell's acquaintance, for otherwise there seems nothing to distinguish "I have a pain" from "I am in pain", sufficiently for the first to justify the second. (The belief "I am in pain" will need to be justified to count as knowledge, on the sort of view being considered.) Knowledge by acquaintance will on this view yield propositional knowledge, the knowledge that I am in pain. But then it seems that I must be deriving the knowledge "I am in pain" from the thing with which I am

The Inner and the Outer 73

acquainted—and how can a *thing* entail or justify a proposition, namely "I am in pain"? Surely only a proposition can entail or justify a proposition? It may be replied on Russell's behalf that the relation of acquaintance holds between me and a *fact*. But the early Wittgenstein's assertion that *fact* is a formal concept here seems unanswerable; for what can "I am acquainted with the fact that p" mean if not simply "I know (directly and immediately) that p"? And "I know that p" can hardly be used to justify (the belief) "p". One cannot derive the knowledge that p from knowledge that p.

These remarks are relevant to the idea of the inner process, for *process* appears to be more akin to *fact* than to *thing*. One can return to the same thing, re-identify it, have a proper name for it; a thing can, as they say, be "wholly present" at different times. This last does not hold of processes or events, hence Hume's characterization of his impressions and ideas as "fleeting" and "perishing". I might have an exactly similar experience of a blue circle in my visual field on two separate occasions, but for Hume it is a fiction that is embodied in the report, "Here is the very same thing (e.g. a blue ball)", since *of course* the second experience—an event—is different from the first! For all that Hume's argument is dubious, *event* and *process* are different logical categories from *thing*, event-terms and process-terms being essentially derived from verbs, such as "think" and "remember". And for these reasons, "I am acquainted with a process of remembering" surely says no more than "I know (directly and immediately) that I remember something". Russellian acquaintance with an inner process thus cannot explain first-personal psychological knowledge.

3. THOUGHT AND WILL AS INVOLVING INNER PROCESSES

I have been discussing some of the grounds that there are for "setting one's face against the picture of the 'inner process'". These grounds, though often expounded with reference to sensations like pain, were sufficiently general to apply also to thoughts and intentions. But the picture of the inner process is as ramified as is the idea of a psychological state, as multifarious as are our psychological concepts; and we find specific versions of the picture cropping up in connection with specific concepts, such as *thinking* or *intending*.

In the case of thinking, it is very tempting to see it as an inner process that *accompanies* various outer activities, such as speaking or making a cake, and which by accompanying them renders them intelligent. For what is it that distinguishes the human being who says "Polly, put the kettle on" from the parrot who squawks the same thing, if not something going on in the human being that doesn't go on in the parrot? (Note the assumption here that the important thing must be something you could find by homing in on "what was happening just then"—i.e. that it must be a *process*.) But the idea that in speaking words you simultaneously think the thought(s) conveyed by the words raises absurd difficulties. Does the thinking take the same

74　*The Inner and the Outer*

length of time as the speaking? In that case, you would only find out what you thought when you had finished your sentence, which might after all be quite a long one, complete with Proustian sub-clauses . . . And it would be obscure why you spoke these words rather than those: "so as to convey my thought" seems unavailable as an answer, given that you discover what you think as you speak. But then won't your words as it were come as a surprise to you?

> "Did you think as you read the sentence?"—"Yes, I did think as I read it; every word was important to me."
> That is not the usual experience.[14] One is not usually half-astonished to hear oneself say something; one doesn't follow one's own talk with attention; for one ordinarily talks voluntarily, not involuntarily. (Z 92)

Maybe then you think the whole thought before you start speaking, the spoken sentence being somehow produced or caused by the thought? But isn't it too neat to say that there should be one thought per sentence? Couldn't a clause like "When he had arrived . . ." be the product of a thought, the thought of his arriving? In that case, a complex utterance would seem to be caused, one bit at a time, by a series of thoughts; but then, as before, you would only find out what your overall thought was at, or near, the end of your sentence. And what about non-assertoric utterances? Is the order "Shut the door!" to be deemed intelligent because of an accompanying thought, "Shut the door!"? (No *thought that p* will be available.) Are we in fact to posit a species of thought for every species of speech-act? Is the greeting "Hello" accompanied by the thought "Hello"? Thoughts now seem to be nothing more than shadows of linguistic forms.

In the face of such questions one of Wittgenstein's main pieces of advice is to remind ourselves of the great variety and complexity actually to be found in our concepts, a variety we can forget if we hold up for inspection a single word, like "thinking".

> 'Thinking', a widely ramified concept. A concept that comprises many manifestations of life. The *phenomena* of thinking are widely scattered . . .
> Remember that our language might possess a variety of different words: one for 'thinking out loud'; one for thinking as one talks to oneself in the imagination; one for a pause during which something or other floats before the mind, after which, however, we are able to give a confident answer.
> One word for a thought expressed in a sentence; one for the lightning thought which I may later 'clothe in words'; one for wordless thinking as one works. (Z 110, 122)

The picture of thought as an inner process goes naturally with the nagging question, "But how was I able to do that (intelligent, complex) thing, unless

The Inner and the Outer 75

I had *thought* what to do?" If necessary, we treat the thought we had allegedly had as a "lightning thought", in which case, as hinted earlier, there is a worrying indeterminacy as to *how much* of my performance must result from a single thought, as well as a danger that the relation between thought and performance be taken as simply causal. These problems need not beset us in the case of "the lightning thought which I may later 'cloth in words', for the temptation now is to speak of the subsequent performance as being a *report* of the earlier thought, not merely something to be explained by reference to the earlier thought. Here, though, there appears to be the question, "What grounds are there, what evidence is there, for making that report?" Memory often yields nothing much that would justify saying "At that moment I thought such-and-such", beyond something or other's having "floated before the mind".

If there is a possible question about what evidence you have for saying that you thought that p, there is likewise a possible question about what evidence you have for saying that you were about to do X (e.g. say certain things). If a thought-as-inner-process is what renders a certain subsequent act or performance intelligent, there will be cases where that subsequent act or performance is prevented from happening; and it will be natural to explain your ability to say what it was you had been going to do by alleging that you know what results the thought-as-inner-process *would* have had (if not prevented). But (i) do you even recall such a thought as having occurred?, and (ii) how can you tell what *would* have followed on it? The former question must often, if not usually, be answered "No"—hence the desire to speak of the "lightning thought". The latter question seems to require some appeal to inductive evidence, but such evidence will clearly be lacking in the case of novel and unprecedented actions—though "I was just about to call the police" may be as certain a statement as any.[15] Moreover such inductive evidence should be good for anyone to use, so long as I tell them about it (i.e. tell them of what I remember having happened within me)—cf. Z 41. Maybe indeed they could use it better than I can use it myself. But of course it isn't like that: "I was about to call the police" is not susceptible of this kind of uncertainty. If uncertainty surrounds such a statement, it relates typically to the sincerity or genuineness of the speaker, and the difference between issues of truth and issues of truthfulness (sincerity, etc.) is one that Wittgenstein rightly makes much of.[16]

Wittgenstein in several places considers the phenomenon of *having been about to*. A first-person statement, "I was about to . . ." may sometimes be like a third-person statement, "He/she/it was about to . . .", in being justified (if it is) by reference to evidence. For example: "I was about to have a seizure, the doctor told me—but they gave me an injection just in time." As we have seen, it is different with statements like, "I was about to say . . ." The ability to come out with such statements Wittgenstein sees as akin to, or related to, the ability to continue doing something after an interruption.

76   *The Inner and the Outer*

"Interrupt a man in quite unpremeditated and fluent talk. Then ask him what he was going to say; and in many cases he will be able to continue the sentence he had begun." (Z 38) We might wonder how it is possible for a person to have this ability: *how does he do it*? And now the temptation arises to say: "For that, what he was going to say must already have swum into view before his mind." But it is surely the other way around: "Is not that phenomenon [of the man's being able to continue] perhaps the ground of our saying that the continuation had swum into his mental view?"

In doing any task of more than momentary duration you might pause (e.g. for breath) or dawdle, and then continue; and this is really just doing *one thing*, if falteringly. "How is one able to continue doing X?" is then much the same question as "How is one able to do X?" The best answer to the latter is very often: "You were trained to do X", to which may be added, "and you do not need to calculate or consider what you do". A similar answer will be available for "How is one able to continue doing X?" An interruption in doing X might last a long, not a short, time, and that would make for a different sort of phenomenon, in one sense—but for the purposes of our enquiry it makes for a similar or related phenomenon.

The picture to be resisted is that of the *thought* that must have occurred, from which the subsequent actions flowed or were to have flowed, and by the recollection of which a person can later say what they had been about to do. Wittgenstein reminds us of cases were the key event, from which later actions "flow", is something quite public, not a thought at all.

> Think of putting your hand up in school. Need you have rehearsed the answer silently to yourself, in order to have the right to put your hand up? And *what* must have gone on inside you?—Nothing need have. But it is important that you usually know an answer when you put your hand up; and that is the criterion for one's *understanding* of putting one's hand up. (Z 136)

Putting the hand up is something a child can be trained to do. More specifically, a child learns a certain "game", in which a teacher asks a question, and you get the right to answer it by putting your hand up, a right which the teacher can allow you to exercise if s/he wishes, e.g. by saying your name—the overall point being to give the correct answer. Learning a game and playing it are manifestations of human intelligence, which is why Wittgenstein speaks of one's *understanding* of putting one's hand up: you wouldn't have understood, wouldn't have got it, if your habit was to put up your hand in the classroom situation and when given the floor say nothing, or just sing the national anthem. Putting your hand up is the first move in a sequence of moves, a sequence that may not be completed. The ability to say later what your answer would have been is no more puzzling than your ability to actually give the answer when called upon by the teacher. Indeed, they are pretty clearly one and the same ability.

The Inner and the Outer   77

We see what the significance is of someone's putting his hand up, not by considering any processes going on at the same time (e.g. inside him), but by considering the sequence of moves, actual or possible, of which putting the hand up is the first. Analogous remarks apply to someone's subsequently giving an answer when asked to by the teacher, and also to someone's telling us what they were about to say, or would have said. Of course, statements of this latter kind are not always made in the context of a "game" like that of putting the hand up; but they are still manifestations of a complex ability, learnt as part of learning the language, and involving sequences of moves or actions. You learn to produce sentences, that is, to produce the kind of sequence of actions that is embodied in the utterance of a string of words; such a sequence can be interrupted, or prevented before it gets going; you also learn another kind of sequence that is resorted to in such a case, embodied in the continuation/production of an interrupted/prevented sequence with such words as, "I was going to say . . .".[17]

The picture of the thought from which subsequent actions flow is of course akin to, if not often the same as, the picture of the decision or intention from which subsequent actions flow. And "I was about to . . ." may well count as a "confession of intention" (Z 39). Part of Wittgenstein's purpose in discussing "I was about to . . ." is to undermine the picture of intention as an inner process, not just because of the misleading connotations of "process" as referred to in PI 308, but because the grammar of "intend" is utterly different from that of such process-verbs as "swoon", "walk", or (in one sense of the word) "think". His remarks here are often characteristically negative, as:

> "I had the intention of . . ." does not express the memory of an experience. (Any more than "I was on the point of . . .")
> Intention is neither an emotion, a mood, nor yet a sensation or image. It is not a state of consciousness. It does not have a genuine duration. (Z 44, 45)

The "grammatical" differences relate, e.g. to notions of duration and possible intermittence:

> "I have the intention of going away tomorrow."—When have you that intention? The whole time; or intermittently?
> . . . Consider what it would really mean "to have an intention intermittently". It would mean: to have the intention, to abandon it, to resume it, and so on. (Z 46, 47)

Ryle and others have described the difference here as that between episode-concepts and disposition-concepts[18], and the idea that Wittgenstein regarded intention as a kind of disposition is not completely inaccurate—at any rate, insofar as the non-linguistic criteria for the truth of a third-person ascription

78 The Inner and the Outer

of intention will typically be (behavioural) *manifestations* of the intention, in roughly the way in which the criteria for the truth of a disposition-statement (e.g. "X is soluble in water") are manifestations of the disposition (e.g. X's dissolving in water). We will have more to say about this presently. But it is worth noting that this sort of "grammatical" difference between intention and certain other psychological concepts is not the only one Wittgenstein has in mind.

> In what circumstances does one say "This appliance is a brake, but it doesn't work"? That surely means: it does not fulfill its purpose. What is it for it to have this purpose? It might also be said: "It was the *intention* that this should work as a brake." Whose intention? Here intention as a state of mind entirely disappears from view.
>
> Might it not even be imagined that several people had carried out an intention without any one of them having it? In this way a government may have an intention that no *man* has. (*Z* 48)

This is the sort of passage which leads incautious readers to say, "So he thinks that intention is never a state of mind, but always something else." But calling intention a state of mind *may* be appropriate, say in connection with someone's forming the firm resolution to do such-and-such. The mistake comes in thinking that there is an essence to the concept of intention, an essence to be clearly found in certain instances regarded as central or paradigm: the essence of being a *psychological state*. For our picture of a psychological state is almost bound to derive from certain ("psychological") verbs, whose grammar will coincide with that of "intend" only up to a point—for example sensation-verbs (cf. *Z* 47); and in any case, we should be prepared to find that the concept of intention, like others, has a variety of strands, criss-crossing and overlapping, rather than a central necessary and sufficient strand or essence.[19]

But more than all this, examples such as that of the brake with a purpose, or the government with an intention[20], do serve to point to an important feature of the concept of intention, namely its connection with aims, goals, plans, blueprints, designs, and the like, all these being objective things. By the term "objective" I mean to point to such facts as: that different people can discuss and debate a plan or intention, giving reasons for and against it, in a context where there are shared ("objective") standards of what count as good or bad reasons. The purpose of such discussion, very often, is of course to *act*. And the relation between some actual course of action and the plan or intention that had been discussed is internal, and is bound up with the reasons that had been given for proposing, and also for adopting, the plan or intention—those reasons typically being the reasons why the action gets done. These issues were touched upon in Chapter 2, both that of the internal relation between intention and action, and that of reasons for action as central to the concept of intention (pp. 52–3).

The Inner and the Outer 79

In order to be able to say "I was about to . . ." you don't need to remember a mental event from which certain actions would have flowed. But of course there is such a thing as remembering that you formed some intention on some occasion. What would here constitute the forming of an intention? Wittgenstein frequently reminds us how helpful it is in such cases to start by considering the public, especially linguistic, version of the question: if I say, "I'm going to give him tea when he arrives", and later recall this, what makes it correct for me to say that this utterance expressed the formation of an intention? A quick answer is, "The usual function of the utterance". The internal relation between utterance and subsequent action holds in virtue of the unity of a language-game, in the way described in Chapter 2 (sec. 2). But as we saw there, there is a similar explanation of the internal relation between intending (expecting, etc.) and subsequent events, where this intending (expecting, etc.) is taken as consisting in such behaviour as putting out teacups, or walking up and down, or whatever. The behavioural manifestation of an intention or an expectation is internally related to subsequent events in virtue of the *description* we give of such a manifestation, that description being conceptually constrained by actual or possible first-person expressions of intention or expectation. Now remembering that you formed an intention may really be remembering some mental occurrence, either a bit of internal speech or something vaguer, such as certain images or feelings. In a sense this mental event gets to count as the formation of an intention by *fiat*—the *fiat* of the agent, who sets up the internal relation between the earlier event and subsequent (actual or possible) actions. He does this by, as it were, putting words into the mouth of his former self—or thoughts into the mind of his former self—in much the same sort of way that you put words into the mouth of your former self when you tell us what you were *about to* say on an earlier occasion. It would be a dead end to home in on the earlier psychic event—images, sensations, sentences heard with one's mind's ear—in the hope of finding something out about the nature of intention. And this sort of lesson, repeated again and again in connection with different concepts, is one of the main lessons we get from Wittgenstein's philosophy of psychology.

4. CONTEXT AND BEHAVIOUR

The key move is to locate a given phenomenon in a wider context, a wider set of circumstances. This context could be a game or language-game, as in the case of the "game" of putting one's hand up in class—but it could also be, very generally, some set of circumstances to be found in human life, against the backdrop of which an action, event or whatever, has a certain significance for us. The phenomenon, in such a case, is best not regarded as a *process*, in that sense of "process" that goes with the idea of having a nature ascertainable by careful inspection or observation of the process

80 *The Inner and the Outer*

itself. The "wider circumstances": this notion is a crucial one for the later Wittgenstein, and his talk of behaviour can only be understood with this notion in mind.

> "But you talk as if I weren't really expecting, hoping, *now*—as I thought I was. As if what were happening *now* had no deep significance."— What does it mean to say "What is happening now has significance" or "has deep significance"? What is a *deep* feeling? Could someone have a feeling of ardent love or hope for the space of one second—*no matter what* preceded or followed this second?—What is happening now has significance—in these surroundings. The surroundings give it its importance. And the word "hope" refers to a phenomenon in human life. (A smiling mouth smiles only in a human face.) (*PI* 583)

The kind of point he is making is not restricted to psychological concepts:

> A coronation is the picture of pomp and dignity. Cut one minute of this proceeding out of its surroundings: the crown is being placed on the head of the king in his coronation robes.—But in different surroundings gold is the cheapest of metals, its gleam is thought vulgar. There the fabric of the robe is cheap to produce. A crown is a parody of a respectable hat. And so on. (*PI* 584)

This latter example especially concerns our responses to phenomena, as conveyed by terms like "pomp", "dignity", "vulgar", "parody". It of course does *not* follow that Wittgenstein is recommending us to see psychological phenomena such as hope or love simply in terms of the (e.g. emotional) responses of spectators. Evidently the responses of the agents or participants matter too! But we can say something like this: where a complex phenomenon is important or significant for us, there it is natural for us to have (i.e. to have developed) a set of concepts, interconnected and interdependent, relating to that phenomenon, such that it is impossible to understand one concept in isolation from the others—and likewise impossible to appreciate one bit of the phenomenon in isolation from the other bits. The notion of *significance*, as invoked in *PI* 583, is a broad one. It can even encompass monetary value: "in different surroundings the institution of money doesn't exist either". (*PI* 584) A bank note, taken in isolation from the background of banks, customs of buying and selling, etc., is just a piece of paper.

We have already seen this line of thought at work, when in the last chapter[21] we found Wittgenstein saying of the proposition "I am going to take two powders now" that "the antecedents of this proposition were different", i.e. different from those of the proposition "In half-an-hour I shall be sick"; where by *antecedents* "I mean the thoughts, actions and so on which led up to it." (*PI* 631) The surroundings of an utterance are its antecedents, but also what comes later, and also what goes on around and about it—the bigger picture, generally speaking.

The Inner and the Outer 81

This is the context in which we find him saying, famously: "An 'inner process' stands in need of outward criteria." (*PI* 580) Such criteria are among the *surroundings* of whatever we decide to call an inner process.

Wittgenstein's use of the term "criteria" has come in for a lot of discussion. What exactly does he mean by it? In the *Blue Book*, the term is introduced in opposition to the term "symptoms", and Wittgenstein asks us to imagine that "X has the bacillus so-and-so[22] in his blood" counts as stating "the criterion, or what we may call the defining criterion of angina", while "X has an inflamed throat" states a symptom of angina.

> I call "symptom" a phenomenon of which experience has taught us that it coincided, in some way or other, with the phenomenon which is our defining criterion. Then to say "A man has angina if this bacillus is found in him" is a tautology or it is a loose way of stating the definition of "angina". But to say, "A man has angina whenever he has an inflamed throat" is to make a hypothesis. (*BB* 25)

He goes on to remark that it may not be very clear-cut what are to count as symptoms and what as criteria, this very often being a matter for decision or stipulation; such vagueness or indeterminacy in language "need not be a deplorable lack of clarity", having to do with the *practical* nature of language-use. If we don't need precise boundaries for some concept, it is fine for that concept to lack them. This is a familiar Wittgensteinian theme.

In so far as some statement does count as giving criteria, and not symptoms, it is akin to a definition, or a "loose definition". The word "loose" here is not just pointing to the sort of vagueness or indeterminacy we have just mentioned. For there is another aspect of the practical nature of language-use which is embodied in the notion of criteria, namely defeasibility. In learning the concept of fear you must come to see certain sorts of behaviour, etc. as giving grounds for saying "X is afraid", such as running away, or screaming, or shaking—especially where these are embedded in a situation in which something can be taken as threatening X, such as a ferocious animal, or a fire. (Such a situation constitutes the "surroundings" of the behaviour.) It is a necessary truth that X's running away and screaming count as good grounds for saying "X is afraid", given that X is a human being. But "good grounds" doesn't mean "sufficient conditions", and the necessity just referred to doesn't yield an entailment. For of course X could be pretending, or acting in a play, or doing it for a bet, or indeed manifesting some other psychological state, such as hysterical effervescence (in which case, the running probably isn't running *away*). Certain things will then count as defeating the original statement, "X is afraid", such things as X's collapsing in a fit of giggles and our finding out that he'd just been let out of school for the summer holidays.

It is tempting to think that we must in principle be able to list the set of possible defeating conditions, as also the set of possible behaviours and

82   *The Inner and the Outer*

situations, in such a way as to arrive at a proper definition of "afraid"—a proper definition being one that gives necessary and sufficient conditions. But this temptation has its source in a simplistic picture of language and its purpose. A good antidote to that picture is the reflection that there is often very good practical sense in taking as one's default position that circumstances are normal, where what constitutes normality is of course dependent on the context; and that there will thus be full warrant in saying or doing something without one's having *first* ruled out those possible defeating circumstances which would render the situation abnormal—for you need only cross bridges when you come to them. These remarks apply to human practices, like buying and selling: buying a pair of socks would become unfeasible if you *first* had to establish that the socks were the property of the vendor, that your own coins were not counterfeit, that the vendor really knew what "buy" means, and so on. Language gets used as an intrinsic part of such practices, and much use of language itself constitutes a practice in the relevant sense.[23]

Screaming and running away are a paradigm expression of fear, and count among the criteria for the ascription of "afraid" to someone. But they are defeasible criteria. The question now arises why we should have a concept, *fear*, with this sort of shape: how does it come about that this concept is associated with criteria and not, say, with necessary and sufficient conditions? The answer will surely not resemble the answer we might give to the analogous question regarding such institutional concepts as *buy, sell, supply, owe*, etc., which likewise partake of open-ended defeasibility. If the use of "fear" and related terms is to be regarded as a practice, what features of that practice explain its being criteria-based?

Part of the answer has to do with the instinctive and pre-linguistic reactions to and interactions with other human beings that are the soil in which many psychological expressions have their roots. Various complex phenomena involving behaviour belong to our natural history, our "form of life", e.g. the phenomenon of fearful behaviour in the face of threat. Many things count as threats to us, and many kinds of response count as fearful responses. And the phrase "count as" is akin to "are seen by us as": in normal individuals, the sights and sounds of another person being scared simply strike one a certain way, which is to say that one responds in an instinctive manner to those sights and sounds. We may be "infected" by fear ourselves, or respond protectively to the other, or . . . And it is on the back of our capacity for such responses that we acquire a mastery of the third-person use of concepts like *fear*. (A lack of such interpersonal responses, as in severe autism, is an obstacle to acquiring psychological concepts.) Thus "fear" cannot be analysed into components such that it is through recognition of these components that we ascribe the term, for our primitive responses do not work via recognition and inference, even if at some ("subconscious") level the component facts work on us through our senses. Behavioural criteria do not amount to a checklist.

The Inner and the Outer 83

It is certainly possible to be convinced by evidence that someone is in such-and-such a state of mind, that, for instance, he is not pretending. But 'evidence' here includes 'imponderable' [*unwägbare*] evidence . . .
Imponderable evidence includes subtleties of glance, of gesture, of tone.
I may recognize a genuine loving look, distinguish it from a pretended one (and here there can, of course, be a 'ponderable' confirmation of my judgment). But I may be quite incapable of describing the difference. And this not because the languages I know have no words for it. For why not introduce new words?—If I were a very talented painter I might conceivably represent the genuine and the simulated glance in pictures. (*PI* ii, p. 228)

The painted representations of the genuine and the simulated glances will be successful insofar as a normal human viewer will be struck a certain way, i.e. in the way that seeing those glances in real life would cause one to be struck.[24] Being able to be struck in this way comes *before* being able accurately to describe the various "subtleties of glance, of gesture, of tone", if indeed one ever acquires the latter capacity.

Thus behavioural criteria, and also those circumstances that defeat or undermine judgments invoking such criteria, often partake of the "imponderable" quality Wittgenstein is referring to. This is one of the things that makes it impossible to give a *list* of those criteria in a given case, unless one is permitted uninformative and circular descriptions of them—as, "the criteria of fear include avoidance-behaviour in connection with the feared object". (What is "avoidance"?—and which object is the "feared" one?—and what constitutes "connection"? These questions are resistant to hand-waving talk of causal chains.)

What sort of behavioural criteria are at issue when we turn to thought and action?

It would be nonsensical to talk of the criteria for just *acting*. Acting is not something you do, any more than is doing. Our question is, rather: by what criteria does someone count, e.g., as writing a letter, or walking? The notions we are discussing are those of voluntary action and of intentional action.[25] Let us begin with intentional action. The criteria for judging that Mary is writing a letter are both behavioural and linguistic, in the following sense: Mary must be doing certain things, such as holding a pen, making word-shapes with it on a piece of paper . . . none of which yet suffice to say she is writing a letter, this being what is vouchsafed by Mary's actual or possible answer to the question "What are you doing?" The central role of this linguistic criterion is most clearly recognised and elaborated on by Anscombe, rather than by Wittgenstein, but there is every reason to think that the master would follow his pupil in this matter. Of course, the answer (actual or possible) to "What are you doing?" has to be a sincere answer, which raises a further kind of question, what the criteria for pretence are in such cases. But now it might be asked, "How does Mary's say-so come to have this criterial role?"

84   *The Inner and the Outer*

To begin with, it is a noteworthy fact that what Mary would say she's doing will typically be the same as what we would say she's doing. And this is an example of the sort of empirical fact that underlies the possibility of a language-game, by enabling "agreement in judgements"[26]. It is an empirical fact that people can say what they're doing, and that others can say the same thing of them. But it is a criterion of Mary's writing a letter that Mary says she's writing a letter. (After all, all that she may ever end up *doing* is covering half a sheet of paper—for she may be prevented from finishing.) So the connection between what a person does and what she says she's doing is not purely contingent. Nevertheless, it is contingent that our accounts of what we are doing are sufficiently in step with our actions to enable those accounts to play the criterial role that they do play. The practice of giving an account of what one is doing depends for its continued existence on the empirical fact that people do not (very often) naturally and spontaneously say bizarre things about what they are up to (e.g. "I'm making soup", said by the letter-writer). And bizarreness is here largely determined by what observers can make sense of. The account given by the person herself and the account given by other people hold one another in check.

What a human being must learn is to be able to make a certain sort of statement involving the future that (unless something goes wrong) gets "fulfilled". And the relation of statement to subsequent deeds and outcomes may be regarded in the same light as the relation of any action which is part of a learnt procedure to later elements in that procedure. We have already encountered the example of the child who learns the "game" of putting the hand up and subsequently giving an answer. This game has been mastered when the child often enough *does* give what can be taken for an answer after having put up his hand; and the "game" of announcing or expressing your intentions has been mastered, roughly speaking, when you often enough do the thing whose description you gave in the earlier statement of intention. That description will typically involve the future, even if it is given in the context of a present tensed statement ("I am writing a letter")—which is why I here speak of a procedure with earlier and later parts. But there are of course answers to "What are you doing?" that relate purely to the present, as, "I am having a bath". Note, however, that the intelligibility of such statements is not unconnected with their surroundings, in the form of what led up to them: if you had been dragged from your desk, stripped, and thrown into the bath, for you to say "I am having a bath" would be at the very least to put a brave face on things.

The phrase "learnt procedure" is not of course meant to imply the sort of invariance to be found in a procedure like putting your socks on. When you follow up saying "I'll kill that man" by killing that man, this whole "procedure" may be something you've never done before. But there are many learnt procedures (games, tasks, etc.) which involve this sort of flexibility and consequent room for novelty. The child who puts up her hand and gives the answer "367" may never have had to do with that question or that answer

The Inner and the Outer   85

before; nevertheless, we can speak of a single game or activity here. The procedure at issue with intentional actions is to be described schematically: it is following up saying "I will φ" (or something equivalent) by later φing.

The point or purpose of a language-game in which people express their intentions, and where those expressions have a criterial role, is not hard to see—though perhaps one should say *purposes*, not *purpose*. One salient purpose was mentioned in the last chapter[27]: that of enabling others to predict what you will do. The difference between expressions of intention and straight predictions, like "I am going to be sick", as we saw, has to do with their surroundings, including the different kinds of reasons that are given in justification of the statements. A person does not justify an expression of intention by giving evidence for its truth, and a question like "How do you *know* you intend to go to Paris?" is typically absurd. Connected with this is the fact that in expressing your intention you are not reporting something found within you, an inner process of intending. When it comes to intention, the picture of the inner process is not just misleading, it is grossly so.

What about *voluntary* actions, movements, and so on? The category of the voluntary is wider than that of the intentional, though it includes it. Unsurprisingly, Wittgenstein subjects to extended criticism the idea of a *feeling* of voluntariness, or an inner act or process that explains or constitutes voluntariness. But he gives us positive remarks also; and these pursue (at least) three lines of thought, invoking three kinds of "mark" of voluntariness: (i) the absence of surprise when you do X; (ii) the circumstances or surroundings in which X is to be found; (iii) the possibility of doing X in response to a request or order, etc. These marks are not intended, either separately or together, to supply necessary and/or sufficient conditions, for reasons that should by now be familiar. One thing that is apparent from his discussion of voluntariness is that no first-person "expression of voluntariness" plays any analogous role to that played by first-person expressions of intention: with voluntary action (*qua* voluntary action) the first-person perspective does not play the central role that it plays with regard to intentional action, though it plays *a* role, in connection with (i), since the first-personal linguistic expression of (lack of) surprise is presumably a criterion of (lack of) surprise. It is to this mark of the voluntary that I now turn.

> Examine the following description of a voluntary action: "I form the decision to pull the bell at 5 o'clock, and when it strikes 5, my arm makes this movement."—Is that the correct description, and not *this* one: ". . . and when it strikes 5, I raise my arm"?—One would like to supplement the first description: "and see! my arm goes up when it strikes 5." And this "and see!" is precisely what doesn't belong here. I do not say "See, my arm is going up!" when I raise it.
>
> So one might say: voluntary movement is marked by the absence of surprise. And now I do not mean you to ask "But *why* isn't one surprised here?" (*PI* 627, 628)

86   *The Inner and the Outer*

The example given here is of an intentional action, pulling a bell, but the point being made applies equally to such merely voluntary actions as fiddling with a pencil or uncrossing your legs.

It seems that the absence of surprise can't be a necessary condition of voluntariness in general: a bad darts player may be very surprised to succeed in hitting a bullseye, but since that was his aim could one really deny that his doing so was voluntary? And all sorts of things about what you do might be surprising in one way or another, e.g. if you find that in uncrossing your legs you produce a loud rasping noise. The latter sort of case can admittedly be ruled out by restricting surprise to *surprise at the fact that you did X*, where the question is whether what you did was voluntary under the description *doing X*. That still leaves the bad darts player. But note that Wittgenstein speaks of voluntary movement in the above passage, not of voluntary action (a much wider category), and as far as the darts player's moving his arm goes, there will presumably be no surprise. As for the question whether his hitting the bull's eye is voluntary, it seems in any case not to admit of a straightforward answer. For where the achievement of a goal X is doubtful, it is surely wrong or at least misleading for the agent, if asked "What are you doing?", to reply "I am bringing about X" (e.g. "I am hitting that bullseye" said by the bad darts player)[28]; which makes it difficult to say without qualification that the person brought about X intentionally, or indeed voluntarily, when he succeeded in his aim. Perhaps any verdict either way would be stipulative, especially by the lights of ordinary usage.

Now I said that the darts player's moving his arm would come as no surprise; but if you tried to move a limb after its having been paralysed for a bit, you might well be surprised when you succeed, despite this being a voluntary movement. So even as restricted to bodily movements, the absence of surprise cannot be regarded as a necessary condition of voluntariness. But Wittgenstein is not in the business of supplying necessary or sufficient conditions. That the absence of surprise is not *sufficient* for a movement to be voluntary is seen from such cases as that of the person who has for a long time suffered from a facial tic, which therefore comes as no surprise when it comes.

When someone shows no surprise at some occurrence, this will often be because (to that person) an occurrence of that sort is unsurprising, and there will be features of the occurrence which make it so, and which could be mentioned by the person in explanation of his insouciance. As, "The boiler always makes that noise", or "He did *say* he would borrow the car". It is not like that when you show no surprise at your arm's going up, and this I take it is why Wittgenstein writes: "And now I do not mean you to ask 'But *why* isn't one surprised here?'" You would not, e.g. say "My arm always does that in this situation", nor yet "I always do that in this situation". Your lack of surprise is primarily a feature of *how you behave*, and in fact is just one of the features of your behaviour which we associate with

The Inner and the Outer   87

the idea of voluntariness. Wittgenstein refers to various such features, for example when he writes: "There is a peculiar combined play of movements, words, facial expressions etc., as of expressions of reluctance, or of readiness, which characterize the voluntary movements of the normal human being." (*RPP* vol. I, 841)

Complementary features characterize involuntary movements. And there are also features of (in)voluntary movements which, though connected with behaviour, are not straightforwardly "behavioural": "An involuntary movement is, *for example*, one that one can't prevent; or one that one doesn't know of; or one that happens when one purposely relaxes one's muscles in order not to influence the movement." (*RPP* vol. I, 761)

If we are trying to say what (in)voluntariness is, we will in the end have simply to mention such variegated features as these. (Note Wittgenstein's italicized *"for example"* in the last quotation.) And the term "features" here includes types of action, e.g. eating or stamping your feet:

> How do I know whether the child eats, drinks, walks, etc. voluntarily or involuntarily? Do I ask the child what it feels? No; eating, as anyone does eat, *is* voluntary . . .
> A child stamps its feet with rage: isn't that voluntary? And do I know anything about its sensations of movement, when it is doing this? *Stamping with rage is voluntary.* Coming when one is called, in the normal surroundings, is voluntary. Involuntary walking, going for a walk, eating, speaking, singing, would be walking, eating, speaking, etc. in an abnormal surrounding. E.g. when one is *unconscious*: if for the rest one is behaving like someone in narcosis; or when the movement goes on and one doesn't know anything about it as soon as one shuts one's eyes; or if one can't adjust the movement however much one wants to; etc. (*RPP* vol. I, 763, 902)

The method of elucidating concepts by means of an open-ended list of examples may remind us of Wittgenstein's remarks on "family resemblance concepts" (*PI* 66–7). In connection with those things we call games he says that "if you look at them you will not see something that is common to *all*, but similarities, relationships, and a whole series of them at that". Is this his message when it comes to the things we call (in)voluntary? The answer, I think, must be that he might well have thought that *voluntary* and *involuntary* are family resemblance concepts, but that he could just as well have been saying, "These various features we *know* to be criteria of (in)voluntariness, and if you want to look for something common to all of them, or just to many of them, feel free to do so; but even if you succeed, this may bring no more philosophical enlightenment than was already vouchsafed us by having noted those various features".

The point that we *know* that, e.g. stamping with rage is voluntary is of course useful in resisting the idea that voluntariness must consist in an inner

88 *The Inner and the Outer*

feeling or process, knowable only to the agent himself. Wittgenstein asks, "If someone were to tell us that with *him* eating was involuntary—what evidence would make one believe this?" (*RPP* vol. I, 764); a good example of his leaving the thinking to the reader[29], for he is not ruling out that *something* might induce us to believe such a person, but is evidently inviting us to see (in attempting to answer his question) that whatever it would be would be extremely out of the ordinary, extremely abnormal.

The quotation from *RPP* vol. I, 902 mentions normal and abnormal surroundings, and we here meet with the second of the three marks of (in)voluntariness (see p. 85, above). I have already discussed the general importance of the notion of surroundings or background circumstances. A question arises whether there is a sort of tension between this mark of (in)voluntariness and the third mark, relating to the (im)possibility of doing X in response to a request or order, etc. For this third mark could be a mark of *particular* (in)voluntary acts only in a potential way: thus a ground for saying that my fiddling with a pencil was voluntary will be that it *could* have been done in response to the order "Fiddle with that pencil". But where normal surroundings already dictate that such-and-such behaviour just *is* voluntary, can we additionally cite the mere possibility of its having been done in response to an order? What would adding this condition achieve? Something like this appears to be what is in Wittgenstein's mind when he asks, "Are, e.g., my normal movements in walking 'voluntary' in a *non-potential* sense?" (*RPP* vol. I, 901)

In fact, however, we should regard the feature *can be done in response to an order* as characterizing a kind of action, or class of actions, not particular actions. (It is *can be*, not *could have been*.) Wittgenstein is not as in love with counterfactual analyses as are some modern philosophers; his use of "can" is closely tied to "do" and "does":

> What, then, are the tokens of involuntary movement? They don't happen in obedience to orders, like voluntary actions. There is "Come here!" "Go over there!" "Make this movement with your arm," but not "Have your heart beat faster." (*RPP* vol. I, 840)

What is the *interest* of this mark of voluntariness? Part of the interest is in the connection that exists between the voluntary and the intentional. (One who obeys an order does so intentionally.)

> Voluntariness hangs together with intentionalness. And therefore with decision as well. One does not decide on an attack of angina and then have it.
>
> One brings on [*ruft hervor*] a sneeze in oneself or a fit of coughing, but not a voluntary movement.[30] And the will does not bring on sneezing, nor yet walking. (*RPP* vol. I, 805, 806)

The Inner and the Outer   89

"Bringing on" means something like "causing" or "producing". If you decide to do X and do it, you typically do not "bring it on"—you just do it. For if you bring something on, you typically do so *by* doing something else: e.g. you tickle your nose with a feather and in this way bring on some sneezing.[31] A philosopher might try to answer "How did you walk?" by saying "I decided to walk", or "I willed my legs to move", thus allegedly citing a cause—an event of deciding, or of willing. But as we saw in the last chapter, a concept like *decide* (*intend*, *will*, etc.) is governed by the existence of internal relations between decisions (etc.) and actions, in a way that is incompatible with causality of the sort that connects nose-tickling and sneezing. Moreover, if you do X by doing Y, using Y as a means to X, then you do Y intentionally and "do Y" will be the name of an action, concerning which the question "How did you do it?" will be appropriate (given that it had to be appropriate in connection with doing X). But "How did you will your legs to move?" had better not be answered by "I willed . . ."—that way lies an infinite regress. " 'Willing' is not the name of an action; and so not the name of any voluntary action either." (*PI* 613) "I just did will them to move", on the other hand, invites two responses: (i) "Then couldn't it be that you *just* moved them?", and (ii) "How do you know? Was there an experience of willing?" The reply to the latter will very often have to be, "No—I felt nothing of the sort".[32]

I will end this section by briefly mentioning a question addressed by Wittgenstein that is of considerable interest, namely: which *mental* phenomena are subject to the will? The following passage brings out the sorts of issues at stake:

> An aspect is subject to the will. If something appears blue to me, I cannot see it red, and it makes no sense to say "See it red"; whereas it does make sense to say "See it as . . ." [e.g. "See *this* as foreground, and *that* as background."] And that the aspect is voluntary (at least to a certain extent) seems to be essential to it, as it is essential to imaging that *it* is voluntary . . . For this hangs together with the aspect's not 'teaching us something about the external world'. One may teach the words "red" and "blue" by saying "This is red and not blue"; but one can't teach someone the meaning of "figure" and "ground" by pointing to an ambiguous figure. (*RPP* vol. I, 899)

The passage is also useful in showing that Wittgenstein is certainly *not* a behaviourist in the sense of someone whose psychology admits reference only to publicly observable behaviour or activity. We might well want to call *seeing the figure as a face* an "inner process"; it is certainly not constituted by observable behaviour, as, e.g. being angry (often) is. For all that, an inner process stands in need of outer criteria. The sort of outer criteria relevant to seeing-as (or aspect-perception) are discussed by Wittgenstein in the *Philosophical Investigations*, II, xi.

90   *The Inner and the Outer*

5.   *IN THE BEGINNING WAS THE DEED*

That the concepts of the intentional and the voluntary should be tied up with behaviour is not so surprising, given that the two terms are paradigmatically predicated of action, and also that, e.g., an intention is typically an intention *to φ*. With thought and judgement things look different. Before we can proceed with this question, however, we need to distinguish the two concepts of *thought* that are embodied in two such statements as "Alison thinks that Paris is south of Moscow" and "Alison is thinking out a solution to that maths puzzle". The latter use of "thinks" describes some episode or ongoing process, while the former use describes a settled state or disposition—roughly—and is synonymous with "believes". We can mark this distinction with the two German verbs, *glauben* (to believe) and *nachdenken* (to think of/about/etc.).

Though the particular example of thinking out a solution may be called episodic, this doesn't go for all uses of "think" (*nachdenken*), as our earlier discussion of the "lightning thought" brought out. And looking for a common feature in all thinking is something Wittgenstein would anyway discourage: "'Thinking', a widely ramified concept. A concept that comprises many manifestations of life." (Z 110) For Wittgenstein, the ways in which thinking is connected with behaviour are many and varied. If we are to say anything general here on Wittgenstein's behalf, perhaps it will simply be along these lines: the concept of thinking, like that of pain or of hope, is learnt by learning how to use certain clusters of words ("think", "doubt", etc.), in whatever language, where such word use is tied up with phenomena of human life, both instinctive and sophisticated, and where this word use has a *point* for us, or rather many points and purposes—such purposes as are not capturable, e.g. by some aetiolated notion of "communication". For a child to learn how to use "think", both in the first-person and in the second- or third-persons, he must be introduced to the word's use in various situations, and must come to show his competence with the word in detectable ways, ways that will for instance differentiate him from a parrot. These "detectable ways" do in fact involve non-linguistic behaviour in a wide sense of that term, but a more salient notion than behaviour here is that of the "wider circumstances".

Maybe these remarks will be accused of being *too* general. But if we are to achieve more detail, more substance, we will have to descend to those particular kinds of thinking of whose existence Wittgenstein reminds us when he writes: "Remember that our language might possess a variety of different words: one for 'thinking out loud'; one for thinking as one talks to oneself in the imagination; one for a pause during which something or other floats before the mind, after which, however, we are able to give a confident answer . . . [etc.]" (Z 122) If our purpose is to end up with a theory the linchpin of which is a statement of the form "Thinking is X", we will fail to produce anything both true and enlightening, and the desire to propound

The Inner and the Outer   91

such a theory merely shows that craving for generality which Wittgenstein saw at the bottom of much philosophizing. A true and enlightening account does just turn out to be complex and messy. Rather than saying more on this topic than I have already said, let me turn to thinking in the sense of believing (*glauben*), for what Wittgenstein has to say about the connection between thought and action, in *this* sense of "thought", merits our attention.

In *On Certainty* there occurs the following quotation from Goethe: ". . . and write with confidence 'In the beginning was the deed'". ("*Im Anfang war die Tat.*") One of the objects of critique in this work[33] is the idea that the foundations of our system of beliefs must be propositions that serve to justify those beliefs. Wittgenstein argues that justification is something that takes place *within* a practice, the criteria for what counts as good or adequate justification being determined by the nature and point of the practice. One who learns that practice (learns how to make moves within the practice) does not first have to learn how the practice is itself justified, and indeed for many practices it makes no sense to ask what "justifies" them.[34]

What is meant by "practice" here? (The term is mine, not Wittgenstein's; in this context, he tends to use the simile of a "game".) A practice may be, for example, scientific enquiry, or historical discourse, or planning the day's activities, or cooking—or we might stand back in order to subsume a lot of experimental and other activities under the title of a practice, namely "natural science". You learn a practice or technique by doing: as Aristotle said, you learn to play the flute *by* playing the flute. Where the practice is one involving language use, one who is in the process of learning it will already be in the business of asserting things, and *ipso facto* believing them, such as "Here's an egg" and "If I turn this tap, the pan will fill with water". Of course, if the person is learning, he will in the first instance typically just *repeat* what he hears; and this is the primitive form of acquiring beliefs.

When a child learns how to boil an egg, she does not first of all need to be persuaded that the egg really exists (is not a figment, etc.). Indeed the proposition "That apparent egg might not be real" can only be understood by one already able to use and apply the word "egg", where such application involves interacting with eggs in various ways—fetching them, identifying them, boiling them. These interactions with eggs are *actions*—including linguistic actions—and what a child must be able to do, in order to learn, is act and interact in various ways, ways which (of course) count as manifesting intelligence. What philosophers or psychologists are liable to classify as "basic beliefs about the world" are in fact basic capacities, especially capacities to *do* certain things; and these capacities not only need not, but cannot, rely on any "basic beliefs". In the beginning is the deed.

Wittgenstein writes: "I want to regard man here as an animal; as a primitive being to which one grants instinct but not ratiocination . . . Language did not emerge from some kind of ratiocination." (*OC* 475) The word here translated as "ratiocination", interestingly, is the French *Raisonnement*,

92 The Inner and the Outer

and a good example of the picture of *Raisonnement* which Wittgenstein is attacking can be found in the work of the Swiss-French psychologist Jean Piaget. In *The Construction of Reality in the Child*[35] Piaget writes:

> Hence it is natural that at this [early] developmental level the external world does not seem formed by permanent objects, that neither space nor time is yet organised in groups and objective series, and that causality is not spatialised or located in things. In other words, at first the universe consists in mobile and plastic perceptual images centred about personal activity. But it is self-evident that to the extent that this activity is undifferentiated from the things it constantly assimilates to itself it remains unaware of its own subjectivity; the external world therefore begins by being confused with the sensations of a self unaware of itself, before the two factors become detached from one another and are organised correlatively.
>
> On the other hand, in proportion as the schemata are multiplied and differentiated by their reciprocal assimilations as well as their progressive accommodation to the diversities of reality, the accommodation is dissociated from assimilation little by little . . . From this time on, the universe is built up into an aggregate of permanent objects connected by causal relations that are independent of the subject and are placed in objective space and time . . . The self thus becomes aware of itself, at least in its practical action, and discovers itself as a cause among other causes and as an object subject to the same laws as other objects.

For Piaget, in the mind of a young infant "the external world . . . begins by being confused with the sensations of a self unaware of itself", a confusion later transcended when the child builds up (a representation of) the universe as "an aggregate of permanent objects". The earlier belief or viewpoint is posited as explaining various things the younger infant cannot yet *do*, such as locate a hidden object. But how could a young infant so much as think the thought, "These objects are not permanent, they are not really distinct from my own (or: from these) sensations"? The same goes for the older child: what does it mean to say that he views the objects around him as permanent? What is *true* is that he, e.g. goes to fetch a toy from behind a screen, and similar things, as a dog goes to dig up a bone or a cat goes back to its accustomed basket. Does the developing kitten "discover itself as an object subject to the same laws as other objects"? Or does it, as it grows older, just go in for more, and more sophisticated, feline activities?

We could, if we like, say that the thought "The objects around me are permanent" is *embodied* in such actions as locating hidden objects. This is one way of employing the concept *thought*. Confusion only arises when we slide from this way of talking to another way of talking, legitimate in its own domain, in which a person's thoughts can justify what they do or say, can serve as reasons or grounds. Basic capacities for action are ungrounded,

The Inner and the Outer   93

and since that includes basic capacities for assertion—the capacity to say "Here's an egg" in the right situation, for example—many "basic beliefs" are in the same way ungrounded. In this respect the concept of belief is unlike that of knowledge. (cf. *OC* 550) The attempt to cast "basic beliefs" as forms of knowledge, i.e. as justified or justifiable in the sort of way that might withstand skepticism, is misguided—as comes out in this characteristically pregnant dialogue:

> "I know that this is a hand."—And what is a hand?—"Well, *this*, for example." (*OC* 268)

I have described "basic beliefs" as being embodied in such assertions as "Here's an egg". And "embodied in" is more appropriate than "expressed by" in the case of the child who is learning language, for it is not as if the child finds she has been given just the right form of words to express her already-formed belief: what could make those sounds coming from Mummy's lips just the right ones for that job? No, at this stage, as I have said, the phenomenon is much more akin to (if not often a case of) repetition or imitation, of what Mummy says and does.

Assertion is a species of intentional action. And behaviourist philosophers may regard it as a manifestation of belief more or less on a par with other, non-linguistic, actions and behaviours, seeing beliefs as multitrack dispositions (i.e. dispositions with a variety of kinds of manifestation). Wittgenstein's account of the relation between assertion and belief cannot be viewed as behaviourist in this sense. If "In the beginning was the deed" alludes to non- or pre-linguistic acts, this is because Wittgenstein is especially concerned with the ungroundedness of language-use and of language-games—their lacking the need for justification, in the form of beliefs or knowledge had by language-learners or language-users generally. You don't need any such justificatory beliefs; rather you need to be able to do various things, and to learn to do various things. *Among* the things you learn to do, of course, is to assert that so-and-so. Now a particular belief is a belief with a particular content, and it is the sentence that appears in the assertion that paradigmatically determines that content; the content is not in this sense *determined* by any array of actual and/or possible non-linguistic behaviours. For the way to specify the content of a belief is by producing the sentence, and this specifying is not akin to indicating something by describing it, as one might describe a material object: in thus specifying a belief one gives, states, what is essential to it. (The belief that p is different from the belief that q.)[36]

This claim about belief-content is not reductive. We can and do speak of unasserted beliefs, of insincere or lying assertions, of animals' beliefs, and so on. The claim can be roughly summed up by saying that sincere assertion that p is the central criterion of belief that p. Donald Davidson has argued that an animal cannot have a belief at all, since there is no principled reason,

94   *The Inner and the Outer*

e.g. to claim that Fido thinks a cat is up that tree *rather than* thinking that a ginger cat is on the lowest branch of it. The distinctness of the two hypothetical beliefs could only be grounded in two distinct linguistic contents, i.e. two distinct possible assertions, and Fido is incapable of linguistic assertion. I have already (47–8) discussed Wittgenstein's more liberal approach to animal psychology, an approach that makes subtler use of the fact mentioned, that the distinctness of two beliefs of the sort in question can only be grounded in two distinct linguistic contents. Crucial to this greater liberality is Wittgenstein's use of the notion of a criterion.

"But if the criterion of belief is sincere assertion, don't we have a vicious circle? For isn't a sincere assertion simply one that expresses the person's actual belief?"—When the child learning English says "Here's an egg", shall we call that a sincere assertion? The important thing, you might say, is that it is *not* play-acting, nor a joke, nor a slip of the tongue, nor . . . And learning to do something, by imitation, repetition and the like, necessarily involves starting with (attempts at) proper moves, rather than somehow deviant ones. Someone who had never hitherto learnt the rules of any game, and was learning how to play chess, could not *begin* by intentionally making what he took to be illegal moves. For what would give him the idea that they were illegal? (What would give him the idea "illegal"?) He could of course do something with the hope or aim of making his teacher (for some reason) annoyed, such as moving twice, or indeed tipping the board over; but then he wouldn't even be cooperating, participating, in pupil-teacher activity. In the same way, the child's first assertions are necessarily not lies, or bits of word-play, or hypocritical, or sarcastic. These are all in their different ways attempts to "seem what you are not", and in general the ability to seem to φ presupposes the ability to φ (where φ-ing is a sort of intentional action). A child doesn't even know what asserting *is* except in the sense of being capable of making assertions.

Among the requirements I just mentioned in connection with a child's utterance managing to count as expressing his or her belief was that the utterance not involve a slip of the tongue. A slip of the tongue is not a case of "seeming what you are not", so merits separate treatment from lying etc. Why and when would we say that a child's utterance was a slip of the tongue? We would appeal to the wider circumstances: such facts as that the child already and elsewhere showed competence with the word in question, that she took back what she'd said, laughed at it, and so on. In the absence of any such facts, the supposition that what she said might have been a slip of the tongue is no better than the corresponding supposition as regards Chamberlain's "This country is at war with Germany".

Of course, grown-ups can and often do make insincere or otherwise deviant assertions, which is why it is natural to characterize the criterion of belief as "sincere" assertion. But as with the child, the point is that the assertion *not* be deviant in some way, and its being non-deviant is necessarily the default position, as well as the conceptually prior one. I discussed this concept of the default position above (81–3), in connection with the defeasibility and open-endedness of psychological criteria. As was argued there, an important part of the rationale for our anchoring a concept by means of a default position—i.e. the position, or "supposition", that there be no defeating circumstances—is that to use a concept is always to be engaged in some form of human practice, and practices have (many and various) points and purposes for us, which very often require that we only cross bridges when we come to them. Buying a pair of socks would become unfeasible if you first had to establish that the socks were the property of the vendor, that your own coins were not counterfeit, that the vendor really knew what "buy" means, and so on.

These remarks indicate one way in which non-deviant assertion is explanatorily prior to deviant assertion, as it would not be did the two phenomena differ merely in whether the belief standing behind a given utterance were "appropriate" to it—whatever that could mean. But more than this, there is the general fact that a learner's first moves are deeds, lacking justification.[37] The assertoric moves of the practiced language-user are different in kind from those of the learner in so far as the practiced language-user is expected to be able to answer "Why do you say that?", "Do you really think so?", and similar questions—that is, she is expected to be able to "justify" her assertions, or at any rate some of them. (You do not normally have to be able to justify the assertion "My name is N", and you might well be unable to.) To justify an assertion that p *is* to justify your belief that p, and doing the former is not merely an indirect way of doing the latter. The adult's "Here's an egg" does not differ from the small child's "Here's an egg" in having an appropriate belief (a "psychological state") standing behind it, a belief whose credentials are independently open to question. And there is a clear sense in which the child's assertion is already all that it should be, given that it's made in the right sort of circumstances, etc. The differences between the two utterances have to do with the *further* possibilities connected with the adult's utterance, possibilities of giving justifications, etc.

Thus a sincere assertion, considered as the central criterion of belief, is not best explained as an assertion behind which stands a belief corresponding to it; it is, rather, to be thought of as an uncorrupt, or non-deviant, assertion. Hence no vicious circle threatens our account.

The picture of assertion as a human practice with a point, or rather many points, is I think what lies behind a remark of Wittgenstein's in *On Certainty* that might seem otherwise puzzling. Wittgenstein is discussing the statement "I can't be making a mistake", a statement that he is trying to show can be (as it were) within its rights, despite the conceivability both of philosophical-sceptical scenarios and of the sorts of radical change of view which we actually know of, from experience or history.[38] An example might be "I can't be making a mistake; I was with him today" (*OC* 635)—perhaps

96　*The Inner and the Outer*

having just said that Smith had grown a beard, and having received incredulous stares. Wittgenstein writes at one point in his discussion:

> Admittedly one can imagine a case—and cases do exist—where after the "awakening" one never has any more doubt which was imagination and which was reality. But such a case, or its possibility, doesn't discredit the proposition "I can't be wrong."
>
> For otherwise, wouldn't all assertion be discredited in this way? (OC 643, 644)

In order for the human practice of assertion, of making assertoric moves, to be a practical possibility, it is necessary that a speaker be able to assert something with as much confidence as is possible within the language-game, despite not being in a position to rule out sceptical scenarios. Indeed, one cannot in general rule out such scenarios, in the sense of *showing* them not to hold, and a requirement that one should do so (or be able to do so) before committing oneself to some proposition would thus be a futile requirement. The phrase "with as much confidence as is possible" does not relate to a subjective feeling so much as to a level or degree of public commitment, a commitment to what one has said that does *without* the addition of qualifications or caveats. Sticking out your neck is an essentially public act.

We can thus see what Wittgenstein means when a little earlier he writes:

> "I can't etc. [be making a mistake]" shows my assertion its place in the game.[39] But it relates essentially to *me*, not to the game in general.
>
> If I am wrong in my assertion that doesn't detract from the usefulness of the language-game. (OC 637)

"I can't be making a mistake" doesn't relate to the game in general, for of course it must be admitted of moves in this game that they *can* be mistaken, whatever the confidence with which they are made. And one's actually being mistaken on occasion doesn't detract from the usefulness of the game, any more than actual mistaken judgements by umpires and referees detract from the playability of tennis or soccer. (Things would of course be different if mistakes became a lot commoner than non-mistakes.) So "I can't be making a mistake" turns out to have a non-threatening and genuine rationale as itself a move in the game of assertion, somewhat akin to the stance of implacability shown by an umpire or referee.

But what if, having received the incredulous stares, you went off by yourself, muttering or just thinking, "Well . . . I mean . . . I just *can't* be mistaken! I was with Smith this morning. He definitely had a beard"? You do not here make any move in a language-game, on the face of it. Isn't the question now really about belief, not about assertion?—But now the question of being "within one's rights" looks a little peculiar: can we really ask "Were you within your rights to think that thought?" Philosophers might want to

The Inner and the Outer 97

talk about "epistemic virtue", but it does not look so clear how one would argue for the thought's having been epistemically virtuous, or on the other hand vicious, at any rate without some sort of (e.g. Cartesian) fiat. And a lot depends on what my imaginary thought-ascription amounts to. It might be that what we are calling a thought was something like a subjective feeling, a sort of "Dammit all! . . ." feeling, perhaps accompanied by a particular sort of frown and tilt of the head. Or it might be that the form of words "can't be mistaken" gets used in your own retrospective report—or expression—of what you had earlier thought[40], so that we are invited to regard the thought in the light of an assertion, "I can't be mistaken!", an assertion which had it been made could indeed have been absolutely within its rights (if Wittgenstein is correct).

The phenomenon of assertion can be seen as straddling our categories of Thought and Will, for it is both the paradigm expression of belief and a species of intentional action. Wittgenstein's explorations in *On Certainty* (and elsewhere) often bring together these two aspects of assertion, in a way that lends support to the general idea that a thinker is a doer, and a doer is a thinker.

But what sort of entity *is* a doer, or a thinker? It is to this question that we now turn.

NOTES

1. See 37, above.
2. Cf. Descartes' use of *prosequi*, discussed above, 18–19.
3. See, e.g. *PI* 611–619.
4. In the case of thinking, there is an additional argument, namely that embodied in Descartes's *cogito*, which can be succinctly rendered: "If you think that you think, then you do think—and so your thought (that you think) is true". Note, however, that this argument will not work in the form, "If you think that you think that p, then you do think that p". If "I think (or: am thinking)" were always short for "I think that p", for some p, then Descartes's claim that he cannot rationally doubt that he is thinking would be undermined: "If I doubt that I think that p, then for all that—since doubting is a kind of thinking—I must be thinking that p" is just false. But Descartes can claim that the unqualified "I think" may be short for "I think that something is the case", i.e. "For some p, I think that p"—in which case, his argument lives to fight another day.
5. As we saw in Ch. 1, Frege held that in grasping a Thought one has an idea (a private mental item), which idea somehow "aims at" the Thought in question. So Frege is among those who share the view being considered here, that the analysis of "N thinks that p" involves a transitive verb (e.g. "has") taking an inner item or process for its object.
6. See Russell 1917.
7. This is *not* to say that the only meaningful uses of indicative sentences are assertive, in the sense of "presenting as true". (Poetry, jokes, pretence . . .)
8. e.g. Joseph Butler, who wrote of the "loose and popular" and "strict and philosophical" meanings of the word "identity". See Butler 1849, 305.

98 The Inner and the Outer

9. Hacker 1990, 84.—Norman Malcolm, in "The Privacy of Experience", having argued that "there is no sense of the expression 'same pain' such that it is impossible for two people to have the same pain", concedes in a footnote that "this remark may not be literally true", and goes on to describe as a "secondary sense" of "same/different headache" the sense in which, e.g. two people will have different headaches—or, as Malcolm prefers, two instances or cases of headache. See Malcolm 1977, 121–2.

10. At *PI* ii, 222 Wittgenstein indicates that "One can feel pain in another's body" can be compared with "A rose has teeth", the latter being counted by him as "not absurd", given a certain proposed interpretation of the sentence—"because one has no notion in advance where to look for teeth in a rose", and hence no reason for ruling out such a proposed interpretation. There is a sense in which "One can feel pain in another's body" *awaits interpretation.*—Similar remarks presumably apply to "One can feel the pain another person is feeling in his knee/hand/etc.", which represents a version of "Another person can feel my pains".

11. It might be wondered whether we should really speak of *counting* different people's pains: should we say that there are two headaches just because two people both have a headache? Well, "How many headaches do we need to treat?" is certainly a question that could be asked, e.g. by a nurse with a given supply of paracetamol.

12. But see fn. 10, above.

13. The best course in fact would probably be to distinguish two propositions or would-be propositions corresponding to "Only I can have my pains", one of which is meaningful, the other of which—the would-be proposition—is not. Whether it was the proposition or the would-be proposition that was at issue would depend on how the person saying "Only I can have my pains" expatiated on the statement.

14. "Experience" is crossed out in the typescript.

15. This issue is essentially the same as the one mentioned in Ch. 1 concerning an alleged external relation between intention and action; see 20.

16. e.g. *PI*, pp. 222–3.

17. The account of this phrase which I have been sketching is derived especially from what Wittgenstein writes in *Zettel*. In those passages of the *Investigations* that discuss having been about to, we do not find the same use of such questions as "How does a child learn to use the expression 'I was just on the point of throwing then'?" (*Z* 42): we find less stress on the issue of what someone can do, who can say what they were about to do or say, and more stress on the language-game as something *not* to be explained "by means of our experiences". (*PI* 655) This can lead the reader of *PI* to come away thinking that Wittgenstein's main ideas here are almost entirely negative, directed above all at the dispelling of philosophical illusions. That of course is a central aim of these passages, and it is the one brought out in Hacker's discussion of them (Hacker 1996, 625–30). But even in *PI*, the language-game is not regarded as a brute phenomenon; we are encouraged to consider the purpose(s) or point(s) which these ways of talking have for us. (See *PI* 656, 659.)

18. The distinction will not explain all the "grammatical differences" in this area: intermittent intention and intermittent attention (to something) have different grammatical features, though *attention* is surely not episode as opposed to disposition.

19. Some philosophers have posited *trying* as the mental process essential to intentional or voluntary action; certainly, "try" looks more like a process-verb than "intend". (Compare "For several minutes he tried to open the can" and "For several minutes he intended to open the can".) Wittgenstein writes "When

I raise my arm I do not usually *try* to raise it". (*PI* 622) But devotees of trying have found a champion in Paul Grice, who invokes his theory of "implicature" to argue that "I tried to raise my arm" would be true though misleading, rather than false or senseless, as said by someone who has raised his arm in the normal way. (Grice 1989, Ch. 1–3) For two Wittgensteinian responses, see Hacker 1996, 568–75, and Schroeder 2006, 221–4.

20. One can supply instances of intentions which a government could have without any individual having them: an intention to go to war would be such an instance. For only nations, as represented by governments (in modern times), *can* be at war with one another; individuals cannot, however much they may contribute to a war effort. Aristotle's notion of "the thing wanted" (*ho orekton*), as governing a practical syllogism, is useful here. A government official may act in the light of a "thing wanted", where it is not he or she who wants that thing, but the government. See also Anscombe's discussion of the "ironical slave", in Anscombe 2005, 136–9.

21. p. 52.

22. His English is here unduly influenced by his German: the English word "angina" is not the name of any infection.

23. Anscombe illustrates the point being made here in her article "On Brute Facts". (Anscombe 1981c)

24. Not in "just the same way", of course: you know that it's only a picture. I here pass over the interesting and important question of the emotive power of representations.

25. The uses in ordinary language of "voluntary" and "intentional" are probably less clear-cut than the following discussion might suggest, and there is a sense in which I am employing these words in a restricted, possibly even semi-technical, way. (Thus, I am pretty firmly associating "intentional" with the giving of reasons.) But despite J. L. Austin's warnings on this topic, such uses of these terms are not mere stipulative uses, divorced from the very problems—problems arising out of our thought and talk—that give point to philosophical discussion. Wittgenstein's use of "(un)willkürlich" corresponds to (and is translated by) "(in)voluntarily" as that word is used in philosophy, and also for that matter in physiology, and hence is wider than the rather narrow use indicated by Austin when he writes that "[the] 'opposite', or rather 'opposites', of 'voluntarily' might be 'under constraint' of some sort, duress or obligation or influence: the opposite of 'involuntarily' might be 'deliberately' or 'on purpose' or the like". See Austin 1979, 191.

26. See *PI* 241–2.

27. See 54–5.

28. cf. Anscombe 1963, 40.

29. The possible reader, that is. The remarks posthumously published as *RPP* vol. I may not have been definitely intended for publication.

30. As always, what we are given here is not a universal generalization, for as Wittgenstein elsewhere says, you can on occasion bring on a voluntary action such as swimming, e.g. by jumping into the water. He actually says ". . . I bring about the act of willing by jumping into the water" (*PI* 613), but this remark is attended by the implicit rider, "If we are to talk in this way of *willing* things . . .". In the swimming example, the voluntariness of the swimming movements is clearly not down to your having jumped into the water: *this* sort of bringing on won't help us in understanding voluntariness.

31. What about the actor who can make himself weep during an affecting scene? Is he bringing on the weeping? If so, does he bring it on *by* doing something else? (Why say so?) Is such weeping voluntary or involuntary? Does the actor *decide* to weep? . . .

100 *The Inner and the Outer*

32. cf. p. 75, above.
33. "Work" is perhaps a little misleading: *On Certainty* is the title given by the editors to a collection of some of Wittgenstein's last writings, first-draft material existing in loose sheets and notebooks.
34. It does not follow from this that every practice, discourse, etc. is immune from criticism. After all, a practice, in the sense here meant, may be a sub-practice of some broader practice.
35. Piaget 1955.
36. These remarks are not undermined by the fact that third-personal belief-reports stand in a complex and flexible relation to the assertions made by those expressing their beliefs, arising from the use of (e.g. reflexive) pronouns, *de re* constructions, paraphrase, etc. You can't necessarily read off the original assertion from such a report as "Martha said that she earns twice what I do"; Martha may only have said "My salary is $100,000 a year". It is clearly this last sentence that canonically specifies Martha's belief, not the third person report.
37. This of course does not mean that these moves cannot be *correct* moves: "To use a word without a justification does not mean to use it without right". (PI 289)
38. Cf. OC 643: ". . . and cases do exist . . ."
39. Here we may take "shows" (*weist*) to mean "assigns to".
40. The topic of such retrospective reports/expressions was discussed in sec. 3 of this chapter.

4 The Subject
Grammar vs. Metaphysics

1. WHAT IS IT THAT THINKS OR WILLS?

In Chapter 1 I referred to "relational" accounts of thought and will, using the term especially for accounts that claim that such verbs as "think" and "intend" are logically transitive, as I put it. Not all these accounts posited a genuine subject for such verbs, since some of them regarded the Subject ("I") as a fiction; but even these accounts tended to commit themselves to relations holding between ideas (perceptions, volitions, etc.) and the objects, whatever these were, of thinking, willing, and so on.

Philosophical accounts which embrace the view that thinking and willing have a genuine subject fall into two main types: those which take the subject to be the Subject, and which privilege the first-person viewpoint, as expressed by "I think" etc.; and those which take the subject to be a human being (or other animal or embodied thing), and which consequently tend to see nothing special in the first-person viewpoint. There are also hybrid accounts, according to which the first-personal use of, e.g. "think" applies to a Subject, while third-personal uses of the verb, being linked to observable behaviour, apply to human beings or bodies.

If we ask of the later Wittgenstein whether he takes the subject of "think", "intend", etc. to be the Subject, or a human being, or both, or neither, what answer should we give?

This question brings to the fore the enormous difference between Wittgenstein and other philosophers as regards philosophical method. For many a philosopher will want to say that our topic here is a metaphysical one, in the sense that we want to know what kind of entity or entities—if any—think or will. Is it a mind? Or an animal? Or a brain? Or is it sometimes one thing, sometimes another? Or can thinking just "go on", without any Thinker? All these questions, for Wittgenstein, are most likely (though not absolutely certainly) signs that the philosopher is going about things in the wrong way, by searching for the entity or entities, or indeed lack thereof, the identification of which will shed the light we want shed on the nature of thought and will.

But, it will be objected, doesn't he himself tell us what sort of entity it is that might think? For doesn't he write: "We only say of a human being and what

102 *The Subject*

is like one that it thinks?" (*PI* 360) And since we must make allowances for Wittgenstein's peculiar habit of referring to "what we say"—as if we might not be wrong!—can't we in fact interpret this statement as meaning, "Only human beings and what are like them think"? The objector, having thus nailed Wittgenstein with a definite philosophical commitment, will probably disregard as whimsy what comes next: "We also say it of dolls and no doubt of spirits too."[1] This statement can indeed appear confusing, with its "also". Part of what is going on is that Wittgenstein is giving instances of entities that are "like human beings"—dolls and (no doubt/perhaps even) ghosts. But of course the sense in which we "say of" a doll that it thinks does not involve our *believing* that it thinks; the "we" here is surely not intended to refer only to children absolutely in the grip of fantasy. So what can we learn from the examples of dolls and ghosts?

In the course of making up a story or a game, we might say that a doll can think, when we would never do the same for a bit of fluff; and the reason is that it is natural for us to move from applying "think" to people to applying it, e.g. to a thing made of wool with what look like arms, legs, a head, etc. If saying of a doll that it thinks were simply attributing "thinks" (whose meaning we somehow grasp as a self-sufficient idea) to a doll—*attributing* being some basic act of the mind, say—then it would be just as natural or intelligible to say of a piece of fluff that it thinks, even if only in a game. Which it is not. "This bit of fluff is doing mental arithmetic" would most likely occur as an instance of that kind of surreal humour which involves producing actual nonsense. The use of "think" is anchored to the conceptually central case of human beings, and of course a child who learns the use of verbs like "think" and "intend" learns them primarily in application to fellow human beings. He will also learn, or come, to apply them to creatures whose behaviour (in a broad sense) strikes us as like human behaviour[2], such application involving those implications and commitments characteristic of ordinary assertion, e.g. the commitment to "actual belief". This commitment is made manifest in such things as saying "No!" to the dog whose demeanour shows its intention of jumping onto the dinner table. All this is in contrast to the use of words made in the course of a game or fantasy, for instance involving a doll. Perhaps a young child does not yet firmly distinguish these latter uses from what I have called ordinary assertion, but of course it is a part of linguistic training that one come to make that distinction. (Correlative with this is the fact that a young child may not yet firmly distinguish stories from histories, fantasy from reality: the phenomenon in question is a mix of the epistemological and the linguistic.)

Someone might ask, "And does the word 'think' mean *the same* or not when applied to these other creatures—dogs, sparrows, toads, and the rest?" The question presupposes, what is false, that "means the same" itself has a single, univocal use, and in particular that a word or expression means the same in two contexts if the thing (object, concept, mode, property . . .) picked out by it "in the world" is the same in both cases—e.g. *the property of thinking*.

The Subject 103

An extended use of a word is both like and unlike the initial use, and while we will generally say "It's the same *word*", there is no reason why we should tie ourselves to the assertion that it does (or doesn't) mean exactly the same in the different contexts of use. For a word is like a tool, e.g. a pen; shall we say that a pen is performing the same function, or a different one, when the person who has been writing words with it then uses it to cross out one of those words? "Different! For isn't writing different from crossing out?" That would be one way of answering the question, but so would, "The same! For all these actions comprise the writing of a message. When he crosses words out he hasn't *stopped* writing." And yet of course there is a sense in which writing words is prior to crossing them out, and the central and defining function of a pen is not to cross words out, but to write them. In an analogous way, the central and defining use of "think" is in application to human beings. To say of a horse that it is thinking involves, not some *hypothesis* in which one says of the horse "just what" one says of a person, but a (to some extent imaginative) extension of the concept of thinking beyond its central application. This concept is notably more anthropocentric than that of pain, though with the latter also, the further one gets from the central case of the human, the more dubious is its application.

This is all very well, but in the end isn't Wittgenstein in fact telling us that, at least in paradigm cases and using words literally and assertively, it is only human beings and what are like them that think? He is.—So he is rejecting the idea that it is the Subject that thinks?—True, if by "Subject" we mean something like the referent of "I". (More of this anon.)—So when someone says, "I am thinking", he is talking about a particular human being, and saying of it that it is thinking?—The answer to *this* depends on how we take the phrase "talk about", and no amount of philosophical alchemy can turn this linguistic question into a metaphysical one.

If Jane truly says, "I am thinking", then it follows that a certain human being, Jane, is thinking; and the answer to Jane's question, "What sort of thing is thinking if I am thinking?" is: "A human being". If these facts are enough for Jane to be talking about a human being when she says, "I am thinking", then to be sure, she is talking about a human being when she says that. But what she says is not equivalent to, "This human being is thinking"; not just because the same sentence, "I am thinking", could be uttered by an intelligent non-human, but also because demonstrative phrases of the form "This F" serve to pick out or identify things in ways that "I" does not. Assimilating "I" to demonstrative phrases or to other referring expressions, e.g. proper names, is liable to lead to certain philosophical dead ends.

An example of such assimilation can be found in Descartes's famous argument to the conclusion that he is an immaterial thinking thing. Descartes recognizes the non-equivalence of "I am thinking" and "This human being (or human body) is thinking", but since he assumes that "I" is like other singular terms in serving to pick out or refer to a particular entity, he infers that there is such an entity and that it is something *other than* a particular

104   *The Subject*

human being. His argument for the non-equivalence of "I am thinking" and "This human being is thinking" relies on the thought that "This human being" commits him to an existential claim which can be doubted, while "I" does not. And there is a kinship, of sorts, between this thought and what Wittgenstein is saying. The difference is that whereas Descartes, by assuming the referential function of "I", is led to say that its use involves an existential claim which *cannot* be doubted, Wittgenstein says rather that the use of "I", in "I am thinking", involves no existential claim at all[3]—even if the fact of such an utterance's being *true* entails an existential proposition. He also invokes a notion of possible error (in connection with the use e.g. of "This F") that is unlike Descartes's notion of error, as we shall see.

2.   "I" AS SUBJECT AND "I" AS OBJECT

In the *Blue Book* Wittgenstein writes:

> There are two different cases in the use of the word "I" (or "my") which I might call "the use as object" and "the use as subject". Examples of the first kind of use are these: "My arm is broken", "I have grown six inches" [etc.] . . . Examples of the second kind are: "*I* see so-and-so", "*I* hear so-and-so", "*I* try to lift my arm", "*I* think it will rain", "*I* have toothache". One can point to the difference between these two categories by saying: The cases of the first category involve the recognition of a particular person, and there is in these cases the possibility of an error, or as I should rather put it: The possibility of an error has been provided for . . . On the other hand, there is no question of recognizing a person when I say I have toothache. To ask "are you sure that it's *you* who have pains?" would be nonsensical. (*BB* 66–7)

Wittgenstein's notion of the use of "I" as subject is a descendant of the notion espoused by him in the *Tractatus*, of the metaphysical subject as a limit of the world, rather than something *in* the world (see *TLP* 5.63–5.64). Where the earlier Wittgenstein says, "There is no such thing as the subject that thinks or entertains ideas" (*TLP* 5.631), the Wittgenstein of the *Blue Book* argues that the function of "I" as subject is not to pick out or identify anything, a claim he attempts to clarify by a comparison with the use of "I" as object. The use of "I" as object is akin to the use of expressions, such as proper names, whose function is to identify or pick out objects—akin to it in providing for the possibility of error, and in particular the possibility of error through misidentification. "It is possible that, say in an accident, I should feel a pain in my arm, see a broken arm at my side, and think it is mine, when really it is my neighbour's." (67) If I say "I have a broken arm", I achieve truth as regards the predicate ("have a broken arm"), since someone does indeed have a broken arm, and—rather gruesomely—I can see this; but I misidentify

The Subject 105

the owner of the arm as *me*. The function of "I" in this sentence was to pick out or identify whoever had the broken arm, e.g. Jack, and it failed in that function: it got the wrong person[4]. And this sort of error is impossible with sentences like "I am thinking" or "I have toothache".

But why is it impossible, unless because of an infallible Cartesian capacity to identify myself (or my Self) *correctly*? Here is Wittgenstein:

> . . . it is as impossible that in making the statement "I have toothache" I should have mistaken another person for myself, as it is to moan with pain by mistake, having mistaken someone else for me. To say "I have pain" is no more a statement *about* a particular person than moaning is. (*BB* 67)

The use of "about" *here* is linked to the notion of identifying or recognizing someone, in the way in which you might identify or recognize your brother—by his appearance, voice, etc. You don't go *by* any features that you happen to have when you use "I" as subject. Going *by* certain features involves the possibility of error, where error (i.e. misidentification) is analogous to a bad or unsuccessful move in a game. To identify, to recognize, to pick out, are all human acts, acts which have a purpose or *telos* and which therefore may fail in their purpose[5], as one may fail to score in a pin game (*BB* 67): for your senses (or analogous faculties) may deceive you that the features to go by are indeed present[6]. By contrast, with the use of "I" as subject, the reason why error through misidentification is impossible is that "the move which we might be inclined to think of as an error, a 'bad move', is no move of the game at all."

The comparison of "I have a toothache" with a moan does not, of course, have a direct analogue for "I am thinking". Thinking does not have a "natural expression", of the sort that serves as conceptually criterial: furrowing your brows, scratching your head, and so on, are symptoms of thought, not criteria of it. This distinction was explained in Chapter 3 (pp. 81–3), and from the ensuing discussion it is possible to glean what Wittgenstein would most likely have said *was* the, or a, central criterion of present thinking (*nachdenken*), namely the linguistic avowal, "I am thinking". This fact is connected with the intentionality of thought, something which, as we saw in Chapter 2 (sec. 2), is explained via the internal relations (e.g. between thought and fact) created by language—not that this entails that only language-using creatures can be said to think. So in order to show that "I am thinking" involves no identification, recognition, or what have you, it seems that Wittgenstein would have to adduce facts, e.g. about its use, how it is learnt, etc., which do not boil down to ones concerning "natural expressions".

Of course it might be said that we have already mentioned the salient fact about the use of "I" as subject, namely that one does not go by any features one has, in the way one goes by features of something one is identifying. "Don't think, but look!" might be the appropriate injunction here: do you

106 *The Subject*

find yourself homing in on any features of yourself, or conception of yourself, when you say "I am thinking"? But in addition to this injunction, an injunction very easily ignored in philosophy, we can attempt a *reductio ad absurdum*: given some alleged features by which one identifies oneself when saying/thinking "I am thinking", we then aim to show how these features land us with the possibility of misidentification, or even of reference-failure (so that "I am F" is void, for lack of any referent of "I")—or with some other absurdity.

Wittgenstein's approach to this question has more the nature of the injunction, "Don't think, but look!", than of any attempted *reductio*. For the latter, we can turn to Anscombe's famous discussion, very much in the spirit of Wittgenstein, in the article "The First Person". Here Anscombe considers the assimilation of "I" to a demonstrative[7], and concludes that "*if* 'I' is a referring expression, then Descartes was right about what the referent was."[8] The reasoning behind this conclusion is as follows. In using a demonstrative phrase meaningfully, there must at least exist something for the phrase to "latch on to", even when the phrase involves misidentification or reference-failure, as is illustrated by Anscombe thus:

> Someone comes with a box and says "This is all that is left of poor Jones". The answer to "this what?" is "this parcel of ashes"; but unknown to the speaker the box is empty. What "this" has to have, if used correctly, is something that it *latches on to* (as I will put it): in this example it is the box. . . . The referent and what "this" latches on to may coincide, as when I say "this buzzing in my ears is dreadful", or, after listening to a speech, "That was splendid!" But they do not have to coincide, and the referent is the object of which the predicate is predicated where "this" or "that" is a subject. (Anscombe 1981a, 28)

If "I", in "I am thinking", involved identification in the manner of "this F", it would need to be immune from reference failure, and the only way to get such guaranteed reference would be by having a referent whose existence was indubitable. "The thinker of these thoughts" seems the only possible contender: here, *these thoughts* are what are latched on to, and the thinker of the thoughts is meant to be indubitable if the thoughts themselves are—unlike Jones's ashes and the box. How so? Because you cannot have thinking without a thinker. But what is a "thinker"? This term cannot be short for "A such-and-such [e.g. human being] that thinks"—for the sortal concept involved in that case would be *such-and-such* (e.g. *human being*), and there would be no indubitability as to existence, and hence no guaranteed reference. The thinker of these thoughts must, in fact, be none other than the Cartesian Ego, whose very essence is to think. But, as Anscombe says, Descartes's theory faces its own absurdities: "His position has, however, the intolerable difficulty of requiring an identification of the same referent in different 'I'-thoughts."[9] She here points towards the well-known problem that the existence of Descartes's Subject is only guaranteed for as long as "I am

The Subject 107

thinking" lasts; for different thoughts at different times there is no guarantee of the unity of the thinker.

Thus Anscombe. Her argument aims to undermine the assimilation of e.g. "I am thinking" with "This F is thinking", by showing up the problems surrounding any choice of "F". As I will be suggesting later on, the argument goes too far, in particular in claiming that one can doubt that one is a human being. But I think Anscombe is right to see "I" as functioning quite differently from "This F" (for any "F"), both because its use entails nothing about Fs—it ascribes Fness to nothing—but also because it is not connected with the phenomenon of pointing (indicating, etc.) in the way in which demonstrative expressions like "this" are.

This latter issue is one addressed by Wittgenstein in the *Blue Book*. He imagines someone saying: "But surely the word 'I' in the mouth of a man refers to the man who says it; it points to himself; and very often the man who says it actually points to himself with his finger." (*BB* 67) And he responds:

> But it was quite superfluous to point to himself. He might just as well only have raised his hand. It would be wrong to say that when someone points to the sun with his hand, he is pointing both to the sun and himself because it is *he* who points; on the other hand, he may by pointing attract attention both to the sun and to himself.

We must distinguish between pointing to something and drawing (or attracting) attention to something. Let us begin with pointing. You do not, in the relevant sense, point to everything to which an imaginary straight line may be drawn from the tip of your extended index finger. Pointing is an intentional action of a conventional kind[10], and involves among other things the capacity of the pointer to say or otherwise make clear what he is pointing to, if called upon to—even if only by doing some more, but different, pointing. (Thus, to use a favourite example of Wittgenstein's, one may point to a colour, or alternatively to a shape, *by* pointing to a red circle; the two physical acts are indistinguishable, and it is one's actual or possible further explanations, linguistic or non-linguistic, that determine "what was being pointed to".) Drawing attention to something may or may not be intentional. Even where it is intentional, it need not be done *by* pointing, or by performing any act the conventional meaning (function) of which is to draw someone's attention to some specifiable thing. You can draw attention, intentionally or unintentionally, to your flashy new shoes by putting your feet up on the table.

When it is a case of drawing attention to yourself, you typically do this whenever you speak, if you are in the presence of others, and you typically do so intentionally. But of course it would be wrong to say that the function of (any of) the various words you used was therefore to draw attention to you, the speaker. When you use "I" in conversation you intentionally draw attention to yourself in the sense of aiming to be heard and understood, just as when speaking more generally; but in addition, through this act of drawing

108 *The Subject*

attention to yourself you aim to get your listener(s) to have some thought of the form "N is F"—where you are N, e.g. Jane, and you have said "I am F", e.g. "I am thinking".[11] As Wittgenstein says, you could also achieve this latter kind of aim by raising your hand, for instance in response to "Who wants some more chocolate?" In such a context, your gesture may well be said to *mean* "I want some more chocolate", its function being to get the other person to have some true thought of the form "N wants some more chocolate", by dint of their perceiving who is making the gesture.

Note that these remarks apply equally to the use of "I" as subject and to its use as object, though it is clear from the context that Wittgenstein is thinking only of the use of "I" as subject. In the above quotation, he writes that "it was quite superfluous to point to himself. He might just as well only have raised his hand." And this surely goes for "I have a broken arm" as much as for "I am thinking": the listener knows, e.g. that it is Harry who is being said to have a broken arm because the listener's attention is drawn to Harry's speaking or hand-raising (i.e. to the speaking or hand-raising of the person he knows to be Harry). Even where there is error through misidentification, the fact that it is error arises out of this: since it is Harry speaking, and since Harry's arm is not broken, his statement "I have a broken arm" is false. Wittgenstein writes, "The man who cries out with pain, or says that he has pain, *doesn't choose the mouth which says it*" (*BB* 68), but nor does the man who says he has a broken arm choose the mouth which says it.

I have been considering the ways in which the use of "I" appears to be independent of the phenomenon of pointing or indicating, and thus different from the use of "this F". This was one of two differences alleged above (p. 107), the other one residing in the (alleged) fact that the use of "I" entails nothing about Fs. It might be thought that the Wittgenstein of the *Blue Book* would restrict this latter claim to the use of "I" as subject, for when using "I" as object, he would say, you do go by certain features which (you think) you have. But if it is true, as I have said, that in "I have a broken arm" you draw attention to yourself in the same sort of way as does one who raises his hand in answer to a "Who?" question, then it would seem that the communicative function of "I" as object is quite independent of the grounds the speaker has for saying "I", these grounds relating to those "features which (he thinks) he has". So perhaps the use of "I" as object entails nothing about Fs, as I put it.

We will evidently need to go more deeply into the question of the relationship between "I" and "this F". But before doing so, I want to look briefly at proper names.

For all that has been said, won't "I" resemble a proper name? After all, in many instances you do not *go by* any features of a thing or person when you use its name in an assertion, and the question, "But are you sure it is X that is F, and not something else?" will be inapposite. "Moscow is probably very cold at this time of year" would be an example; when I say this, it is most unlikely that I do, so on account of having *recognized* Moscow, say from film

The Subject 109

footage. Moreover, the use of proper names seems to be independent of pointing gestures and the like in just the same way as is the use of "I". If I pointed to Smith while saying "Smith is very rich", my gesture would be superfluous (unless I was telling you who Smith was, on top of calling him rich). There is, however, a strong case for saying that a proper name is as it were anchored by the possibility of adducing certain features of the referent and/or of pointing to it, picking it out, recognizing it. That a name has a (sufficiently) determinate meaning, distinct from those of other names, seems to require this possibility. An example of an account of proper names which relies on that thought would be John Searle's, as outlined in his "Proper Names"[12], an account clearly influenced by Wittgenstein (e.g. the remarks at *PI* 79).

The determinacy of the meaning of "I" in utterances containing it is indeed *indirectly* grounded in possibilities of adducing features and of pointing, etc., insofar as a central part of its function is, as I have said, to get another person to have a thought of the form "N is F", where "N" will have to be associated with criteria of identity. For those criteria of identity are bound up with possibilities of adducing features, of pointing, etc. But in so far as in using "I" one *draws attention* to oneself, this being distinguishable from pointing to oneself, such criteria of identity play no part in a speaker's use of "I".[13] If I say, "Mrs Jones is on the rampage again", and you ask, "But who is Mrs Jones?", I will (*pace* Kripke) need to be able to say *something* descriptive, or indeed point out Mrs Jones to you, if I am to be regarded as knowing what I'm talking about. By contrast, if I say "I'm thinking", or "I have a broken arm", and you ask, "But who are you?", your question has a quite different import (after all, by hearing me speak you are almost certainly in a position to frame an identifying description "X" with which to think, e.g. "X is thinking"); and it is possible that (through amnesia, say) I can only answer, "I don't know who I am", without this at all impugning my use of "I".

Let us return now to the comparison of "I" with "This F", e.g. "This human being". The use of "this" (and still more of "that") is bound up with the act of pointing, and equivalent acts; it often requires a supplementary act of pointing, or similar, if the speaker is to be understood. Let us imagine that you respond to "Who wants some more chocolate?" by calling out "This person!" If "this" is being used as it is in, say, "This car belongs to my dad", then the question could in principle be asked, "Which person?", analogous to "Which car?" In both cases, the question might be a silly one, e.g. if there's nobody else in the room, or if we're sitting in a car (so that unless I point out of the window to another car, I'm to be taken as indicating the one we're in). No need to point, in either case—but this is a contingent fact about the situation. If there are others in the room and you call out "This person!", you could in fact be asked "Which one?"; but given the nature of the context, and your probable demeanour, you will most likely be taken to have done something equivalent to raising your hand or shouting "Hello-o!". Your use of "this", in other words, will not be quite the same as the use of it in "This car belongs to my dad"—still less "This

110   *The Subject*

person [pointing to your neighbour] wants more chocolate". The function of "this", in what might be called its standard sense and when applied to material objects, is bound up with pointing and other demonstrative gestures, whereas the function of "I"—either as subject or as object—is not, as we have seen.

A question arises whether the use of "This human being" might further differ from that of "I" in involving the possibility of reference-failure. Even though in using "I" as object one goes by certain features, so that misidentification becomes possible (according to Wittgenstein), still, so long as someone manages to say or think "I am F" at all, the existence of the person who is talking or thinking about himself—as we might as well put it—is guaranteed, and in that sense so is the immunity to reference-failure of "I" in his utterance/thought. (This way of putting things is intended to embody agnosticism on the question whether the function of "I" is to refer.) But, as Anscombe's example of Jones's ashes shows, "This F" (or "These . . .") can fail of reference even where something is successfully latched on to. What about the particular case of "This human being" or "This person"? How could *these* expressions fail to refer? In fact we might ask the same of "This car", in "This car belongs to my dad": if we're both sitting in the car, how could I fail to refer successfully? The traditional answer is something like, "You could be dreaming, or hallucinating; or a fake car could have been built and substituted for the car in the garage (etc.)". And it may be alleged that something similar can be made out for "This human being": I might have been told I was a human being from an early age, when in fact I am some sort of humanoid—or I might be in Anscombe's sensory deprivation tank, unable to perceive my body at all and with no sensations to "latch on to", so that "the possibility will perhaps strike me that there is . . . nothing that I am."[14]

If we are, on the face of it, both sitting in a car and you say, "You could be dreaming, or hallucinating; or a fake car could have been built and substituted for the car in the garage", will this lead me to doubt that I'm sitting in a car? No; for I will only begin actually to doubt this if I become inclined to think that I *am* dreaming or hallucinating, or whatever. I can perhaps imagine becoming inclined to think such stuff (e.g. in altered circumstances)—but it is not in general true that "we are in doubt because it is possible for us to *imagine* a doubt." (*PI* 84) There may then be a sense in which, in the actual situation, I cannot—cannot psychologically, cannot rationally—doubt that I'm in a car, nor that I refer to a car by means of "This car". But for all that, there is a describable situation, e.g. involving a practical joke using a fake car, in which I would actually be wrong, a situation for whose actuality I could be given rationally convincing grounds. In *this* sense of "possibility", there is a possibility of reference-failure when using "This car", and such a possibility might of course "strike one" when sitting in a car. Does anything like this hold of "This human being" or "This person"?

It is far from clear that I can describe evidence such that if it turned up I should have good reason to say, "So I am not a human being after all". To describe such "evidence" one would have to imply that there had been

The Subject 111

a lot of collusive deception (for what motives?) from other people concerning where I came from and who my forebears were, or alternatively that my memory had deceived me hugely about such things. Or perhaps my parents and grandparents were also unwitting humanoids? But how did we get here, then? And can one fail to be a human being despite being enormously like one (think of all my visits to doctors, dentists, etc.)? What sort of biology would embrace that? In fact, if biologists started using certain tests to differentiate "real human beings" from people like me and my family, I, and no doubt others, would simply regard the new tests as no better than ones purporting to show that Australian aboriginals were not really human. The concept *human being* is not the sole property of biologists, but is an ancient and entrenched common concept. In sum, any putative evidence that I was not a human being would surely strike me, and no doubt others, either as a hoax or as a piece of pseudo-science. The anti-sceptical tactic used here is of course one that is adumbrated and employed by Wittgenstein, especially in *On Certainty*.

The case of Anscombe's sensory deprivation tank is rather different. The problem here, if Anscombe is right, is that "This human being" can't get off the ground at all, for lack of anything for "This" to latch on to. One cannot point to anything, or mentally focus on any current perceptions or sensations, by which one might explain to oneself (as it were) which human being one meant by "this one". To call this a case of reference-failure is in one way misleading, since what we have is not a singular term with a bona fide meaning that fails to refer to anything (like, say, "Zeus"), so much as a sign, "This human being", that fails to mean anything, i.e. fails to be a symbol at all. The case is similar to the one described by Wittgenstein thus: "Imagine that you were telephoning someone and you said to him: 'This table is too tall', and pointed to the table." (*PI* 670) If the purported statement "This table is too tall" is to be understood as inclusive of the pointing gesture, and simultaneously as addressed to another person, then it is a failed or would-be statement. What you said and did could only together amount to a statement if you had in fact been talking to yourself—and the pointing gesture would then of course be superfluous. But talking or thinking to yourself is no help in the sensory deprivation tank, where you are in the same position as the person at the other end of the telephone, despite its being you that are doing the talking. For one in the sensory deprivation tank, "This human being is thinking" and "This human being has two legs" are neither of them any better than was "This table is too tall".

We may admit the difference between "I" and "This human being" without making the further inference made by Anscombe, that one can coherently think "There is nothing that I am". For there may be reasons why "I am something", or "I am embodied", are non-contingently true, reasons having to do with the preconditions of there being such an expression as "I". These preconditions are connected with that function of "I" which I have mentioned, of getting another person to have a true thought of the form "N is F", where "N" must

112   *The Subject*

be associated with criteria of identity. Anscombe writes of her first-personal judgements that she "probably learnt to have them through learning to say what she had done, was doing, etc.—an amazing feat of imitation."[15] The capacity to say "I kicked the ball", "I am leaving", "I am hungry", and so on, is acquired—like all such linguistic capacities—through imitating those around you. *Imitation* is as protean a notion as *same* (as in "do the same thing"); the imitation in question is directed and constrained by what others say to you and about you. Smith's I-thoughts have to be sufficiently in sync with others' judgements about Smith if he is to count as having mastered the sense of "I". And others' judgements about Smith are necessarily tied to the identity of the thing that Smith is: an embodied human being. Hence Smith's use of "I" is also tied to the identity of that same embodied human being.

We have been looking at ways in which the use of "I", either as subject or as object, differs from that of demonstratives ("This F") and from that of proper names. More could be said on these themes; I have not, for example, discussed definite descriptions, such as "The person thinking these thoughts" or "The person speaking these words". The reader can probably infer the sort of thing Wittgenstein would say in response to any attempted assimilation of "I" to such descriptions. It should, I think, have emerged from our discussion that what is of importance is how like or unlike the use of "I" is to the uses of other kinds of terms: we do not need to worry too much whether it is right and proper to call "I" a "referring expression", this being after all a technical term. As Hacker says: "What matters crucially is that one be aware of the differences [in uses]; and if thereafter, one still wants to say that 'I' is nevertheless a kind of referring expression or, better perhaps, a degenerate referring expression, nothing need hang on that preference as long as one does not assimilate the function of the word 'I' to an inappropriate paradigm of reference."[16] But an issue which does need attending to is whether Wittgenstein was right, in the *Blue Book*, to make the distinction between the two uses of "I", and in particular whether he was right to posit a use of "I" as object. The distinction is not one to be found in those passages which he later wrote concerning "I", in the *Philosophical Investigations* (esp. 404–11). And it seems fair to say that in any case Wittgenstein's main interest is in the use of "I" as subject, i.e. in the use where it makes no sense to impute error through misidentification.

Wittgenstein's example of the man who says "I have a broken arm", seeing the broken arm beside him, perhaps in some sort of melée of human bodies, is intended to show the possibility of error through misidentification. But it may be suggested that what is misidentified is not the person himself, but his arm: he mistakes someone else's arm for his own, and it looks odd to say that he mistakes someone else for himself, given that he doesn't perceive that "someone else". How is this matter to be decided? Perhaps the surest method is to come up with an example in which it is the man's whole body, or his person (as the phrase is), which gets misidentified by him. If while standing in a queue at the bank you look up at a figure on the closed-circuit

The Subject 113

TV screen and say, "Oh dear, I am stooping these days", do you not intend to refer to the person on the screen, but fail to do so if that person is in fact your neighbour in the bank queue? And why not go on: "The person you actually refer to is yourself; you have misidentified another as yourself"? Here at least, Wittgenstein might argue, is a pure case of the use of "I" as object. To deny this, we should seem to have to argue that your statement amounted to "Oh dear, the human body (or human being) that I have (or am (identical with?)) is stooping these days", where what you misidentify the person on the screen *as* is not yourself[17], but your body, or even the human being that you are. This would raise the interesting question what the status is of a proposition like, "I am (identical with?) such-and-such a human being".

I will leave the matter of "I" as object there, since as I have said it is really "I" as subject that Wittgenstein is interested in. When it comes to "I am thinking", a comparison with "I have a toothache" would be inadequate, as we have seen (above, 105), on account of the fact that whereas the latter may arguably be regarded as moan-like, the former can hardly be seen as akin to any "natural expression", of the sort that serves as conceptually criterial. If I am right, Wittgenstein would most likely have regarded the linguistic utterance, "I am thinking", as itself the, or a, central criterion of present thinking (*nachdenken*), something which is connected with the intentionality of thought. On the face of it, the same would seem to go for expressions of intention, such as "I am going to take two powders now": the relation between such an utterance and its fulfilment (e.g. one's taking the powders) is, for Wittgenstein, an internal one, and is a case of the two related phenomena "making contact in language", a topic that was discussed in Chapter 2, sec. 2. For this reason, one may, like Anscombe, worry about Wittgenstein's talk of the natural expression of an intention in *PI* 647: "What is the natural expression [*Ausdruck*] of an intention?—Look at a cat when it stalks a bird; or a beast when it wants to escape."[18] Perhaps if we are to characterize such animal behaviour as the natural expression of something, that something should be *desire* rather than *intention*. This is not to say that animals can't have intentions, intentions which we ascribe to them on the basis of their behaviour—but that behavioural manifestations of intention are not natural expressions of intention in the way in which moaning is a natural (and criterial) expression of pain. Of course, Wittgenstein's purpose in *PI* 647, as the surrounding context makes clear, is to throw doubt on the idea that an intention consists in an "inner experience"; so his example of animal behaviour is presumably meant to serve as a reminder (even if imperfectly described) of how we confidently ascribe intentions without feeling any qualms about what's going on "within" the creature in question. For an intention may be embodied in what is visibly done: "I can see what she's doing, she's writing a letter", or "I can see what the lion's doing, it's chasing the antelope". In so far as you can frequently see what a creature is doing, what it's up to, you can see what it intends, what it's after.

114   *The Subject*

3. COMPARISON OF FIRST-PERSONAL
WITH OTHER-PERSONAL USES

One of the main points of Wittgenstein's discussion of the first-personal uses of "think", "intend", etc. is to show up the asymmetry, as it is often called, between first-personal uses and third- (or second-) personal uses of such verbs. At the beginning of this chapter I referred to the philosophical method that so radically distinguishes Wittgenstein from more metaphysically minded philosophers, of the sort that begin their enquiry, or a part of it, with a question like, "What sort of entity or entities think, or intend?" There is a similar impulse to begin one's enquiry, or a part of it, with the question, "What sort of mental state is thinking, or intending?" Adopting that question is naturally liable to lead to one's viewing "I am thinking" and "Jack is thinking" as essentially doing the same sort of thing: ascribing a certain sort of mental state to a person. The philosophy is then meant to consist in saying what this state *is*. But such an approach, apart from anything else, initially leaves many philosophical puzzles untouched, such as that concerning a person's "authority" as to what and whether he is thinking; and the temptation is now almost irresistible simply to add metaphysical ingredients to the basic picture, the picture of a person's enjoying (or having, or instantiating . . .) a mental state. Such an added ingredient might, e.g. be Descartes's natural light of infallible introspection.

The basic picture, in short, is liable to be too basic, too simple-minded. This simplicity generates compensatory complexities, typically dressed in metaphysical garb (Descartes's natural light *et al.*) By contrast, if we start by bearing in mind those philosophical questions and puzzles that got us interested in thought, will, and so on, in the first place—and these are many and varied—we shall be more likely to be impressed straight away by the differences between the first person and the third/second person uses of "think", "intend", etc., and so will be in a position to be open-minded about what might explain those differences. For it need not be "metaphysical facts about the mental state of thinking/intending" that explain them.

An important lesson at this stage is that it is not as if *experience* (even very early experience) taught me that I, like other people, seem to know best what I am thinking, or what I mean to do. The knowledge that people *do* "know best" in this way cannot be justified by evidence that they do, in the normal sense of evidence. It would be absurd to say, "You know, when Jack says he's thinking about food, or that he plans to holiday in France, he (almost?) always gets it right—he *is* thinking about food, or planning to holiday in France!" What could confirm Jack's reports, after all? The idea that we have a reliable report at all here evidently comes under pressure, but it is a fact that addiction to the basic picture of ascribing mental states to persons or entities can put you in a state of denial concerning that pressure.

Now is the time to mention the suspicion that Wittgenstein again and again directs towards phrases like "mental state", "state of mind", etc. (*Zustand*

The Subject 115

der Seele, Seelenzustand, etc.). He does not think that such phrases inevitably bring confusion, and the use of one in a given context might be unexceptionable. Consider the following:

> We say "I am expecting him", when we will believe that he will come, though his coming does not occupy our thoughts. (Here "I am expecting him" would mean "I should be surprised if he didn't come" and that will not be called the description of a state of mind [*Beschreibung eines Seelenzustands*].) But we also say "I am expecting him" when it is supposed to mean: I am eagerly awaiting him. We could imagine a language in which different verbs were consistently used in these cases. (*PI* 577)

(NB: it would be wrong-headed to start worrying about Wittgenstein's use of "mean" [*heißen*] in this passage; the verb has a variety of uses (see above, e.g. 49) and here means roughly "amounts to".) When "I am expecting him" means "I am eagerly awaiting him", when, that is, I am conveying that his coming occupies my thoughts, we could capture this by saying that what I supplied was a description of my state of mind—or even, in Philospherese, a description of a state of my mind. At any rate, we might well want to say so in order to *distinguish* such a case from that in which "I am expecting him" amounts to "I should be surprised if he didn't come". The word "state" has various possible connotations, and the connotations it here has enable us to point up a distinction, something Wittgenstein regards as important in fighting the craving for generality so endemic in philosophy. If, succumbing to that craving, we simply spoke of both uses of "I am expecting him" as ascribing a mental state to a person, we should have covered over a real distinction, not only between ways of talking, but—of course—between real-life phenomena.[19]

The sort of trouble using that crutch can get you into is well illustrated by Moore's Paradox, the paradox embodied in a statement like "I believe it's going to rain, and it will not rain". For if "I believe it's going to rain" ascribes a mental state to someone, is a statement about someone's state of mind, how

116   *The Subject*

can it conflict with "It will not rain", which is surely about the weather? My mind and the weather are two quite independent things! Wittgenstein remarks:

> Moore's paradox can be put like this: the expression "I believe that this is the case" is used like the assertion "This is the case"; and yet the *hypothesis* that I believe this is the case is not used like the hypothesis that this is the case.
>
> So it *looks* as if the assertion "I believe" were not the assertion of what is supposed in the hypothesis "I believe"!
>
> Similarly: the statement "I believe it's going to rain" has a meaning like, that is to say a use like, "It's going to rain", but the meaning of "I believed then that it was going to rain", is not like that of "It did rain then". (*PI* ii, p. 190)

Why should, e.g. the facts mentioned in the last sentence, about meaning-(dis)similarity, worry us? They will worry us if we are attached to a picture of the meaning of a predicative word, here "believe", according to which it is the same in different contexts in virtue of ascribing (or referring to . . .) *the same state* ("in the world") in each context. And Wittgenstein's imaginary interlocutor immediately gives voice to his attachment to such a picture: "But surely 'I believed' must tell of just the same thing in the past as 'I believe' in the present!"

To which Wittgenstein replies: "Surely $\sqrt{-1}$ must mean just the same in relation to -1, as $\sqrt{1}$ means in relation to 1! This means nothing at all." Of course it can be said that "believe" means the same in "I believe that p" and "I did then believe that p". This is in virtue of the fact that there is a complex of interrelated uses of "believe", a complex which itself strikes us—who are its creators and implementers—as unified, on account especially of those interrelations of use. (Think of the unity of a currency, such as sterling.) Or in other words, the unity of the language-game is what underlies the unity of meaning of the embedded word, "believe". This idea was expounded in Chapter 2 in connection with the sameness of meaning of, e.g. "he will come" as it appears in "I expect that he will come" and the simple "He will come" (see 41–2). By contrast, one who says "But surely 'I believed' must tell of just the same thing in the past as 'I believe' in the present!" in a way gets things back to front, for he will most likely want to account for the unity of the language-game containing "believe" by reference to the unity in meaning of that word in different contexts, something he will then feel impelled to explain by talk of "just the same thing"—*believing*—existing or subsisting in the relevant different portions of reality (e.g. in the past and in the present). Such a philosopher may well try to explain himself by using phrases like "X means the same *in relation to* the past as Y does *in relation to* the present"—which as Wittgenstein says, really means nothing at all. And he will be lumbered with such paradoxes as Moore's.

The Subject 117

Turning then to what Wittgenstein has to say about the first-personal vs. third/second-personal uses of "think", "intend", and the like, we are prepared with a likely answer to the question: "But in view of these big differences in what you call the *use* of 'think', as it occurs in the first person or the third person, how—given your assimilation of use and meaning—can you make out that the verb means the same in both cases? Aren't you in fact committed to calling 'think' ambiguous, like the word 'bank', or 'row'?" The answer is: the complex of interrelated uses of "think", including those of "I think" and "Jack thinks", is a unified complex. Consider that part of the function of "I am F" which I have already adverted to, of enabling or getting another to have a true thought of the form "N is F". Wittgenstein's talk of drawing the attention of another to something (as opposed to pointing to it) is clearly in keeping with this view of the function of "I", since if I draw another's attention to myself, whether by speaking, moaning, or whatever, I get him to have some thought of the form "N is F", e.g. "Roger is in pain". Here would be a case of an interconnection of uses: say, of "I am in pain" and "Roger is in pain"—the first person and the third person.

An instance of just this interconnection was discussed in Chapter 2 (54–5), namely that between someone's expression of intention, "I'm going to do X", and another's "N is going to do X". The former statement, as we saw, is not on all fours with other kinds of prediction, for reasons especially having to do with what grounds one might give for one's expression of intention. And it casts light on the use and meaning of "I'm going to do X" to point out the *usefulness* of our being often able to predict a person's actions from her expressions of intention, that is, of our being able to get from a first-person to a third-person statement, from an expression of intention to a straight prediction; this is evidently part of the point of the language-game of expressing decisions or intentions.

Among the "big differences" between the first and third/second-person uses of verbs like "think" and "intend" perhaps the most notable is that of the typical groundlessness of first-person uses, contrasted with the possibility of giving grounds when it comes to the other uses. You do not go by any features you happen to have when using "I" as subject; and nor do you typically go by any phenomena—sensations, feelings, outward behaviour, movements of the larynx, or whatever—when using a verb like "think" in the first person. These two facts are surely connected. The groundlessness associated with first-person uses of "think", etc. is something that came out in our discussion of "inner processes" in Chapter 3. Among the facts there mentioned (see 75–7) was the human ability to learn the use, e.g. of "I was just about to say . . .", an ability that turns out not to have to do with inner processes recalled in memory, but which may rather be seen as an instance, or relative, of the more general ability to continue interrupted procedures.

Remember that there are many uses of words which must be seen as ungrounded: apart from the obvious cases, like "of" and "in" (only a hyperempiricist would now look for the sensation or idea which I need to recognize

118 *The Subject*

in order to use these words), there are cases like "red". As to the latter, Wittgenstein's observation that in order to obey "Imagine a red patch", you do not have first to imagine a red patch to serve you as a pattern (*BB* 3) provides as good an inoculation as any against the sort of regress and absurdity that threatens when we demand to know what grounds or justification a person has for using some word.

But for me to know when to use "Jack is thinking", "Sally means to sing after supper", etc., I must know what sorts of grounds are appropriate for making such assertions, and I must very often be in a position to indicate such grounds. Grounds can here include both criteria and symptoms, in the sense of those expressions earlier discussed (Chapter 3, 81–3). But it may be that I judge that a person e.g. intends something or other, only on the basis of what Wittgenstein would call "imponderable evidence"—the sort of evidence that "includes subtleties of glance, of gesture, of tone" (*PI*, ii, p. 228). Perhaps I judge that the rather drunken guest to my right is any moment now going to start trying to chat up the pretty girl opposite him; I go by something in the movements of his eyes, in the stance of his body, in the change in his speech patterns—all taken in the context of that well-known human situation—but if asked informatively to describe those movements, that stance, that change, I should be able to say almost nothing of interest. In the sense in which the first-personal expression of intention "I am going to do X" typically *lacks* grounds, we can say that my judgement about the drunken guest has grounds, albeit "imponderable" ones, for I do *go by* his eye movements, stance and speech, in coming to my conclusion (or in just being hit by it). And that much I could probably tell you, after all.

A moment ago I mentioned the fact that one often lacks grounds or justification for *using* a word or expression, such as "of" or indeed "red". But isn't my present topic that of the grounds, or lack thereof, for making certain ("psychological") *assertions*, the notion of grounds being here connected with the aim of assertion, namely truth? You can have grounds or justification for asserting "There are some red apples in the cupboard", e.g. "I saw them there", where this statement gives an enquirer evidence for the truth of the first assertion, even if you lack grounds for using the word "red"—at any rate in the sense that you can't answer the question "But why do you call that colour red?" by citing grounds for your choice of word. (Indeed you can hardly be said to *choose* the word "red" at all, in ordinary circumstances.) You could perhaps give some other sort of answer to this last question, as Wittgenstein imagines when he writes: "How do I know that this colour is red?—It would be an answer to say: 'I have learnt English'." (*PI* 381) And the possibility of this sort of answer points to another sense of "justified", such that you are justified in using a word because it's the right word for you to use there, something which typically has to do with your making yourself understood. Making yourself understood in turn has to do with using words in line with general usage, so that being justified in using a word, say "red", in *this* sense is a matter of being linguistically competent. The difference

The Subject 119

between the two notions of justification is alluded to by Wittgenstein at *PI* 289: "To use a word without a justification [*ohne Rechtfertigung*] does not mean to use it without right [*zu Unrecht*]." You can be warranted in using the word "red" despite lacking a justification [*Rechtfertigung*], i.e. despite being unable to *give* a justification.

It is, however, very often a part of linguistic competence with an expression that you know when it is justified to make certain assertions employing it—that is to say, you must know when there is a need for you to be able to *give* a justification for such an assertion, and know what sort of thing will meet that need. Saying "I saw them in the cupboard" might be a case in point. If a child was unable to cotton on to the rules of such language-games as that of responding to "How do you know?" questions, her competence with many words would be so radically incomplete as to amount to incompetence. And competence with the third-personal use of "think" or "intend" in this way involves knowing what count as good grounds for using these words assertively, these grounds adverting either to criteria or to symptoms, or to some yet more indirect species of evidence. By contrast, in the face of "I'm thinking how to put up that shelf" the question "How do you know you are?" is akin to "How do you know that colour is red?" If it is asking for grounds of the sort that connect with the aim of assertion, truth, in the way in which giving criteria or symptoms does, then it is a pointless question, since the first-personal present-tense use of "think" is immediate in the same way as is the assertive use of "red" in paradigm conditions (e.g. when looking at a ripe tomato in daylight); while if it is asking why the person has chosen the particular word "think", here too no answer will be available, unless indeed it is "I have learnt English".

4. BODY AND SOUL

Our examination of the peculiarities attaching to "I think", "I intend", and so on, has involved description of the use of "I" in such statements, not description of any special features or faculties had by the entity supposedly referred to by "I". (Indeed, one of our findings has been that the function of "I" in "I think" etc. is significantly unlike that of a proper name or demonstrative expression, and in that sense is not to refer to anything at all.) Our examination, in fact, has been not a metaphysical one, but what Wittgenstein would call a grammatical one. But in the course of this examination various ways of addressing traditional philosophical puzzles have suggested themselves. Thus, to take one example, the incompatibility of "I think it's raining" and "It isn't raining" within a single utterance looks to be easier to account for once we jettison the idea that the former is simply, as it were, the first-person version of, e.g. "Jill thinks it's raining", whose function is to *ascribe a mental state to something*. Moore's paradox, by the way, has an analogue for expressions of intention: "I plan to cook dinner this evening, but I won't cook

120   *The Subject*

dinner this evening" surely involves much the same sort of self-contradiction as does Moore's statement, something that will be hard to account for if (relying on an undifferentiated notion of *aboutness*) we regard one conjunct as being about my current mental state and the other as being about a future culinary event.

If one effect of this grammatical investigation has been to show up as a myth the philosophical Subject, Descartes's Ego, the self-knowing Self, then a correlative effect has been to instate, or reinstate, the human being as thinker and actor. One crucial part of the function of "I", as has been stressed, is that its use in "I am F" enables another to form a judgement of the form "N is F", where "N" will pick out the speaker *as* the sort of thing the speaker is—for the use of a name is bound up with criteria of (re-)identification, i.e. criteria determining when we have the same such-and-such as before or elsewhere. And until such time as we encounter aliens or angels, this *such-and-such* will be a human being. Moreover, when we are dealing with the use of "I" as subject, in statements involving such verbs as "think" and "intend", these verbs themselves have their paradigm application to human beings (see 101–3, above).

I have already quoted Wittgenstein's "We only say of a human being and what is like one that it thinks" (*PI* 360); he is more compendious at *PI* 281, writing: "It comes to this: only of a living human being and what resembles (behaves like) a living human being can one say: it has sensations; it sees; is blind; hears; is deaf; is conscious or unconscious." This list is notable in including such opposing pairs as "sees" and "is blind". What might be called the negative member of the pair is not equivalent merely to the logical negation of the positive member: "Socks do not see" doesn't mean "Socks are blind". The negative predicate in such cases often signifies a privation: a creature is only blind if it is *meant* to see, i.e. if the normal specimen of that kind of creature has eyes and sees. Hence the range of (kinds of) things that can be blind is the same as the range of (kinds of) things that can see.[20] And that natural languages have such pairs of predicates is an indication of our interest not only in the central case of the human being, but in this idea of what is *meant* to be—in other words, in teleology. It is often possible to explain why we have certain concepts, and why they have the shape they do, by reference to our interests and concerns, something which is stressed by Wittgenstein in various places; and it is hardly surprising that those interests and concerns should include facts about ourselves, i.e. about human beings, and about matters teleological, matters that intersect in all sorts of ways with human action and practical thinking.

At the beginning of Chapter 1 I spoke of three dualisms characteristic of modern philosophy: dualism of mind and body, dualism of inner and outer and dualism of thought and will. And I spoke of the last of these as embodying a picture of Man, as at once passive (acted upon by the world) and active (acting upon the world). But this picture was typically not so much a picture of Man as a picture of the Mind; as a result of which accounting for human agency and activity has frequently resembled attempting to build a bridge while remaining on one side of the river, as I expressed it. In the course of the last three chapters we have seen how Wittgenstein's thought bears upon these three dualisms. A multi-faceted critique of the dualisms of mind/body and of inner/outer yields a view of the dualism of thought and will which does indeed see these as attributes, not of a Mind, but of a human being (and of what resembles a human being). And not only agency and activity, but thought and belief also, no longer appear to involve a metaphysical gap between subject and world which must somehow be bridged or closed, for the human being who thinks and acts is a part of that world, her thinking and acting are phenomena within the world—and the metaphysical gap we imagine to ourselves is but a shadow cast by language.

That we are not minds or souls inhabiting or possessing human bodies is part of the point of Wittgenstein's remark, "The human body is the best picture of the human soul". (*PI* ii, p. 178) As we have seen[21], Wittgenstein in various places talks of a "picture" as a sort of medium through which, or metaphor by which, we are inclined to view some topic. It is often helpful to be aware of the influence of such pictures when doing philosophy, and it may also be helpful to put forward new or clarifying pictures. For a picture may or may not lead us astray, and whether it does will depend on what use is made of it, what service it performs for us. Now we might well think that the remark just quoted concerns a picture in something like this sense, a picture that expresses a view of thought, intention, and so on, as above all embodied in human beings and in human behaviour—and that is surely at least a part of what Wittgenstein is driving at. But he is notably more tolerant of, and indeed sympathetic towards, those pictures, notions, and claims which are to be found *outside philosophy*, according to his way of thinking—such as are associated with religious thinking, for example. And of course the notion of an immortal human soul belongs among these. A little before the remark just quoted we find:

> Religion teaches that the soul can exist when the body has disintegrated. Now do I understand this teaching?—Of course I understand it—I can imagine plenty of things in connexion with it. And haven't pictures of these things been painted? And why should such a picture be only an imperfect rendering of the spoken doctrine? Why should it not do the *same* service as the words? And it is the service which is the point. (*PI* ii, p. 178)

It might well be thought that his critique of the dualisms of mind and body and of inner and outer would leave little room for a meaningful proposition, "A soul can exist without its body"—given that "soul" signifies something like "entity that thinks, wills, and so on, and that informs a human person", a signification to which Wittgenstein would appear to consent in the passages surrounding this one. And he surely feels it incumbent on him to consider the teaching of religion concerning the soul precisely because what he has said appears to undermine its sensefulness; hence his question, "Now

122   *The Subject*

do I understand this teaching?" His answer, "Of course I understand it—I can imagine plenty of things in connexion with it", appears, as far as it goes, to employ a very liberal notion of understanding, and therefore of its correlate, meaningfulness. This notion of meaningfulness would hardly suffice on its own if we were attempting to show that the religious teaching was significant in a way that Lewis Carroll's "Jabberwocky" isn't. But he then seems to suggest what *sort* of thing it is that he can imagine in connexion with the teaching, by alluding to paintings of souls, souls perhaps leaving their bodies at death. What kind of paintings? The answer is surely given a couple of lines later: "The human body is the best picture of the human soul." (Think of those mediaeval depictions of a homuncular soul leaving the mouth of the dying person.) Is then the teaching that the soul can exist when the body has disintegrated something best grasped via a picture of the soul as a human body? The proposal has an air of paradox about it; and unfortunately Wittgenstein leaves us in the dark what "service" is done by the paintings he has in mind—presumably something more than that of inducing religious reflection.

Wittgenstein's view of thought and will, and of the other activities of the soul (to put it in those terms), has a clear kinship with Aristotle's. Aristotle called the soul the form of the body, his concept of form encompassing not only shape but also characteristic functions and activities. And for Aristotle, just as for Wittgenstein, the idea of a disembodied soul appears prima facie to be ruled out: the idea seems to be like that of the shape of a pear which persists, *as that pear's shape*, even after the pear has been eaten. The universal quality, *pear-shaped*, might indeed be thought to be around after the demise of the pear, given, e.g. that other pears can partake of it, but the idea of a personal soul is not intended to be the idea of what is common to all living human beings; there is purportedly a one-one (not a one-many) correlation between souls and bodies. That is why there needs to be a *teaching* that the soul can survive the death of the body. Nevertheless, Christian thinkers—notably Aquinas—who have taken Aristotle's view of the soul on board have attempted to show that this view is after all compatible with the thesis of disembodied existence, if only for the period between death and resurrection. The efforts of those thinkers take up much more space than do Wittgenstein's sketch-like thoughts on this topic, but whether they are any more successful in their aim is something that is beyond the remit of this chapter. In the case of Wittgenstein's philosophy, what in the end confronts us as the paradigm subject of thought and will is not a soul, nor is it a mere body in the sense of a conglomerate of physical particles—it is a living human being.

NOTES

1. In German, "Wir sagen es auch von Puppen und wohl auch von Geistern."
2. The nature of behavioural criteria for psychological concepts was discussed in Chapter 3 (81–3).

The Subject 123

3. G. E. Moore records Wittgenstein as having quoted "with apparent approval" Lichtenberg's statement, "Instead of 'I think' we ought to say 'It thinks'"—the "it" being the (obviously non-referring) impersonal pronoun. See Moore 1959, 309.

4. Note a certain flexibility in the notion of a function here; for we could also say (always assuming that there is such a thing as the use of "I" as object), "The function of 'I' in this sentence was to pick out the speaker"—as we might say that the function of "Socrates" in some sentence was to pick out Socrates. *Such* "functions" are ones that a word can't fail to perform, so long as a word is taken to be a symbol, not a sign (in the phraseology of the *Tractatus*).

5. This is true of recognizing in the sense that recognition consists in forming a (true) judgement of the form "That is X", where "X" *picks out or identifies* something.

6. For a discussion of putatively infallible introspective faculties, see Chapter 3, 65–6.

7. She also considers its assimilation to a proper name, A. This name is written on a person's wrist, so that direct verification of "A is F"—by the person himself or by another—will involve observation of that wrist and its connection with the person. Such a procedure introduces the possibility of error, thus throwing doubt on the assimilation of "I" to "A".

8. Anscombe 1981a, 31.

9. Anscombe 1981a, 31.

10. Such phenomena as pointing or using arrows are so familiar that it can be tempting to think of them as intrinsically or naturally demonstrative, something touched on by Wittgenstein more than once; see *PI* 454, and also *PI* 85, with its famous comparison (in the mouth of the interlocutor) of a rule and a signpost, to which Wittgenstein replies: "But where is it said which way I am to follow it; whether in the direction of its finger or (e.g.) in the opposite one?" Try pointing to its food bowl in the presence of a cat; the cat will most likely take an interest in your finger, not the bowl.

11. This point survives the observation that you don't *draw* the attention of a listener who is already listening to you (e.g. by your sixth use of "I" in that monologue). What is important is that the listener perceives who it is that is speaking/raising his/her hand/etc.

12. Searle 1967. The claim that the use of a name has to be anchored in possible descriptions, pointings, etc., has famously been denied, in particular by Saul Kripke in his *Naming and Necessity*. A midway position might allow for what Putnam called "linguistic division of labour", whereby in order to count as competent in the use of a name it is sufficient to have "got" (in the right way . . .) the name from people who *can* adduce descriptions, etc. Unfortunately, I do not have space to consider any of these possibilities here.

13. This is compatible with saying that in order to be able to use "I" one must be aware of the connection between "I am F" and "N is F", and hence of the involvement of criteria of identity of some sort: i.e. those associated with "N", whatever they are. And, as we shall see, one cannot but know that the *general* criteria of identity governing names like "N" are those for a human being. But one is not, in using "I", committed to being able to answer or determine an answer to "Who are you?"

14. Anscombe 1981a, 34.

15. Anscombe 1981a, 34.

16. Hacker 1990, 493.

17. This use of "yourself", like other such uses of "-self" in the text, is a case of the so-called indirect reflexive (i.e. the indirect speech correlate of the direct speech "I"), since it follows the verb "misidentify". Hector-Neri Castaneda

124 *The Subject*

was one of the first to see the importance for any examination of the first person of the indirect reflexive; see Castaneda 1967.

18. See above, 54.

19. A curious example of a philosophical use of 'mental state' is that made by Timothy Williamson, who has presented the thesis that 'knowledge is a mental state' (Williamson 2000). This turns out to mean not much more than that 'S knows that p' can't be analysed into necessary and sufficient conditions, and that knowing is 'similar' in various respects to things we call mental states, so that we should call it a mental state also. Unsurprisingly, there is little discussion of the differences between 'I know' and 'He knows'.

20. Note that Wittgenstein says, "only of a living human being and what resembles (behaves like) a living human . . .", not "only and always . . ." (We have a conditional, not a biconditional.) So some things that in the relevant sense resemble human beings may not count either as seeing or as blind; though to call a Belize Land Crab or a Grotto Salamander blind is not nonsensical in the way that "Socks are blind" is.

21. See especially Ch. 3, sec. 1.

5 Aftermath and Legacy

1. THE THEORIZERS STRIKE BACK

In Chapter 1 I discussed the views of some of Wittgenstein's philosophical predecessors concerning thought and will, bringing out various problems inherent in those views. Among these problems were: (i) that of giving a satisfactory answer to Parmenides's challenge, "How is false thought (or unfulfilled intention) possible?"; (ii) that of explaining how an inner item (thought, volition, idea . . .) could *represent* anything; (iii) that of explaining a person's authority concerning her thoughts and intentions. In considering these problems we encountered attempted solutions, further problems, seeming dead ends. Wittgenstein's views about thought and will were expounded in the last three chapters, views which evolved during the course of his life. His mature position can be seen to have coped with or avoided the difficulties attaching to the traditional accounts, in various ways. The notions of "intrinsic" representation, of an inner state, of introspective knowledge, as also of merely causal relations holding between intention and fulfilment or thought and fact, are all examined and criticised by Wittgenstein. So are more general underlying philosophical tendencies, such as the tendency to see the single or essential function of "psychological" statements as being that of *ascribing mental states*. In place of the notions and pictures that have been attacked Wittgenstein gives us a complex and multifaceted account, in which are stressed such things as the *point* of (certain of) our language-games, often in terms of the sort of creature we are, i.e. human beings.

In this chapter, I will be considering such questions as "How were Wittgenstein's views received?", and "How do the views of more recent philosophers and philosophical schools relate to Wittgenstein's views?" The answers to these questions could have involved many names and much detail, but what follows will not be encyclopedic. I have decided to aim for a general thematic picture of Wittgenstein's reception, coupled with more detailed philosophical discussion of particular authors. This means I have had to omit discussion of various important figures, such as Gilbert Ryle (who can, however, be seen as having developed his views in parallel with

126 *Aftermath and Legacy*

Wittgenstein rather than in clear response to him). And when I speak of Wittgenstein's views I will generally mean the later Wittgenstein's views.

In the period immediately following his death, Wittgenstein's influence continued to be, as it had been already while he was alive, very considerable; and there were many philosophers whose work owed its direction and method above all to him. But other trends in English-speaking philosophy were making themselves more and more felt, some of which simply manifested an ignorance of Wittgenstein's philosophy, but others of which were actively hostile to it. The whole topic of anti-Wittgensteinianism in philosophy is a large and sociologically interesting one.[1] Part of its interest relates precisely to this *hostility*, for while such post-war philosophers as Austin and Ryle may have become unfashionable, and possibly sniggered at in some quarters, they have not by and large attracted the sort of opprobrium reserved for Wittgenstein and his more evident followers. (Indeed, Austin was himself rather hostile to Wittgenstein's work.) There are a number of factors that help to explain this hostility, of which I will mention just two: first, Wittgenstein's talk of philosophical confusion, nonsense, etc.; second, his views on the relationship between philosophy and natural science.

"My aim is: to teach you to pass from a piece of disguised nonsense to something that is patent nonsense." (*PI* 464.) Implicit in this remark is a picture of what the typical situation is in philosophy, together with an expression of an aim, an aim deemed suitable for remedying that situation. And the situation referred to is that in which the real or imaginary interlocutor is saying or implying something nonsensical. Now Wittgenstein had already, in the *Tractatus*, expressed the thought that philosophical propositions are typically nonsensical (*unsinnig*)—but he had had the good manners to include his own propositions in that generalization (see *TLP* 6.54). And although there is continuity between the earlier and later philosophy, the degree of which is still the subject of lively debate, I think it is clear enough that he has in the later work dropped the idea that his own, or the "correct sort", of philosophy must, always or typically, manifest itself in nonsense. Rather, the therapeutic method consists in showing how various statements made in philosophy boil down to nonsense; and this method, when enacted in real life, is liable to cause offence. A philosopher would generally much prefer his opponent to meet his "P" with a straightforward "Not P", however brusquely uttered, for after all their positions will in that case be strictly symmetrical. Each will be playing by the same rules—namely, to assert a theory and to attack theories inconsistent with it. But if, on stating some favourite proposition, you receive the response "What you've said hasn't made sense", you may well feel unfairly stymied, and may also feel that you're being made out to be a fool. This response has undoubtedly been often felt by those at the receiving end of Wittgensteinian methods.[2] The response perhaps shows a lack of awareness of the later Wittgenstein's positive attitude to nonsense (and here we do have a degree of continuity with the earlier work), as expressed in this remark, from 1949: "For a philosopher there is more grass growing down in the valleys of silliness [*Dummheit*] than up on the barren heights of cleverness." (*CV* 80e)[3] The fool is evidently the one who stays up on the barren heights of cleverness—the one who will not risk his statements falling into absurdity, who makes sure his back is covered, e.g. by confining himself to technical tinkering or anodyne abstraction. A familiar enough figure.

Apart from being liable to cause offence, the picture of philosophical problems as typically arising from conceptual confusion meets with another kind of resistance: it is felt to belittle philosophy itself, to depict it as incapable of any positive contribution to our knowledge of the world. For any useful philosophical work would appear to have only negative value, the value of getting rid of confusions. And in doing this, it would only tell us things we already knew: "Philosophy simply puts everything before us, and neither explains nor deduces anything.—Since everything lies open to view there is nothing to explain. For what is hidden, for example, is of no interest to us." (*PI* 126)

Wittgenstein's primary motive in making such remarks is to pull us away from alternative views of the nature of philosophy, views he thinks mistaken; and it is possible that he consequently presents a view that appears unnecessarily restrictive, even (perhaps *particularly*) by his own lights. "Philosophy" may well, after all, be something of a family resemblance concept, and it seems pointless to *rule out* the possibility that a philosopher might, without changing the subject, take an interest in what's hidden, or more generally in things not known to everyone. Nevertheless, it is clearly central to Wittgenstein's conception of philosophy, as manifest in his own work, that to approach those problems which have come down to us as belonging to philosophy as if they were problems about the nature or essence of "things out there" is both characteristic of philosophers (and indeed of human beings when they take to philosophizing) and wrongheaded. It is this sort of assertion that many people feel belittles philosophy. For what had seemed exciting, or profound, or grand, about philosophy was precisely its claim to uncover the nature of things, to depict and delineate the most fundamental categories—and to do this by the sheer power of thought!

This last account of what philosophy is can be summed up by the word *metaphysics*. "What *we* do is to bring words back from their metaphysical to their everyday use", writes Wittgenstein in *PI* 116; and a characteristic move of his is to substitute a grammatical enquiry for a would-be metaphysical one: "*Essence* is expressed by grammar." (*PI* 371) For philosophers drawn to the giddy heights to which Plato and Kant had seemed to beckon us, such statements have an almost scandalous air. The resurgence of metaphysical system-building in the last few decades has of necessity gone with a fierce rejection of Wittgensteinian notions, since if there is any truth in those notions, the products of these various research programmes are quite likely to be elaborately kitted-out castles in the air.

128 *Aftermath and Legacy*

The view that philosophy's importance depends on its claim to be describing general features of Reality, where such description takes the form of a theory (or theories) expressed in generalizations, is a view shared with the metaphysical approach I have just mentioned by the scientistic approach: that approach to philosophical problems which regards them as essentially the same kinds of problems as those tackled in the natural sciences, and hence to be dealt with by means essentially similar to the means adopted in science. Here we must mention the second of the two factors I mentioned above, as helping to account for the backlash against Wittgenstein's philosophy—his view of the relationship between philosophy and science. It is a theme that runs through his work from the early to the late writings: that philosophy is to be sharply distinguished from natural science both as regards subject matter (philosophy not really having one at all) and as regards method.

Now scientism in philosophy is no more a phenomenon of the last few decades than is the metaphysical approach; it can for example be detected in the British empiricists, John Locke and David Hume, the latter's *Treatise* famously bearing the subtitle "An ATTEMPT to introduce the experimental Method of Reasoning into MORAL SUBJECTS". A later British empiricist, Bertrand Russell, spoke at one point[4] of philosophical problems being problems the solution to which was obscure so long as no advances in science enabled people to tackle them properly, alleging that it was characteristic of such problems to be reclassified as scientific once such advances had been made. Perhaps the biggest difference between Hume and Russell concerning this issue lies in what they take an experimental or scientific enquiry to look like. Hume's "experimental method" was basically that of psychological introspection, and while Russell was certainly a devotee of introspection, his notion of scientific method was altogether more modern, as one might put it, even just as applied to the realm of psychology. (We have already seen in Chapter 1 how he was influenced by behaviouristic theories of mind.) And the developments of modern science clearly lend to modern scientism a different flavour from earlier versions.

Modern scientism about philosophy has mainly North American roots. Its origins lie partly in American pragmatism, partly in logical positivism, several of whose representatives—Carnap, Schlick, and others—came over to America in the early decades of the twentieth century from a politically troubled Europe. The Ohio-born Willard van Orman Quine met several of the logical positivists when he travelled to Europe in 1932/3, later writing that "no one has influenced my philosophical thought more than Carnap"[5], and it is probably Quine who is most associated with the modern view of philosophy as "continuous with science".

Quine's main argument for this view[6] centres on a rejection of the analytic/synthetic distinction. He takes it that the claim that philosophy is concerned with purely conceptual investigations goes with the claim that philosophical propositions are (typically) analytic—in which case the former claim is undermined to the extent that the analytic/synthetic distinction is undermined. But a more potent factor for scientism, I think, has been Quine's quite general picture of a theory and its "ontological commitments". According to this picture, a theory—scientific, philosophical, or what have you—may be assessed in terms of what kinds of thing must exist for it to be true. The model for this picture is evidently the sort (or a sort) of theory to be found in the natural sciences. And yet the picture has proved amenable to the metaphysical impulse, an impulse that might at first glance have been thought at odds with scientism. For a theory, even of natural science, may turn out to be ontologically committed to kinds of things not explicitly mentioned in the theory. A provisional licence thus becomes available to the metaphysical philosopher, a licence to expatiate on kinds of entity above and beyond atoms, force fields, genes, and the rest. Quine himself embraces sets, as "required" for the truth of mathematical theories; his disciple Donald Davidson claims to reveal by Quinean means our ontological commitment to events as concrete particulars; and David Lewis, again employing the characteristic machinery of existential quantifiers interpreted à la Quine as "objectual", has discerned for us a whole universe of co-existing possible worlds, dimly visible in such ordinary sentences as "If you heat a lump of butter it melts", as aeons of past time may be visible in the rings of a tree trunk.

We should pause to consider this matter of existential quantification. Quine distinguishes the *objectual* from the *substitutional* interpretations of the existential quantifier ("There exists . . ."), and argues that only on the first interpretation can a theory be seen as making substantive claims.[7] On Quine's objectual interpretation, "There are cats" means "There is at least one object which is a cat", while on the substitutional interpretation it means "There is at least one true substitution-instance of 'x is a cat'".[8] What about, e.g. "There are properties"? One might regard this as merely a logical generalization from sentences like "Fido and Snapper share a property", and the latter as a logical generalization from a sentence like "Fido and Snapper are both dogs", taking the latter to refer to (be about, pick out . . .) only Fido and Snapper—and not even implicitly the property *doghood*, or the set of dogs, or the Fregean concept *dog*. Such a view of things would go naturally with a substitutional reading of "Fido and Snapper share a property", i.e. as meaning "There is at least one true substitution-instance of 'Fido is F and Snapper is F'"; while on a substitutional reading "There are properties" will mean something like "There is at least one true substitution-instance of 'x is F' (or of 'x is not F')". This latter reading will of course be regarded by Quine as not really substantive. The substantive reading would translate the sentence as meaning "There exist certain abstract objects, to wit *properties*", and would give the green light to a metaphysical enquiry into the nature of these entities. (Possible findings include: they exist entire in each of their instances; they are sometimes related to one another by laws of contingent necessitation which make statements of laws of nature

130   *Aftermath and Legacy*

true; they correspond only to those predicates to be found in "our best science"; and so on.)

Now an anti-metaphysical philosopher like Wittgenstein might say that there is less to "There are properties" than meets the eye, and congratulate Quine on seeing that there is a way of expressing this fact in the terms of symbolic logic: higher-order quantification, involving bound variables of the category of predicate, sentence, etc., may best be interpreted in a substitutional fashion, and at any rate should *not* be interpreted in an objectual fashion.[9] (It is a matter for debate whether Quine's two interpretations exhaust the possibilities.) But at this point the dialectic is quite likely to become confused. For Quine does not claim to show that there's anything *wrong* with substitutionally-interpreted existential statements, merely arguing that they won't count as substantive in the way that the propositions of a theory must be substantive. And a Wittgensteinian philosopher might agree, saying: "There are properties" is indeed not part of a *theory*—adding that the same goes for "People feel pain", "16 has just one positive square root", "Stuff happens", or "There's many a slip 'twixt cup and lip'". Such statements are typically either very obvious everyday statements (possibly bedrock propositions) or grammatical propositions, in Wittgenstein's sense of that phrase. But this agreement will not be appreciated by the scientistic or metaphysical philosopher. Such a philosopher may want to object to substitutional or similarly deflationary interpretations of what we say on the grounds that such interpretations disallow a theory-oriented ("substantive") approach to those sayings, while arguing for the theory-oriented approach by reference to the Quinean view that everything that we say is part of some theory, with its own ontological commitments. But evidently the possibility of deflationary interpretations itself casts doubt on this latter view. One cannot *both* argue against deflationary interpretations of what we say by appeal to the "Everything is a theory" theory *and* argue for this theory by appeal to a presumption of non-deflationary as against deflationary interpretations of what we say.

I have discussed the Quinean version of scientism in philosophy at such length for two reasons. First, because scientism is a, if not the, dominant flavour of post-Wittgensteinian philosophy of mind, so that modern theories of thought, belief, will and intention tend implicitly or explicitly to adopt a stance of subservience towards scientific psychology, in a way that is at odds with Wittgenstein's approach. Secondly, it does seem that the modern assumption that philosophy is continuous with science has, if questioned, not much to back it up besides those original arguments of Quine's, or variants of them (e.g. in Putnam's earlier work). The attack on the analytic/synthetic distinction has not, of course, gone unquestioned[10], and it is in any case doubtful how many scientistic philosophers would nowadays base their position on that attack. On the other hand, the picture of philosophizing, and of -izing more generally, as a species of theory-construction, assessable in terms of ontological commitments, does seem to be just that: a picture.

Aftermath and Legacy   131

And as I have indicated, the invocation of this picture by those attacking Wittgenstein's conception of philosophy runs the risk of begging the question in a fairly obvious way, especially given Quine's own directions for how to produce "non-substantive" (substitutionalist) versions of various traditionally metaphysical propositions.

It seems likely in fact that the main reasons for the prevalence of scientism in philosophy have to do with the status of science in our (especially Western) culture. The natural sciences and their practitioners enjoy considerable kudos, and professional philosophers are both impressed by the "scientific paradigm" and, all too often, tempted on that account to cast their subject as a cousin or handmaiden of science, even if this involves a degree of wishful thinking.[11]

2.   SCIENCE AND SCIENTISM: SOME SKIRMISHES

Turning now to Wittgenstein's legacy, we can see some of the above themes played out in application to the topics of thought and will, and more generally to the philosophy of psychology, if we look at how a Wittgensteinian philosopher like Norman Malcolm has reacted to (putatively) scientific theories, such as Chomsky's theory of generative grammars, comparing his approach with that of such anti-Wittgensteinians as C.S. Chihara and J.A. Fodor.

Malcolm, like Wittgenstein, regarded various scientific approaches to the mind as running real risks of conceptual confusion, and he was not afraid to point out those risks to practising scientists. At a colloquium held at Rice University he attempted to steer between the Scylla of dualism, represented by C.R. Rogers, and the Charybdis of behaviourism, represented by B.F. Skinner—both Rogers and Skinner being psychologists. His arguments owe much to Wittgenstein, and for me to spell them out here would in effect be to repeat points made in earlier chapters of this book.[12] At one point Malcolm praises Noam Chomsky's critique of Skinner's programme, but it is to Chomsky that he turns in "The Myth of Cognitive Processes and Structures", where, in language that recalls Ryle, he writes *contra* Chomsky that "our understanding of human cognitive powers is not advanced by replacing the stimulus-response mythology with a mythology of inner guidance systems".[13]

Chomskian linguistics is thought by many to be "scientific", at least in spirit, and Chomsky's conception of linguistic ability as requiring explanation in terms of a calculus or set of rules somehow embodied in (the brain of) the individual does manifest a common scientific impulse—one that is often justifiable—namely, the impulse to posit a hidden cause of certain regularly observed phenomena. Now nobody sensible would deny that the human capacity to learn and use language is down to human beings' having brains, and down to structural and other features of those brains. But

132 *Aftermath and Legacy*

Chomsky's "hypothesis" concerning generative grammars does not belong to neuroscience; it seeks to infer an inner mechanism, mirroring the rules embodied in actual language use, from the observed phenomenon of that language use. In fact the mechanism must not only mirror the rules, it must itself embody or even express them: it is itself a "grammar". The rules of actual language use have been *projected inwards*, since nothing less than an image of language itself could possibly explain language.

What sort of explanation does Chomsky have in mind? Qua mechanism, the posited internal grammar is meant to supply causal explanations of people's sayings, writings, acquiescings, etc.—much as the mechanism of a watch explains its telling the time correctly. Qua calculus, or qua grammar, it is meant to supply normative (justificatory) explanations of those phenomena—much as my statement "I was told to shut the door" explains my shutting the door. It is the second aspect of Chomsky's account that Malcolm latches onto.[14] If in using language I need to be following or obeying a pre-existent (somehow embodied or promulgated) rule, I need to know how to interpret that rule. Do I do this by following rules for the interpretation of the symbols constituting the first rule? That way lies an infinite regress. Do I then *just follow* the rule? But if I can do this, why can't I *just follow* linguistic rules when I speak? The dilemma is *echt* Wittgenstein, of course.

It is worth remarking on Chomsky's hoped-for combination of causal and normative explanation. We have already seen in Chapter 2 how two pictures of human behaviour can both thrust themselves upon us, in one of which our actions are *guided*, are justified (or unjustified)—while in the other, they are the effects of prior or current states of the person. I intend to go into the field and pick a red flower. What is it for me to execute my intention? Under the influence of the first picture, we may posit an image, or sample, or instruction, something that guides me and with which my future action will or will not be in conformity; and this conformity will be an internal relation, holding between the image (etc.) and the action (here including the red flower). Under the influence of the second picture, we may think of the intention as a state that causes my flower-picking (or my failure), and may characterize the content of the intention, e.g. as whatever would cause the cessation of my behaviour-cycle. The relation between intention and action is here an external one.

Both pictures, as we saw in Chapter 2, raise acute difficulties, and one might wonder if a theory such as Chomsky's which appears to combine the pictures is in danger of incurring both sets of problems. It is true that the *explanandum* which he is dealing with is rather different from the question what it is for us to execute our intentions; and yet one can see certain parallels between the two sorts of issue. There is a temptation to think of intending to do X as a *state* of the person, a state which *produces* the action of doing X (in favourable circumstances). Don't we after all predict what people will do on the basis of what they intend to do? But from the first-person perspective one seems to be able to "read off" what one is going to do from one's intention, rather than merely predicting it—for one surely has a special authority about what one will do. Chomsky similarly appears to regard linguistic understanding as a state of the person, a state productive of utterances, etc., and which can be inferred by the linguist as a cause is inferred from its effect; while at the same time recognising that if you understand what someone has said, you do not merely *predict*, on the basis of finding this state of understanding within you, that you will, e.g. say certain things by way of explanation of, inference from, or disagreement with, what was said—for in some sense your understanding *guides* you.

It is perhaps above all the picture of the "mental state", of intention or of understanding, which is the main culprit here. It is the picture of a state, expressed by the relevant verb, which can simply be *attributed*, in the third, second or first person: that picture Wittgenstein's critique of which was one of the themes of Chapter 4 (see 114–16). Chomsky is not alone in feeling the need, having posited such a state, to endow it with both external and internal relations to its manifestations. (The internal grammar both produces and justifies linguistic utterances.) Davidson's famous account of "reasons as causes" likewise aims to have the best of both worlds, as we shall see presently. And the fact is that both external relations and internal relations are *in play*, the former, e.g. holding between my walking up and down, muttering "Where is he?", and Jack's knocking on the door—the latter holding between "I expect Jack will come" and "Jack has come". As Wittgenstein put it, "It is in language that an expectation and its fulfilment make contact." We have seen in Chapter 2 how that saying is to be cashed out. Wittgenstein makes room for both internal and external relations, as also for the possibility of predicting people's actions, first-person "authority" as to those actions, and so on—and in doing so, he does not inherit the problems of the two pictures mentioned above so much as neutralise both sets of problems. For he is not hampered by the picture of thought, intention or understanding as an inner state or process.

Malcolm took issue not only with Skinner, Rogers and Chomsky, but also with those scientists who invoked evidence surrounding the phenomenon of REM (rapid eye movement) sleep to hypothesize that dream-experiences occur during episodes of REM sleep. For Malcolm, this hypothesis boils down to nonsense, given that we are operating with the ordinary concept *sleep*, since (he argues) the phenomenon of sleep—or at any rate of deep, undisturbed sleep—is logically incompatible with the sleeper's having such experiences as visual imaginings or feelings of fear, as also with the sleeper's thinking or intending anything. Malcolm lays much stress on the notion of a conceptually central criterion[15], and asks, "What are the criteria of someone's feeling fear, or thinking, or intending, etc.?" and "Could such criteria be manifest when someone is asleep?" Any putative third-person criterion will have to be usable as such in a language-game, and so will have to be either behavioural or linguistic. *Ex hypothesi*, there is no behaviour going on in (sound) sleep; while a person's saying in his sleep, "I am

134 *Aftermath and Legacy*

thinking", "I can see a dragon", "I am asleep", or indeed anything at all, is not saying anything in the relevant sense of "say": there are none of the usual consequences of a linguistic move's having been made, such as being committed to what you have said, being bound by the norm of truth or truthfulness, and the like. What then is the criterion for dreaming? Malcolm replies, naturally enough: it is the dream-report someone gives on waking. Why is this "report" expressed using the past tense? Roughly, because the experience one has on waking is, or is like, a delusive memory, e.g. of having been chased by a dragon. Malcolm derives his arguments—of which I have only given a sketch—largely from Wittgenstein. But it is worth pointing out that another follower of Wittgenstein, Severin Schroeder, has thrown doubt upon Malcolm's conclusions.[16]

Malcolm's arguments in *Dreaming* were attacked by C.S. Chihara and J.A. Fodor in the course of an article[17] generally critical of Wittgenstein's philosophy of psychology, and characteristic of what I have called scientism in its proposal that we should regard people's ordinary assertions about the pains, dreams, thoughts, etc. of others as empirical hypotheses, akin to those made in physics. The authors write:

> Perhaps, what we all learn in learning what such terms as "pain" and "dream" mean are not criterial connections which map those terms severally onto characteristic patterns of behaviour. We may instead form complex conceptual connections which interrelate a wide variety of mental states. It is to such a conceptual system that we appeal when we attempt to explain someone's behaviour . . . In the course of acquiring these mental concepts we develop a variety of beliefs involving them. Such beliefs result in a wide range of expectations about how people are likely to behave . . . On this view, our success in accounting for the behaviour on the basis of which mental predicates are applied might properly be thought of as supplying *evidence* for the existence of the mental processes we postulate . . . The behaviour would be . . . analogous to the cloud-chamber track on the basis of which we detect the presence and motion of charged particles. Correspondingly, the conceptual system is analogous to the physical *theory* in which the properties of those particles are formulated.[18]

Here we have a fairly overt embracing of the idea that such connections as that between being in pain, on the one hand, and groaning or rubbing a part of the body, on the other, are all of them causal and contingent (external) in nature. And the "conceptual system" must already be at least partly in place before the various beliefs and expectations as to behaviour come on the scene[19]; at any rate, if one were to allow these beliefs and expectations a status on a par with the conceptual system itself, rather than being logically posterior, their confirmation could hardly play the role of *evidence* with respect to the system which the authors wish to propose. (The connection between "People in great pain often groan" and "Henry is groaning . . ." would in such a case appear to be just the sort that is predicted by a criterial account of the concept *pain*.) But given a logical priority of conceptual system over beliefs and expectations, it looks as if the meaning of "pain", for Chihara and Fodor, will have to reside entirely in its place in a system of terms, terms whose meanings are also determined by the place of the terms in the system. Perhaps the conceptual system vouchsafes us something like "If x is in pain, then x wants not to be in pain"; but it won't vouchsafe us "If x wants not to be in pain, x will try to do what x thinks will stop the pain"—for *trying to do* is too behavioural. (Of course, *neither* of these statements is universally true, something accountable for by reference to criteria, but not so clearly accountable for by reference to a "conceptual system".) One might in fact wonder what someone can *do* who has learnt "If x is in pain, then x wants not to be in pain", on Chihara's and Fodor's view. It is much as if the person had learnt "If x sturges, then x doesn't wiffle x's sturging". Adding more such axioms, with additional wurging and stiffling, won't magically convert the nonsense into sense.

A clue as to why the authors seem confident that "pain" *et al.* will actually be meaningful, as well as enjoying multiple conceptual interconnections, comes a little later:

> The belief that other people feel pains is not gratuitous even on the view that there are no criteria of pains. On the contrary, it provides the only plausible explanation of the facts I know about the way that they behave in and *vis à vis* the sorts of situations I find painful.[20]

For me, it is a hypothesis that Sally is in pain, but not a hypothesis that *I* am in pain; that is why there is no difficulty for me in knowing which are "the sorts of situations I find painful". I infer Sally's pain from her groaning, but don't infer my own pain from my groaning: I *just know* I'm in pain. I know it because I have it. And I know what "pain" means, presumably, because I'm acquainted with my own sample of it. So now I am at liberty to learn about conceptual connections between "pain" and other terms, whose meaning I have in like manner determined.

We have been here before. (See 66–8, above.) What is of interest is how easily a "scientific" account of psychological concepts falls back, apparently unwittingly, on a view of first-person privileged access characteristic of mind-body dualism. But were we to expunge this latter feature from the account, we should still be left with the problem I have mentioned, of endowing the various interconnected elements in the "conceptual system" with meaning.

There is a suggestion in Chihara and Fodor that the notion of multiple conceptual connections between psychological terms is absent from a Wittgensteinian account—hence their reference to "criterial connections which map those terms *severally* onto characteristic patterns of behaviour"

136 *Aftermath and Legacy*

(my italics). There is no evidence for this suggestion, and indeed it is surely false. Wittgenstein would in addition be happy, I think, to say that conceptual connections between "pain", "want", "believe", etc. are partially determinative of the meanings of those terms, in one central sense of "meanings". The desire to talk of these conceptual connections as binding psychological terms together into a *system* is, of course, alien to Wittgenstein's thought, unless that word is being used in a very liberal and open-ended sense, tantamount to *family*. It seems likely that the comparison by Chihara and Fodor of a "conceptual system" and a "physical theory" is motivated in part by the desire to depict psychological vocabulary as, after all, perfectly respectable.

Certainly, the question whether our ordinary talk of pain, thought, will, etc. *is* fully respectable is a question that has been taken seriously in the post-Wittgensteinian scientistic tradition. This is a natural consequence of buying into Quine's picture of all that we say and think as comprising *theories*. The name that has been given to the alleged theory of mind held by ordinary people is "folk psychology". Unsurprisingly, this theory has been compared unfavourably with proper science—after all, the folk have been pretty remiss when it comes to conducting experiments, collecting statistical results, and so on—with the result that some philosophers have proposed that folk psychology is likely to be false, even to the extent that the "hypotheses" that we think or believe things, want or intend things, feel or suffer things, are all of them false. The name of this position is *eliminativism*.[21] It is a position standing in a long and venerable line of philosophical positions that deny the reality of some large class of things we had all thought real: material objects, time, colours, moral facts, heaps, other minds. Like these other positions, eliminativism can be counted on not actually to make any difference to how its proponents live or to how they talk non-philosophically— at least one hopes not, for their sakes. McTaggart still wore a watch, and no doubt Professor Churchland still says "I think . . ." and "That hurt!" Some will say that these facts do not constitute a philosophical refutation. Perhaps indeed they constitute something more damning. Hume wrote of abstruse philosophy that "when we leave our closet, and engage in the common affairs of life, its conclusions seem to vanish like the phantoms of the night on the appearance of the morning . . ."[22] If there is a clash between what we say in our philosophical closet and what we say in the outside world, we could try emulating Walt Whitman and embrace contradiction—or we could put phantoms and fairy tales behind us.

3. THE INNER PROCESS AND THE BIGGER PICTURE

In the last section I looked at some examples of how the "scientific paradigm" has influenced work in such areas as linguistics and philosophy of psychology, arguably in ways that open the door to Wittgensteinian critiques. In this section I want to turn to the psychology and the philosophy of

Aftermath and Legacy 137

psychology of the last few decades, in order to illustrate the relevance of that particular species of Wittgensteinian critique which insists on the importance of context or surroundings. I will not be thrashing out the arguments here so much as giving examples of certain trends of thought, leaving it to the reader to fill out in detail how considerations from previous chapters might apply to these.

One way of seeing what has been happening in these fields is as either (i) focused on the individual to the exclusion of his environment, or (ii) embracing that environment. The relevance of Wittgenstein's thought to this dichotomy should be evident by now (see, e.g. Chapter 3, sec. 4). To generalise somewhat, philosophers and psychologists to whom (i) applies will quite often be at odds with Wittgenstein in a way in which those to whom (ii) applies will not. Thus it is not so surprising when psychologists who are interested in investigating brain processes assume that a given psychological term must apply to a *process* in exactly the sense I described earlier, in connection with Wittgenstein's remark, "we have a definite concept of what it means to learn to know a process better": i.e. homing in on it, observing it in detail, and describing its nature by describing what is observed.

In an experiment conducted in the 1980s, Benjamin Libet asked each of his subjects to choose a random moment to flick their wrist while he measured the activity in their brain, in particular the build-up of electrical signal called the readiness potential. Apparently it was already known of this readiness potential that it (always? typically?) precedes voluntary physical action; the question that Libet asked himself was how the readiness potential corresponded to a person's "felt intention to move". To determine when the subjects felt the intention to move, he asked them to watch the second hand of a clock and report the position it had had at the moment when they believed they had experienced that feeling. Libet found that the brain activity leading up to the flicking of the wrist began approximately half a second before the time given by the subject as the time when he had felt the intention to move, or experienced the making of the decision. He concluded that a person's belief that his actions occur at the behest of his will is illusory: since the best evidence for when the intention/decision occurred is the subject's say-so ("first-person authority"), that intention/decision is evidently occurring after the neurological cause (the readiness potential), which—being neurological—must be a *sufficient* cause.[23]

It is of course interesting that people can take themselves to understand the question, "When, at what *second*, did you feel (or experience) the intention/decision to flick your wrist?"—though in the course of his experiments, Libet did encounter quite a few subjects who said they didn't know how to answer questions like that one.[24] The picture of the "inner process" is indeed highly seductive. As we have already seen, there is a twofold way with someone in the grip of this sort of picture. You begin with Wittgenstein's "Don't think, but look!" (*PI* 66), and ask the person whether he really is aware of conscious decisions to do X in connection with all his intentional acts

138 *Aftermath and Legacy*

(and how does one count those?)—and if not, whether he is on that account worried that his riding a bike is perhaps quite unintentional, does not occur "at the behest of his will". Secondly, you go into the concepts of the intentional and the voluntary in sufficient detail to show the absurdity of the claims made under the influence of the picture. This sort of thing has been done in connection with experiments like Libet's: the philosopher P.M.S. Hacker and the neuroscientist M.R. Bennett teamed up to write a book[25] with the main aim of unravelling conceptual confusions in neuroscientific psychology. Hacker is a noted Wittgenstein scholar and Wittgensteinian, and so can be seen as continuing the sort of work I described Norman Malcolm as having undertaken in his dialogues with scientists. That there is nothing in neuroscience per se that conflicts with the views of Wittgenstein seems to be shown by M.R. Bennett's collaboration on this project. Another person coming from neuroscience but sceptical of the reductive tendencies of many of its practitioners is Raymond Tallis, author, among other things, of *Why the Mind is Not a Computer: A Pocket Dictionary on Neuromythology.*[26]

I said above that it is perhaps not surprising that psychologists interested in investigating brain processes quite often assume that a given psychological term must apply to an inner process. It is likewise less than startling that social psychologists, developmental psychologists, and the like, should *not* be liable to make such an assumption, but should be more ready to look to the (especially social) environment of a person when wielding psychological concepts. A good example of this is an article by the developmental psychologists Charlie Lewis and Jeremy Carpendale, in which the authors write that "Wittgenstein's philosophy can be applied as a general critique of many current theories of social cognitive development", a remark they back up with a fairly extended resumé of Wittgenstein's ideas, including his ideas on privacy and private language. They then set forth a positive account of children's understanding of and interaction with others, an account very much in the spirit of Wittgenstein but (of course) backed up by, or tied in with, empirical findings. They compare "approaches based on the assumption that the development of an understanding of mind is an individual process of introspection, maturation, or the formation of a theory, with the contrasting position that children acquire culture-specific concepts regarding the mind which are passed on from the social group"; and write:

> Instead of choosing between these two contrasting positions, we begin from a different starting point and endorse an alternative perspective emphasizing the relations between people. . . . Concepts about the mind are not just passed on from the social group, nor are they completely formed by individual child-theorists. Instead, children gradually construct social understanding through the regularities they experience in interacting with others.[27]

Note the use of the word "understanding" in the last sentence, a word to be contrasted with "theory". It is surely not to such psychological research, but rather to research like Libet's, that the remarks in the final section of the *Investigations* apply: ". . . in psychology there are experimental methods and *conceptual confusion* . . . The existence of the experimental method makes us think we have the means of solving the problems which trouble us; though problem and method pass one another by." (*PI*, ii p. 232)[28]

Developmental psychology of the sort represented by Carpendale and Lewis, and social psychology in general, is sometimes referred to in psychological circles as "holistic". More commonly, I believe, this term is applied to a theory or approach that considers the "whole system"—i.e. the whole system of beliefs, attitudes, or whatever, associated with a *single person*. This is also typically how the term is used in the philosophy of psychology. But the relevance of the *environment*, social or natural, to philosophical issues concerning psychological states, etc., is certainly asserted in various accounts, as for example in "externalist" accounts of the content of propositional attitudes (beliefs, intentions, etc.). Might such accounts be seen as exemplifying an environment-embracing tendency within philosophy of mind, as Carpendale and Lewis exemplify such a tendency within psychology?

The most famous form of philosophical externalism about the mind is associated with the work of Putnam, who derives his main argument from an externalist account of linguistic meaning of the sort associated with both Putnam and Kripke. Putnam's catch-phrase "'Meanings' just ain't in the head"[29] sums up an argument which especially stresses the identity of the putative *causes* of a person's beliefs. That it was H_2O with which Oscar had to do in forming certain beliefs he expresses using the word "water" is what determines the content of those beliefs—rather than, e.g. anything Oscar might say or think about the appearance of the stuff in question. If Oscar's "twin" says and thinks just the same things, but has had to do with a qualitatively indistinguishable stuff whose chemical composition is not H_2O, then the twin's beliefs expressed using "water" are not the same as Oscar's. This sort of argument has a degree of affinity with Wittgenstein, but in its negative conclusions more than in its positive ones; the reliance on causal origin to sort things out (to which I will turn later on) is unWittgensteinian, as is the relative lack of interest in how Oscar and those around him would *use* a term like "water".[30] Nevertheless, the externalism (semantic and psychological) of Putnam and others is quite close to Wittgenstein by comparison with the Language of Thought Hypothesis of Jerry Fodor. This latter position is one of the more vivid philosophical instances of the first of the two tendencies I referred to at the beginning of this section (the tendency to focus on the individual to the exclusion of his environment).

We have already encountered Fodor doing his bit in the 1960s to resist the ideas of Wittgenstein. Over the course of his career, despite changes in his views, Fodor has remained true to a basic outlook, at the heart of which is the picture of the inner process. He has been influenced by Chomsky, and like Chomsky (see 131–3, above) he is drawn to the idea of inner states which both cause behaviour and embody features of language: another instance, in

140 *Aftermath and Legacy*

a way, of the desire to combine external and internal relations—though I'm sure Fodor would be officially against the idea of internal relations (in this context). Unlike Chomsky, of course, he takes for his subject-matter not just language and linguistic behaviour, but psychology more generally.

The main components of Fodor's position can be set forth thus[31]:

1. To each propositional attitude A there corresponds a particular psychological relation R, such that (for all propositions P and subjects S) S As that P if and only if there is a mental representation 'P' such that S bears R to 'P', and 'P' means that P.
2. Mental processes, thinking in particular, consist of causal sequences of (occurrences of) mental representations.
3. Mental representations belong to a symbolic system within which they have a combinatorial syntax and semantics, and the operations on representations that constitute thinking are causally sensitive to the syntactic/formal structure of representations.
4. Mental representations are realized by (embodied in) physical properties of the subject that has the propositional attitudes.

Fodor's Language of Thought—sometimes dubbed "Mentalese"—is the system of (constituents of) mental representations, operations upon which constitute the having of propositional attitudes, e.g. thinking.

In terms of the three-way division of views I introduced in Chapter 1, labelled (A), (B) and (C), Fodor's position can be seen as belonging to (B). He differs from a philosopher such as Locke mainly in regarding as purely physical the intermediary which is alleged to exist between the thinking subject and the world. And he is like some other empiricists, e.g. Hume, in believing that the constituents of someone's thought processes stand to one another in the relation of cause and effect. The causal relations involved somehow mirror the rules of syntax etc. which govern the thought-symbols—which is just as well, for otherwise you'd be at constant risk of thinking gobbledygook.

I pointed out in Chapter 1 the need for a proponent of (B) to explain how the intermediary items managed to represent or be *of* "things out there" (which of course had to include unicorns and the like). This is a question which Fodor originally believed could be answered without reference to anything outside the thinking subject, but which (perhaps under the influence of such philosophers as Putnam) he later came to believe should be answered by invoking the external causal origins of the mental representations. But the "central processing" part of the subject's brain-or-equivalent is still independent of external things; this is the part of the system which takes care of logical and syntactical relations, e.g. between various representations. It is to be regarded as a sort of computer, the nature of whose computations can in principle be ascertained by observation of them and of nothing else. The inner process has an intrinsic nature.

Many of the difficulties faced by other proponents of (B) are faced by Fodor's theory, and one does not need to resort especially to Wittgenstein to recognise these difficulties. But Wittgenstein is certainly worth mentioning, if only as the philosopher from whom perhaps Fodor has most spectacularly failed to learn. Quite apart from "the picture of the 'inner process'", the two features of Fodor's theory that really strike one as crying out for Wittgensteinian therapy are (i) the naive correlation of expressions with things or processes, and (ii) an *a priori* reliance on causal connection.

If we look only to surface grammar, we might conclude that in "Jones thinks it's raining", "Karen wants to go shopping", "I wish I had more money", etc., we find Subject—Relation—Object. (Though this would be more simplistic than the analyses given in any actual English grammar.) This is the conclusion effectively governing premise 1 of Fodor's account, above, in which "thinks that" *et al.* get correlated with psychological relations, and "it's raining" *et al.* get correlated with mental representations. This correlation need not be semantic—Fodor's claims need not explicitly pertain to meaning or reference; for all that, they evidently employ a notion of "propositional attitude" that derives from a coarse-grained parsing of surface forms, in which verbs are naively read as relational predicates. (Hence the reification of propositions as mental representations.) As for (ii), it is manifest both in the externalist reliance on causal determinants of meaning and in the positing of causal connections among the representations constituting thought. The latter manoeuvre shows Fodor attempting to use external (causal) relations in an explanation of internal (logical) relations, rather as we found Russell doing in his theory of desire (see Chapter 1). As we have seen, an easy fix is rarely to be had in this way from the concept of cause. The temptation to reach for such a fix is a theme I shall be returning to in sec. 6 of this chapter.

Fodor presents his theory of the Language of Thought as a hypothesis. In the preferred acronymic patois, LOT is the subject of LOTH. And his choice of the word "hypothesis" is an ideological one, the ideology in question being that of Quine. This ideology tells us that philosophy, or good philosophy, is continuous with science. But even if scientism were *true*, it remains the case that a scientific theory (or publication) can be conceptually confused, even gibberish. Fodor's hypothesis may belong squarely within natural science; even so, that would not make it immune from the sorts of critique which philosophers seem to specialize in, not even the sort of critique that smacks of Wittgenstein. I have sketched how I think such a critique might look: it would (at least) advert to (i) the seductive power of surface linguistic forms and (ii) an a priori trust in causal connections. And governing all in LOTH is a philosophical approach that as far as possible eschews the bigger picture, preferring to home in on "what's going on in" the subject. It was after all Fodor who proposed what he called "methodological solipsism" as a research strategy in cognitive science.[32]

142   *Aftermath and Legacy*

4.   ANSCOMBE ON INTENTION

I turn now to what have probably been the two most important contributions to the philosophy of intention in the last sixty years or so, those of Elizabeth Anscombe and of Donald Davidson. This is relevant to the present chapter for two reasons: first, Davidson's extremely influential account is explicitly opposed to the thought of Wittgenstein and of his followers on this topic; second, Anscombe's account may be seen both as greatly elaborating upon themes from Wittgenstein and as presenting the most significant and powerful alternative to Davidsonism.

Anscombe's *Intention*, like other of her writings, is a dense and often difficult piece, and this may in part account for its having been either ignored or misunderstood by many philosophers, while Davidson's essays have been more easily and readily assimilated. Since her death in 2001 this state of affairs has altered, and it is no longer sociologically accurate to call Davidson's the "standard" view, as has for some time been the custom. (Though Davidsonism may still be the *majority* view.) *Intention* is an extremely rich book, covering many themes; I will give a synopsis of some of its arguments, with a view both to showing the influence of her teacher, Wittgenstein, and to preparing the ground for the debate with Davidson.

At the start of the book, Anscombe introduces her subject under three heads:

(A) Expression of intention for the future (e.g. "I'm going to buy some milk")
(B) Intentional action (e.g. my buying of some milk)
(C) Intention in acting, or intention 'with which' (e.g. *to buy some milk*).

The structure of the book corresponds to these themes in this order. There are certain advantages in this division and ordering. For example, it will turn out that the picture of intentions as inner states that cause actions is radically defective, as Wittgenstein had seen; and by postponing any direct discussion of phrases like "the intention to φ" till we get to (C), Anscombe allows us to proceed unhampered by that picture. She is thus able to take such expressions of intention as "I'm going to buy some milk" at face value, i.e. as about future actions, not present mental states.

What then distinguishes "I'm going to buy some milk" from "I'm going to be sick"? Anscombe considers, but rejects, the thought that the latter is a "prediction" while the former is not. Both statements are predictions, if that means statements about the future that can turn out true or false. The clue, she says, lies in the difference in the sorts of reasons or grounds that are given for each statement. This was the view of things we encountered in Chapter 2 (52–3), in connection with Wittgenstein's discussion of the two different claims made in "I am going to take two powders now, and in half-an-hour I shall be sick." Anscombe characterizes the sense of "reason" or "ground" she has in mind by reference to possible responses to the question "Why?"—as in "Why are you going to buy some milk?" Intentional actions "are the actions to which a certain sense of the question 'Why?' is given application".[33] Our task is to elucidate the relevant sense of "Why?"

Anscombe carries out this task partly by delineating the conditions under which "Why?" is refused application, and partly by stating what sorts of answer can be given when the question does have application. Application of the question is refused by means of answers like, "I didn't know I was doing X", and also "I knew I was doing X, but only because I observed that I was" (e.g. making a squeaking noise with my shoes as I walked). The issue implicit here is that of practical knowledge or the lack of it, to which issue we will turn in a moment. Positive answers to "Why?" are categorised by Anscombe as follows: "the answer may (a) simply mention past history, (b) give an interpretation of the action, or (c) mention something future." (24)

Anscombe should probably have said "further" rather than "future" in (c), since the sorts of answer to "Why?" she discusses include ones that give wider descriptions of a present action without adverting to the future— e.g. "Why are you ticking that box?"—"I'm voting for Bloggs" (or "To vote for Bloggs"). Construed thus generally, (c)-type answers give "further intentions", and figure importantly in practical deliberation and practical inference.

Both (a)-type answers and (b)-type answers (purport to) give what Anscombe calls *motives*, the former giving backward-looking motives, the latter, interpretative motives (or "motives-in-general"). An example of a backward-looking motive is the motive of revenge: "Why did you kill him?"—"Because he killed my brother." An example of an interpretative motive is the motive of patriotism: "Why are you singing?"—"It's my country's national anthem". Neither sort of case can be reduced to a "further intention". If you answer "Why did you kill him?" by saying "So as to have my revenge", your answer does not show you to be aiming at some independently specifiable outcome or action-description. For the concept of revenge is explained via such reasons as "Because he killed my brother", not.[34] To avenge a deed is, roughly, to harm someone *because* they have harmed you or yours. Though Anscombe does not point this out, the existence of genuinely backward-looking motives generates prima facie problems for theories, such as Davidson's, which define intentional actions as actions caused by intentions, or by desires (plus beliefs)—since an act of revenge (e.g.) is certainly intentional, but is not done *with* any independently specifiable intention or desire, and *a fortiori* is not caused by any such intention or desire. (That's to say, "Because he killed my brother" doesn't give such an intention or desire; asked "Why are you shooting?" you could of course state a further intention: "So as to kill him"—or express a desire: "I want to kill him".)

However, more than one kind of answer to "Why did you do that?" can mention past history, and some answers cite causes, rather than reasons, in the sense of "reasons" we have been trying to pin down. "As, e.g. when

144   *Aftermath and Legacy*

we give a ready answer to the question 'Why did you knock the cup off the table?'—'I saw such-and-such and it *made me jump.*'" (16) Anscombe labels such causes as seeing a face at the window *mental causes*. These cannot be distinguished from backward-looking motives by alleging that the effect of a mental cause is always involuntary, for it is not; Anscombe illustrates this with "The martial music excites me, that is why I march up and down". Nor are mental causes known to the subject only indirectly, by induction or from general knowledge. They are known directly, something that had been suggested by Wittgenstein in an essay dating from 1937 which Anscombe may have known, in which he writes: "If someone says: 'I am frightened, because he looks so threatening'—this looks as if it were a case of recognizing a cause immediately without repeated experiments."[35] Anscombe suggests that the difference between backward-looking motives and mental causes has to do with the ideas of good and of harm, which are involved in the former but not in the latter.

The distinction between reasons and causes is not a hard and fast one, and there are borderline or complex cases.[36] Nevertheless, the distinction is real, and one way in which the difference typically shows up is in the fact that a person can say straight off what her reasons are, but not what causes an event has—mental causes being a notable exception. And in fact a person will typically be able to say straight off what action she is performing. What is the nature of this ability?

In a famous example, Anscombe imagines someone going out with a shopping list, and returning with a bag whose contents do not correspond to what's on the list. This mismatch does not show that the list is at fault. For "if the list and the things that the man actually buys do not agree, and if this and this alone constitutes a *mistake*, then the mistake is not in the list but in the man's performance". (56) By contrast, a detective whose job it was to record what the shopper bought would produce a list that was in error, given a mismatch between list and bought items. This phenomenon has been dubbed a difference in "direction of fit", a phrase that nowhere occurs in *Intention*, and accounts of which usually differ significantly from what Anscombe says on the topic. For Anscombe, the shopping list example illustrates the difference between *practical knowledge* and *contemplative knowledge*. Knowing what you are about (practical knowledge) is not a case of correctly assessing facts that are prior to and independent of the knowledge. A statement of intention is like a shopping list, and to that extent is also like an order (as Anscombe says, the shopping list could in fact embody an order, if given to the man by his wife); but whereas an order is not false if it doesn't get obeyed, a statement of intention that doesn't get carried out is properly called false. For a statement of intention does *tell* others, e.g. where you will be, and in general what to expect of you; cf. Wittgenstein's "we can often predict a man's actions from his expression of a decision. An important language-game." (*PI* 632) Hence such statements, when they do get carried out, and so come true, count as expressing knowledge, for

Aftermath and Legacy 145

Anscombe. Nevertheless, where there is a discrepancy between what a person does and what he said he meant to do, and if this and this alone constitutes a mistake, then the mistake is not in the statement of intention but in the person's performance.

Connected with this is the by now familiar fact that you do not justify a statement of intention by giving grounds for believing it true, but by giving reasons for doing the thing in question. The epistemic ungroundedness of statements of intention is linked by Anscombe with the ungroundedness of the knowledge a person has of the positions of his limbs. Both kinds of knowledge are non-observational, and with both, there is room for intelligible error: you may fail to do what you set out to do, and you may think your leg is bent when in fact it is straight. By contrast, there is no room for intelligible error about the locations of your pains. If you say your hand hurts and not your foot, but keep rubbing the foot, limping, etc., then it would be "difficult to guess what you could mean" (14)—unless of course you are joking, or are a bad speaker of English, or . . . Anscombe marks the difference she has in mind by saying that you *can say* where your pains are, not that you *know* where they are—but that you do know what you are, or will be, doing. It doesn't follow from this that you know what you intend, since with statements of the form "I intend to φ" there appears to be little or no room for intelligible error. (Or rather, any error here would be pathological, and would not constitute a *mistake*; perhaps subconscious intentions are a case in point.) This seems to show that "I am going to buy some milk" and "I intend to buy some milk" are not exactly equivalent; nor is Anscombe committed to saying that they are. Rather, she is reminding us that the first is as much an expression of intention as the second, and that the first does not "rest on" the second in any way.

In her drawing of philosophical conclusions from facts about what possible statements are intelligible or unintelligible (e.g. "My hand hurts", above), Anscombe resembles Wittgenstein. But in the matter of putative knowledge of the position of one's limbs, or (contrastingly) of the place of a pain, Anscombe is both like and unlike Wittgenstein, in particular because he seems to have changed his mind at various points—at least concerning how best to put things. Thus we find "One *knows* the positions of one's limbs . . . Just as one also knows the place of sensation (pain) in the body" (*RPP* II, 63); but he later wrote:

> "I know where I am feeling pain", "I know that I feel it *here*" is as wrong as "I know that I am in pain". But "I know where you touched my arm" is right. (*OC* 41)

Wittgenstein was, however, clear on the question whether you *go by* anything (any "local signs") when you say where a pain is, his answer being "No"; and—like Anscombe—he gave the same answer to the question whether you go by anything, e.g. kinaesthetic sensations, when you say

146   *Aftermath and Legacy*

what position some limb is in.[37] However, it is not at all clear whether he would have agreed with Anscombe in connecting the ungroundedness of statements of intention with that of knowledge of the positions of limbs.

The arguments and lines of thought I have been expounding show Wittgenstein's influence on his pupil; but there are a number of ways in which Anscombe goes beyond anything to be found in Wittgenstein, both in *Intention* and elsewhere, as: (i) in the use she makes of the idea that actions are only intentional "under a description"; (ii) in laying out the structure to be found in practical reasoning, a structure made manifest through iteration of the question "Why?"—each answer provoking "And why are you aiming at *that*?"; (iii) in examining the notion of a "desirability characterisation", in giving which a person can in principle put a stop to the series of "Why?" questions; (iv) in her comparison of practical reasoning with theoretical reasoning; (v) in delineating the importance for ethics of various of these issues; and in yet other ways. But even where she goes beyond Wittgenstein, Anscombe shows again and again how deeply she is influenced by him, especially in her methods of attacking a problem.

5. DAVIDSON: REASONS AS CAUSES

A few years after the publication of *Intention*, Donald Davidson published his article "Actions, Reasons, and Causes" (1963).[38] *Intention* is mentioned in a footnote of that piece[39], along with books or articles by Ryle, Hampshire, Hart and Honoré, Dray, and "most of the books in the series edited by R.F. Holland, *Studies in Philosophical Psychology*", including ones by Kenny and Melden. What all these works have in common is their rejection of "the ancient—and common-sense—position that rationalization is a species of causal explanation". ("Rationalization" is Davidson's term for an explanation of an action that works by giving the agent's reason(s) for performing the action.)

Davidson is surely right when he says in his Introduction (xii) that an important modern impetus for anti-causalism is to be found in the work of Wittgenstein. The argument which Davidson here attributes to Wittgenstein is "that causal relations are essentially nomological and based on induction while our knowledge that an agent has acted on certain reasons is not usually dependent on induction or knowledge of serious laws." The word "essentially" in this quotation is too strong, since as we have seen (144, above) Wittgenstein, like Anscombe, recognises a species of directly observable, non-inductively known causality—and not just "mental causality" either, as one finds when one reads Wittgenstein's 1937 essay. Still, one could replace "essentially" by "typically" and get something roughly right. But as far as the difference between causal explanation and reasons-based explanation goes, there is a far more challenging point made in Wittgenstein (*et al.*) than the one Davidson mentions. This is a point which Davidson

Aftermath and Legacy   147

does address towards the end of his article, when considering objections to his view:

> It is said that the kind of knowledge one has of one's own reasons in acting is not compatible with the existence of a causal relation between reasons and actions: a person knows his own intentions in acting infallibly, without induction or observation, and no ordinary causal relation can be known in this way. (17–18)

Again, this version of the anti-causalist argument needs adjusting if it is to resemble what Wittgenstein or Anscombe would say. For these philosophers, a person does indeed have a kind of "authority" as to his intentions, if this just means that his expressions of intention have a criterially central status; but it is doubtful whether on that account we should speak of his *knowing* what his intentions are, and if we did we should certainly not go further and call such knowledge infallible. The point can then be made thus: your ability to say what your intentions (or reasons) are or were cannot be based on any *beliefs* as to what actions of yours were, are, will be, or are liable to be, effects of some prior or concurrent state of you (or of anything else).

In response to this claim, Davidson begins by pointing out that you can be wrong about what your real reasons for some action were or are. This phenomenon—or one version of it—is called self-deception, and it supplies one reason for eschewing the word "infallible". Davidson admits that the phenomenon is a rare one, and that it in any case doesn't alter the fact that in stating what your intentions or reasons were or are, "you usually have no evidence and make no observations". But he sees no problem for his view in this fact; for (i) "in order to know that a singular causal statement is true, it is not necessary to know the truth of a law; it is necessary only to know that some law covering the events at hand exists", and (ii) "it is far from evident that induction, and induction alone, yields [such] knowledge". So all I need to know, when I claim that my intention in firing the gun was to hit the target, is that it was this intention that caused the firing, and that there is some natural law covering the two events. If I've never fired a gun before, and have witnessed no one else doing so (having announced the intention of hitting something), then the second piece of knowledge presumably derives entirely from the first; and after all, "one case is often enough, as Hume admitted, to persuade us that a law exists".

But the invocation of Hume seems fantastical. *When* would Hume agree that "one case is enough"? A well-worn example might be putting one's hand in the fire and getting burnt: that is an experiment I don't need to repeat. My inclination to say "The fire hurt me", as also "Fire can hurt you", is probably well-entrenched after a single experience, something that has to do with the nastiness of the experience (and maybe with some evolutionary advantage in my being thus constituted). Does this sort of story

148   *Aftermath and Legacy*

carry over to intentional actions? I find within me an intention, note that my body does certain things, and just can't help thinking the intention caused those things. But all this will have to be true regardless of how nasty, nice or neutral the events in question are, for obviously I can form all sorts of intentions and do all sorts of things. A mystery.

Perhaps it seems less of a mystery when we reflect that the intention to hit the target in some sense *justifies* my firing the gun: firing the gun in that way is a good means to the end of hitting the target. Do I then think, "This intention within me, of hitting the target, has for its content something the achievement of which is made much more likely by . . . yes, by this firing of a gun that I'm doing! So I suppose the intention must be causing the firing." Davidson does seem to want to say some such thing, and he writes: "The justifying role of a reason . . . depends upon the [causal-] explanatory role, but the converse does not hold." We shall see in a moment what lies behind this last remark. But let us first turn to something that Davidson says very little about in "Actions, Reasons, and Causes"—namely, expressions of intention for the future.

If intentions stand in a causal relationship to their corresponding actions, then when I say what I will do "on the basis of" my present intention, I will be making a prediction, similar to my prediction that I will be sick, made on the basis of my having swallowed Wittgenstein's Two Powders. And if I have formed a quite novel intention, the question will arise how I can possibly predict *anything* on the basis of my having it.[40] To say "one case is enough" won't work here, for the obvious reason that this phrase applies to a single case of an observed conjunction of events—and I haven't yet observed what I will do. Again, the justifying role of a reason might occur to us as providing some sort of clue, in so far as that role goes with a correspondence between the *content* of an intention and the action that will fulfil it. I mentioned the fact my intention to hit a target has for its content something made more probable by my firing a gun; and of course my intention to φ quite generally has for its content that which will fulfil it, namely φ-ing. It is this internal relation which Wittgenstein has in mind when he says that it is in language that an expectation (intention, desire, command . . .) and its fulfilment make contact. But Davidson shows little or no awareness of the problem what it *is* for an intention or desire to have a particular content. And a Wittgensteinian line on this would clearly be of no use to him, since that line is incompatible with the idea that you read off, or otherwise predict, what you will do "on the basis of" your intention.

In fact, what Davidson has to say about intentional content appears confused. He writes:

> . . . the event whose occurrence makes "I turned on the light" true cannot be called the object, however intentional, of "I wanted to turn on the light". If I turned on the light, then I must have done it at a precise moment, in a particular way—every detail is fixed. But it makes

Aftermath and Legacy 149

no sense to demand that my want be directed to an action performed at any one moment or done in some unique manner. Any one of an indefinitely large number of actions would satisfy the want and can be considered equally eligible as its object. (6)

Davidson seems to want to say this in order to make room for his claim that the relation between a desire and its fulfilment is causal, and thus non-necessary. And it is true, as he remarks, that "I turned on the light" and "I wanted to turn on the light", are logically independent in the sense that neither sentence entails the other.[41] But you feel like asking, "Is it then a *coincidence* that the same proposition occurs after 'I wanted' as would report what fulfils the want?" The fact emphasised by Wittgenstein in more than one place holds good—that it is the very same proposition that occurs in "I want that p" and "p", as for that matter in "Not p" and "p".[42] Davidson's argument in the above passage is specious, for when we say that my turning on the light was the intentional object of my want, i.e. that the subsequent action was exactly what I wanted to happen, we are not somehow incorporating that action into an earlier mental state (whatever that would mean). Nor are we saying that the action is the direct object of the verb "want", in the way in which a cake can be the direct object of "cut". You can't cut what doesn't exist, but you can evidently want something that will never exist or happen—this sort of fact was discussed in Chapter 1, as connected with the Parmenidean problem of false thought, whose analogue for the will is unfulfilled intention or desire. That my turning on the light was, e.g. done at 11.34 p.m. is quite compatible with its being *what I wanted*, in the only sense that there is of that phrase. On Davidson's view, it would seem that the person who is ordered to mend a fence cannot obey the order: for he, e.g. mends it on a Tuesday, using wood bought from a local shop . . . and he was never ordered to do *that*!

I said above that both Chomsky's theory of generative grammars and Fodor's Language of Thought Hypothesis involve attempts to combine internal (justificatory) and external (causal) relations in one phenomenon. Something like this seems to hold of Davidson also. That the fulfilment of an intention is internally related to the expression of that intention is something he appears not to have noticed he was taking for granted, in ways I have tried to indicate; but there is more to it than that. For another well-known line of thought in Davidson's writings concerns the normativity of rational explanations, something he especially connects with "interpretation".[43] "Normativity" relates to the justificatory role of explanations, both of what people say and of what they do, and Davidson admits happily that this feature of such explanations is incompatible with the sort of law-like generality which he thinks characterizes causal explanations. It is because psychological ascriptions are constrained by canons of normativity that there are no psychological laws—but psychological states may still be causally connected, since other (e.g. neurological) descriptions may apply to

150   *Aftermath and Legacy*

them, involving predicates which do figure in causal laws. So we appear to have both internal (normative, justificatory) and external (causal) relations holding between e.g. intentions and actions.

There has been much discussion whether this position can be saved from incoherence, but I will not here go into that question. I want rather to look at what Davidson has to say about "first-person authority", since it is conceivable that we may there find some sort of answer to the question how it is that I know (or can say) what my present intention is, something that appears obscure in "Actions, Reasons, and Causes" on account of the characterization of intentions in causal terms. If Davidson can give an answer to this question, he may be able also to give some sort of answer to the question how I can know (or say) what I will do.

In "First Person Authority"[44] Davidson argues that a speaker occupies a special position as regards the meaning and meaningfulness of his utterances, arising from the fact that he does not—and indeed cannot—be an interpreter of what he says, whereas those who hear him must be interpreters. As elsewhere, Davidson claims that the positions of two people conversing are in essence the same as those of two people speaking different languages who want to understand one another; and he writes:

> Let one of the imagined pair speak and the other try to understand. . . . The best the speaker can do is to be *interpretable*, that is, to use a finite supply of distinguishable sounds applied consistently to objects and situations he believes are apparent to his hearer. . . . It makes no sense in this situation to wonder whether the speaker is generally getting things wrong. His behaviour may simply not be interpretable. But if it is, then what his words mean is (generally) what he intends them to mean . . . There is a presumption—an unavoidable presumption built into the nature of interpretation—that the speaker usually knows what he means. (Davidson 1984, 111)

The reason all this bears on authority about one's mental states is that there is another presumption operating in the picture, namely that a person sincerely saying something knows that he holds the sentence he utters to be true. If you both know what you meant by a sentence and hold it to be true, then you believe whatever it is you meant by the sentence. Davidson is thus in a position to continue the above quotation by saying, "So there is a presumption that if he knows that he holds a sentence true, he knows what he believes"; and we are to take the antecedent of this conditional to be (generally) true. First-person authority about one's beliefs appears confirmed.

The argument is an interesting one. It can of course be questioned at certain points, e.g. as regards the notion that two people conversing in a familiar language are in a similar position to that of two people who speak different languages who want to understand one another. Be that as it may, how does Davidson's argument bear on authority about one's intentions?

Aftermath and Legacy 151

The article is meant to be about first-person authority about propositional attitudes generally, "like belief, desire, intention; being pleased, astonished, afeared or proud that something is the case; or knowing, remembering, noticing or perceiving that something is the case". (102) However, it is only the first item in this list that Davidson considers (and we have seen what argument he develops about that). His reason for this way of proceeding is that "in almost every instance [of a propositional attitude], if not in all, first person authority rests at least partially on a belief component".

Unfortunately we are given no explanation of this last assertion. What is the belief component in intention, we might ask? One could argue that an expression of intention is just the expression of a belief about what you are doing or will do; but how then are we to exclude "I am trembling" and "I am going to be sick" from the picture? However we do so, the first-person authority attaching to expressions of intention surely doesn't boil down to authority about the content of (certain of) one's beliefs. In the case of expressions of intention for the future, it is not that I know best what I *think* will happen, but rather that I know best what *will* happen. (I am assuming for the sake of argument that first-person authority is best cashed out in terms of knowledge.)

And it seems in fact that the very nature of Davidson's argument for first-person authority about belief makes it untransferable to the case of intention. For the argument relies on the nature of *assertion*, as paradigmatically expressive of belief, tying the phenomenon of assertion to the presumption of interpretability. In the sense in which assertion is a speech-act, there is no species of speech-act which is as such expressive of one's intentions in the way in which assertions are expressive of one's beliefs. Statements of the form "I am φing" or of the form "I am going to φ" do not as such express intentions; to delineate the sub-class of such statements that *do* express intentions, we must (as Wittgenstein and Anscombe both saw) turn to the sorts of grounds or reasons a person might give for what they say. Once these grounds or reasons are in play, we have to take note of the fact that a third-person statement of (another's) intention will have quite other sorts of grounds; and we will be up against the question which Davidson hopes to avoid by talking about mere assertions, rather than about first or third-person utterances—namely, "In virtue of what does a first-person expression of X [belief, intention . . .] involve the *same* state or concept as a third-person ascription of X?" In Davidson's words, "why should we think that a predicate that is sometimes applied on the basis of observation, and sometimes not, is unambiguous?"[45]

We have already seen how Wittgenstein would answer this last question (40–42; 116–17, above). The unity of the language-game grounds the unity of the concept. Davidson on the other hand offers no answer; instead, he puts the question to one side, and turns to another question that *bears upon* the first. And as we have seen, it appears only to bear upon one form of the first question, that form of it that has to do with belief.

152 *Aftermath and Legacy*

We must conclude, then, at least on the basis of those articles I have mentioned, that Davidson gives us no answer to the question how or why I am an authority about what I intend. Nor, it seems, does he say anything that might explain how or why I am an authority about what I will do in the future.

So what, if anything, can be said in favour of Davidson's view of reasons as causes? There is in "Actions, Reasons, and Causes" something that many philosophers are wont to regard as a sort of Master Argument; let us see how convincing it is. Davidson points out that you might have a number of reasons for doing X; when you actually do X, however, you might well do so for just one of those reasons.

> [A] person can have a reason for an action, and perform the action, and yet this reason not be the reason why he did it. Central to the relation between a reason and an action it explains is the idea that the agent performed the action *because* he had the reason. (Davidson 1980, 9)

What does this "because" signify? Davidson proposes that it must signify efficient causality. We want to *explain* someone's action, and causal explanation is something we're anyway familiar with: "cause and effect form the sort of pattern that explains the effect, in a sense of 'explain' that we understand as well as any." (10) This last remark is perhaps rather hopeful, especially in light of the necessity which Davidson soon recognised, of excluding all those possible effects that having a given belief/desire pair (Davidson's postulated cause) could have upon a person—including even some action which on the face of it "fits" the belief/desire pair. In "Freedom to Act"[46], Davidson refers to nonstandard or wayward causal chains connecting a belief/desire pair "in the wrong way" with an action that would otherwise count as being rationalized by that pair; and he admits that it seems difficult to say anything enlightening about what makes for (non)standardness in a causal chain.

The suspicion, of course, is this: that the only way we could or would ever decide that some (e.g. neurological) causal chain was indeed "standard" would be by finding that it was instantiated *when someone acted for a given reason*. For what else would we have to go on? Patterns of neurological causation are not in themselves wayward or the converse; and it won't do to say that the most *common* causal chains count as "standard", since a belief/desire pair might most commonly produce, e.g. trembling, rather than a given action, for example if the action that would be rationalized is very difficult to perform. But if, as I imagined, we home in on a neurological process by seeing that it occurs when someone acts for a given reason, we are evidently operating with some prior, independent criterion of what acting-for-reason-R is.

What might such a criterion be? Severin Schroeder mentions three kinds of possible criterion in his critique of Davidson's argument:

> . . . first, in a given situation it may be perfectly obvious what someone is doing, in a way that amounts to knowing for what reason he is

Aftermath and Legacy 153

acting . . . Secondly, by observing a person's behaviour over a longer period of time (or asking someone who has done so) we learn what considerations tend to weigh with him . . . Finally, and most importantly, one may simply ask the agent to give his reasons.[47]

Our capacity to employ the first and second criteria (or perhaps families of criteria) rests both on a shared human nature and on a large set of background beliefs and items of knowledge. I discussed this in Chapter 3 (83–4), where in addition I tried to sketch how the third, central criterion comes into existence as in a certain sense governing the language-game, while being bound up with the other more purely behavioural criteria. This third criterion is what Anscombe brings to the fore with her question (asked of an agent) "Why?"

It is by means of employing such criteria that we can determine which, of several reasons a person had for doing X, was her actual reason for doing it. There may of course be cases where it is somewhat indeterminate what an agent's "real reason" for doing something was; and there is a large and interesting topic in the offing here, namely that of sincerity or truthfulness. A person's answer to "Why?" will only give her reason for acting if it is sincere. But as Wittgenstein argued in connection with other first-person (esp. "psychological") statements, the possibility of insincerity does not entail that such statements report, truly or falsely, the occurrence of a privately known inner state; after all, a moan or smile can be insincere or phoney, just as much as a statement—and moans and smiles aren't reports.

There are many cases where the description of an action itself implies a special sort of authority in the agent as regards the reason for the action, and where the statement that "there were various reasons for performing that action" is liable to mislead us into thinking that *that action* can be considered in isolation from its reason. A contrite son comes to his parents and says, "Mum, Dad—I apologise for drinking your last bottle of Chateau Latour." Why is he apologising? Because he drank the last bottle of Chateau Latour.—But he had many reasons to apologise to them: he'd also done no housework for a month, had broken his father's CD player, had sworn at his mother . . . So which of these things supplied his real reason for apologising?—But you can't *just apologise*: apologising is always apologising because *p*, or for the fact that *p* (and not any old *p* will do). And we might say that what the son did was apologise-for-drinking-the-last-bottle, and that there weren't several reasons for doing *that*.

Perhaps it was dwelling guiltily on the broken CD player that induced him to get up, go to his parents, and make the apology; but if on that account we say "His reason for saying sorry was that he'd broken the CD player", we are using "reason" in an eccentric manner. We are not in fact giving the boy's (real) reason at all, and this not because of any wayward causation connecting the guilty thoughts and the subsequent apology,

154   *Aftermath and Legacy*

but simply because the boy's apology came with the label *For drinking the last bottle* on it. His apology is a linguistic move having particular consequences (by which I don't simply mean effects): thus, his mother might reply, "We quite forgive you; wine is for drinking in this household, and your apology is very gracious." The forgiveness does not as it were *misfire* just because it was the boy's guilt about the CD player that kick-started him.

One thing that this example brings out is that there can be genuinely backward-looking reasons for action: the son's reason for saying sorry was that he had done such-and-such. It was not, e.g. so that he or his parents would feel better afterwards. (We can assume that he would not be interested in other ways of making them feel better, such as announcing that he was engaged to an heiress.) I mentioned this as a point recognised by Anscombe (143, above), where I added that the existence of backward-looking reasons makes problems for causalist accounts of intention. And not only for such accounts: "expected utility" theories of rational deliberation are likewise thrown into doubt, it would seem.[48]

6.   DIAGNOSIS

What conclusions about the Davidsonian project can be drawn in the light of these various criticisms?

There are perhaps two sources of trouble that ought to be highlighted, each of which, from a Wittgensteinian point of view, might be predicted to be a source of trouble, and each of which is symptomatic of much recent philosophy besides that of Davidson. The first is a tendency to overlook or smooth over differences, in the pursuit of a theory that is both general and economical; the second is a reliance on an idea of efficient causation that is likewise general and undifferentiated, this reliance being at least partly motivated by the belief that the role of efficient causality in the natural sciences makes it a sort of "default concept".

We have already had a rather vivid example of Davidson's overlooking differences, in his arguing to a conclusion about all propositional attitudes from considerations having to do only with belief (151, above). Another example, of significance for the whole theory of reasons as causes, is to be found in his reduction of intention in action to a combination of a belief and a "pro attitude toward actions of a certain kind"[49]. He admits that there is a long list of things that he wants to subsume under "pro attitude": desires, urges, tastes, economic prejudices . . . but is confident that the differences between these things will not matter philosophically. We find him, indeed, sometimes using "desire" instead of "pro attitude"; just what term is used is evidently of not much importance. The important thing is that there be a combination of two items, one cognitive, the other conative. Here we have a version of that dualism of thought and will mentioned at the start of this book. But how are the technical terms, *cognitive* and *conative*,

Aftermath and Legacy 155

introduced? Typically either by means of a list ("desires, passions, decisions, tryings . . .") with the addendum, "and so on", or by some kind of picture or metaphor—as, "the motive force, the pump, that originates all action". The main thing is to end up with two mutually exclusive sets of (mainly "psychological") terms; though it may have to be admitted that there exist terms which are to be factored into a cognitive element and a conative element.

This last remark reminds us that there are two distinct projects that have employed the belief/desire model: the project we have been discussing, of accounting for intentional action, and the more ambitious project of analysing all psychological concepts (or as many as possible) in terms of belief and desire—e.g. analysing *regret that p* as equivalent to *belief that p* plus *desire that not-p*. (In this case, since *p* must be past-tensed relative to the verb "regret", the proposed desire component looks strange, and the analysing philosopher might have to go back to the drawing-board.) The success of the first project does not, of course, depend upon that of the second. Nevertheless, the choice I just described, between two ways of elucidating "cognitive" and "conative", is faced by both projects, at any rate as they are typically explained by their proponents, e.g. Davidson with his use of "pro attitude".

Someone might respond to the first way of proceeding, that of listing some examples and saying ". . . and so on": "But I'm not sure these things can really all be put into two separate lists; or at any rate, I can think of various alternative ways of listing them, e.g. under the headings reason, passion and will." What reply can be made to such a person? A list of the sort in question is meant to be governed by salient similarities among the items, and we can either (i) admit that salient similarity is a matter of "how things strike you", or (ii) try to lay out in advance the respects of similarity—the *ways* in which the items listed are similar. By (i), the "cognitive/conative" lists will lose any presumption to privileged status. What about (ii)? Can one non-question-beggingly say what's common to desires, wishes, sentiments, tastes, etc.?

It is often said that conative states have a different "direction of fit" with the world than cognitive states. Whereas the belief that p is meant to be changed when not-p, the desire that p needn't be. A belief is meant to fit the world[50], but the world is meant to fit a desire—in some sense of "meant to". What sense? Is it something to do with the agent's being disposed to *change* the world, i.e. bring it about that p? But a desire will issue in action only in combination with certain beliefs. You need, e.g. to believe that what's in that glass is water (and not hydrochloric acid) if your desire to quench your thirst will result in your drinking it. But then why not call the *belief* a disposition to perform certain actions, or to "change the world"—in combination with certain desires, naturally?

Beliefs of course can be true or false, unlike desires. But truth-aptness will not do as a criterion for the purportedly psychological distinction between the cognitive and the conative, since it relates rather to the linguistic

156 *Aftermath and Legacy*

category of assertoric sentence. A putatively conative state may be expressed using an assertoric sentence, as "I am going to sack him", an expression of intention which can, at least retrospectively, be called true or false, and which it would beg the question in this context to replace with "I intend to sack him". An appeal to the ordinary uses of "true" will be inconclusive at best: beliefs can be called true, but knowledge surely can't—"What Keith knows is actually *true*" is absurd, by the lights of ordinary usage. And conversely, we happily say that our wishes, conative though they be, sometimes come true.

Thus it seems that the Davidsonian project is in various ways open to a well-known species of Wittgensteinian critique: a craving for generality has resulted in an account of the phenomena that achieves simplicity by means of question-begging stipulations. By contrast, the sheer variety that faces us when we consider the phenomenon of intention is much more evident in Anscombe's account. This comes out in the details of what she says, in her examples, illustrations, and so on—but also in her general statements. Consider her subdivision of positive answers to "Why?" into three types: "the answer may (a) simply mention past history, (b) give an interpretation of the action, or (c) mention something future.[51]" She likewise subdivides answers that refuse application of the question. And when she turns to the concept of the *voluntary*, she is happy to list a few broad kinds of voluntary action or inaction (etc.), with no suggestion that the list is a complete one, but simply as a way of giving some signposts for further enquiries (enquiries which she herself does not there undertake).[52]

More examples could be given of this feature of Anscombe's way of proceeding, in *Intention* and elsewhere. It is a way of proceeding that conforms to Wittgenstein's advice, "Don't think, but look!"; the lists or subdivisions she gives are simply the result of looking at the actual uses of our words, while making sure to avoid a "one-sided diet of examples". (*PI* 593) These lists and subdivisions typically function as *headings* within the enquiry, not as key propositions in a theory: Anscombe's purpose is not to construct some general theory which will manage to "unify" the various subdivisions we began with, but simply to lay out a true, and at the same time illuminating, description of the conceptual terrain—or (as with what she says about voluntariness) just to give pointers towards the laying out of such a description. Of course it is precisely this feature of her philosophy that produces bafflement or dissatisfaction in readers expecting to be given a System. But it is not as if, in reading *Intention*, one has the sensation of being taken on a stroll through more or less familiar linguistic pastures. One has the sensation of being made to think hard about matters which, though not hidden, may never have struck one before in the way they now strike one. The comparison with Wittgenstein is obvious, though in fact the two philosophers are *stylistically* quite different.

I referred above (154) to two sources of trouble in Davidson's project. I turn now to the second of these, namely Davidson's reliance on a general

Aftermath and Legacy 157

and undifferentiated idea of efficient causation. His statement that "cause and effect form the sort of pattern that explains the effect, in a sense of 'explain' that we understand as well as any" is telling. It is not the sort of statement you would expect to find from his mentor Quine. But in this matter it is Davidson, not Quine, who gave voice to the spirit of the times, philosophically speaking. Accounts aiming to solve some philosophical problem, or group of problems, by means of a "causal theory" are now so common as no longer to be noteworthy. We have had causal theories of knowledge, of perception, of memory, of meaning, of reference. Et cetera.

We have also had philosophical critiques based on the thought that if something lacks a causal role, it can't be real: thus, both psychological (esp. "phenomenal") facts/qualities and moral facts/qualities have been indicted on the grounds that were they to exist, either they would have to be causally impotent or they would undermine the presumed sufficiency of physical causality. The second possibility offends against the scientistic spirit, while the first possibility is thought to be a problem particularly by those who adopt a causal theory of knowledge, since how could we hope to know about pains or virtues if they couldn't *cause* us to have beliefs about them? This problem ought to exist also for mathematical facts, but fictionalism about maths is considerably less appealing than fictionalism (or similar) about the mental or the moral, on account of the status of maths as bosom buddy of the natural sciences.

Positive causal theories and negative causal critiques often seem, when examined, to be motivated by an almost pre-Humean faith in causation as a sort of metaphysical *oomph*—something "robust", to use a buzzword— or alternatively as a metaphysical chain, connecting things in a secure and determinate way. (The phrase "causal chain", as in "deviant causal chain", is part of standard philosophical vocabulary.) A philosopher may ask what significant truth can possibly be elicited by Anscombe's question "Why?" unless it be some *state* of the agent, with proper causal credentials, capable of actual metaphysical efficacy; while another may think of the fact that Socrates is the referent of "Socrates" as vouchsafed us by a single, long line of causality, stretching back through the centuries from a particular use of the name to some initial baptism, a line both strong and sure. What comes out in both sorts of case, very often, is an implicit faith in causality as the cement of the universe. And connected with this faith is a view of causation as resting upon "strict laws"[53], i.e. exceptionless generalizations, about which Anscombe wrote: "The truth of this conception is hardly debated. It is, indeed, a bit of *Weltanschauung*: it helps to form a cast of mind which is characteristic of our whole culture."[54] Davidson embraced this conception, which lies at the bottom of his "anomalous monism": since psychological generalizations aren't strict they can't be causal; but psychological explanation has to be causal (see above); so psychological states and events must also be physical, enabling them to fall under strict causal laws.

158 *Aftermath and Legacy*

This bit of *Weltanschauung* is above all a picture—hence those metaphors of pumps and cables which come so readily to mind. And to put dogmatic trust in such a picture can look like a form of superstition. In the *Tractatus* Wittgenstein had gone so far as to write that "Belief in the causal nexus is *superstition*" (*TLP* 5.1361), by which he "didn't mean to say that the belief in the causal nexus was one amongst superstitions but rather that superstition is nothing else than the belief in the causal nexus."[55] It is a bold statement. Whether or not the later Wittgenstein would have concurred with it, he would surely have pointed to the belief in the causal nexus as one of the prime temptations for philosophers, especially for philosophers in whom either the metaphysical or the scientistic impulse (or both) can be found. A few centuries ago, Hume attempted to liberate us, and himself, from addiction to the picture of *causal necessity*. Wittgenstein can be seen as continuing that job, as well as offering other forms of liberation, such as liberation from "the dogmatism into which we fall so easily in doing philosophy" (*PI* 131)—itself a Humean ideal. But it is a notorious fact, both in politics and in intellectual life, that people don't always want the freedom that may be offered to them.

* * * * *

In the Introduction, I described thought and will as two fundamental aspects of the human condition. This can be asserted without embracing a simple input-output model of the human being; for *thought* and *will* are not so much unitary categories as vague but useful headings or pointers, pointing down different pathways of enquiry. "Concepts lead us to make investigations; are the expression of our interest, and direct our interest." (*PI* 570) Wittgenstein was not thinking primarily of philosophical investigations and philosophical interest when he wrote this, but the remark will serve. His own investigations yield a picture which is as rich and complex as is to be expected when the subject matter is such a large tract of human life and human nature. That makes his account resistant to being expressed in the form of a general theory, a theory of the kind that happily accepts some "-ism" for a label. But to any genuinely curious student of philosophy (and that title can in principle apply to anybody) the offer of richness and complexity probably outweighs the attraction of "-isms", which are the bling of philosophy. A theme of this chapter has been the legacy of Wittgenstein's thought on these topics, and as long as there is such a thing as the genuinely curious student of philosophy, I think that legacy is assured.

NOTES

1. I touch on this topic in Teichmann 2011 (Ch. 5).
2. In "Conversations with Wittgenstein", Drury reports W. E. Johnson as saying: "I consider it a disaster for Cambridge that Wittgenstein has returned. A man

incapable of carrying on a discussion. If I say a sentence has meaning for me no one has the right to say it is senseless." (Rhees 1981, 103.) The remark is quoted approvingly by Charles R. Pigden, in "Coercive Theories of Meaning or Why Language Shouldn't Matter (So Much) to Philosophy" (Pigden 2010). For Pigden, Wittgenstein is an arch-offender among those philosophers who make out that philosophical theses are or can be nonsense, and Pigden's accusation of "coercion" well exemplifies the sort of indignant response I am alluding to. He would like Wittgenstein at least to give us "a theory of what makes propositions meaningful", but what he finds in the *Investigations* is "nothing but a mixed bag of metaphors and a vague gesture towards use, plus a rough line round the privileged uses". (16) Whether he would arrive at a more sophisticated understanding if unimpeded by worries about "totalitarianism" is a moot question.

3. A slightly earlier use of this image shows that it is not other people's silliness that is so nourishing, but one's own: "Never stay up on the barren heights of cleverness, but come down into the green valleys of silliness". (*CV* 76e) Wittgenstein's approving attitude to silliness goes beyond the bounds of philosophy; thus he writes: "A typical American film, naïve and silly, can—for all its silliness and even *by means* of it—be instructive. A fatuous, self-conscious English film can teach one nothing". (*CV* 57e) For interested film buffs, the date of this remark is 1947.

4. Russell 1912, Ch. 15.

5. Quine 1966, 203.

6. See, e.g. Quine 1951.

7. See Quine 1969.

8. The analysis needs tinkering with on account of possibly-true sentences like "There exists an unnamed pebble". We could rewrite it thus: "For some p, it's possible to introduce a name, N, such that 'N is an unnamed pebble' would say that p; and p." The possible sentence *would* say (falsely) to be the case what *is* in fact the case. This analysis (due to Dermot Cassidy) raises further questions about "the identity of propositions".

9. This sort of thought is already present in Wittgenstein's discussion of formal concepts in the *Tractatus*: among formal concepts are *object, property, proposition*, etc. (See Ch. 2, 30–31.) The objectual reading of "There are properties" on the face of it involves treating "x is a property" as a genuine first-level predicate, rather than as a formal concept-expression.

10. The first notable dissent coming from Grice and Strawson; see their 1956.

11. I discuss the sociology of scientism, and more generally the similarities and differences between science and philosophy as practices, in Teichmann 2011, Ch. 5.

12. Malcolm's contribution to the colloquium was published as "Behaviourism as a Philosophy of Psychology", in Malcolm 1977 (85–103).

13. Malcolm 1977 (159–69), 169. Chomsky's theories are developed in various places, e.g. Chomsky 1968.

14. Ibid., 168.

15. This notion was discussed in Ch. 3; see 81–3.

16. Malcolm's arguments are to be found in Malcolm 1959. See Schroeder 1997 for the critique.

17. Chihara and Fodor 1968.

18. Ibid., 413.

19. The authors' statement, "In the course of acquiring these mental concepts we develop a variety of beliefs involving them" leaves the question of logical priority/parity unaddressed.

20. Ibid., 414.

21. See Churchland 1981.

160 *Aftermath and Legacy*

22. Hume, *Treatise* Bk. 3, Part I, sec. 1.
23. Libet 1983.
24. You wonder what he would have made of someone who said that he found that his experience of intention came *after* the action; would that idiosyncrasy have simply been included among the experimental data?
25. Bennett and Hacker 2003.
26. Tallis 2004.
27. Carpendale and Lewis 2004, 84.
28. If scepticism is expressed that any *research* could confirm or support the picture of children's understanding of mental concepts presented by Carpendale and Lewis, on the grounds that we will more properly arrive at such a picture through a combination of common knowledge and philosophical reflection, I think the authors are in a position to agree with this last statement ("we will more properly arrive . . ."), proposing for developmental psychology the role of adding much detail to the picture, detail that would for example be of use to educationalists and others.
29. Putnam 1985, 227.
30. Putnam himself came to recognise the problems with his position, and to bring himself into closer alignment with Wittgenstein. See various essays in Putnam 1995.
31. See, e.g. Fodor 1987.
32. See Fodor 1980.
33. Anscombe 1963, 9.
34. Cf. Anscombe 1963, 20.
35. "On Cause and Effect, Intuitive Awareness", from MS 119 in von Wright's catalogue, trans. P. Winch, reprinted in *PO* 371.
36. Anscombe 1963, 23–4.
37. The fact that you can no longer tell the position of your limbs if deprived of such sensations, e.g. through anaesthesia, does not entail that you *go by* those sensations, in the sense of taking them as grounds or evidence for what you say.
38. Davidson 1980, 3–19.
39. Ibid., 3.
40. Cf. Ch. 1, 20.
41. This doesn't go for all verbs: consider "I wrote a letter" and "I wanted to write a letter" (or at any rate "I intended to write a letter"). You can't accidentally write a letter.
42. Cf. Ch. 2, 41.
43. See various essays in Davidson 2001.
44. Davidson 1984.
45. 106. Davidson raises this question several times in the course of his article.
46. In Davidson 1980, 63–81.
47. Schroeder 2001, 153–4.
48. I argue this at greater length in Teichmann 2013.
49. Davidson 1980, 3.
50. In the sense in which this holds of beliefs, it does not hold of imaginings. For those philosophers who want to classify all mental states as either cognitive or conative (or some combination), imagining that p will thus pose a problem: for surely it isn't a conative state?
51. Anscombe 1963, 24.
52. Anscombe 1963, sec. 49.
53. Or *serious* laws, in Davidson's words; see 146, above.
54. Anscombe 1981b, 133.
55. In a letter to Ogden; see von Wright 1973, 31.

References

Anscombe, G.E.M.
1959—*An Introduction to Wittgenstein's Tractatus*, London: Hutchinson, 1959.
1963—*Intention*, 2nd ed., Oxford: Basil Blackwell 1963.
1981a—"The First Person", in *Metaphysics and the Philosophy of Mind. The Collected Philosophical Papers of G.E.M. Anscombe*, Volume II, Oxford: Basil Blackwell, 1981.
1981b—"Causality and Determination", in *Metaphysics and the Philosophy of Mind. The Collected Philosophical Papers of G.E.M. Anscombe*, Volume II, Oxford: Basil Blackwell, 1981.
1981c—"On Brute Facts", in *Ethics, Religion and Politics. The Collected Philosophical Papers of G.E.M. Anscombe*, Volume III, Oxford: Basil Blackwell, 1981.
2005—"Practical Inference", in *Human Life, Action and Ethics*, ed. M. Geach and G. Gormally, St. Andrews Studies in Philosophy and Public Affairs, Exeter: Imprint Academic 2005.
2011—"A Theory of Language?", in *From Plato to Wittgenstein: Essays by G.E.M. Anscombe*, ed. M. Geach and L. Gormally, St. Andrews Studies in Philosophy and Public Affairs, Exeter: Imprint Academic, 2011.
Austin, J. L.
1962—*How to Do Things with Words*, Oxford: Clarendon Press, 1962.
1979—"A Plea for Excuses", in *J .L. Austin: Philosophical Papers*, 3rd ed, ed. J. O. Urmson and G. J. Warnock, Oxford: Clarendon Press 1979.
Ayer, A. J.
1936—*Language, Truth and Logic*, London: Victor Gollancz, 1936.
Bennett, M. R. and P.M.S. Hacker,
2003—*The Philosophical Foundations of Neuroscience*, Malden, MA: Blackwell, 2003.
Berkeley, G.
1710—*The Principles of Human Knowledge*
Butler, J.
1849—"Of Personal Identity", in *The Analogy of Religion*, ed. Samuel Halifax, Oxford: Oxford University Press, 1849.
Carpendale, J.I.M. and C. Lewis.
2004—"Constructing an Understanding of Mind: The Development of Children's Social Understanding within Social Interaction", *Behavioural and Brain Sciences* 27: 79–151.
Castañeda, H.-N.
1967—"On the Logic of Self-Knowledge", *Noûs* 1: 9–21.

162 References

Chihara, C. S and Fodor, J. A.
  1968—"Operationalism and Ordinary Language", in *Wittgenstein: The Philosophical Investigations*, ed. G. Pitcher, London: Macmillan 1968, 384–419.
Child, W.
  2016—"Wittgenstein on Inner-Outer and Avowals", in *The Blackwell Companion to Wittgenstein,* ed. H.-J. Glock and J. Hyman, Oxford: Wiley-Blackwell, 2016 (projected).
Chomsky, N.
  1968—*Language and Mind*, New York: Harcourt, Brace and World, 1968.
Churchland, P. M.
  1981—"Eliminative Materialism and the Propositional Attitudes," *Journal of Philosophy* 78: 67–90.
Crane, T.
  2010—'Wittgenstein and Intentionality', *The Harvard Review of Philosophy*, 17: 88–104.
Davidson, D.
  1980—*Essays on Actions and Events*, New York: Oxford University Press, 1980.
  1984—"First Person Authority", *Dialectica* 38 (2–3): 102–11.
  2001—*Inquiries into Truth and Interpretation*, 2nd ed., Oxford: Oxford University Press, 2001.
Descartes, R.
  1967—*The Philosophical Works of Descartes,* ed. and trans. E. S. Haldane and G.R.T. Ross, Cambridge: Cambridge University Press 1967.
Finkelstein, D.
  2007—"Holism and Animal Minds", in *Wittgenstein and the Moral Life: Essays in Honor of Cora Diamond*, ed. A. Crary, Cambridge, MA: MIT Press 2007.
Fodor, J.
  1980—"Methodological Solipsism Considered as a Research Strategy in Cognitive Science", *Behavioral and Brain Sciences*, 3 63–73.
  1987—*Psychosemantics: The Problem of Meaning in the Philosophy of Mind*, Cambridge, MA: MIT Press 1987.
Frege, G.
  1884—*The Foundations of Arithmetic (Die Grundlagen der Arithmetik)*, 1884.
  1952—*Translations from the Philosophical Writings of Gottlob Frege.* ed. P. Geach and M. Black, Oxford: Blackwell 1952.
  1967—"The Thought: A Logical Inquiry", in *Philosophical Logic,* ed. P. F. Strawson, Oxford: Oxford University Press 1967, 17–38.
Grice, H. P.
  1989—*Studies in the Way of Words*, Cambridge, MA: Harvard University Press 1989.
Grice, H. P. and P. F. Strawson.
  1956—"In Defense of a Dogma", *The Philosophical Review*, 65 (2): 141–58.
Hacker, P.M.S.
  1990—*Wittgenstein: Meaning and Mind, Vol. 3 of An Analytical Commentary on the Philosophical Investigations*, Oxford: Blackwell 1990.
  1996—*Wittgenstein: Mind and Will, Vol. 4 of An Analytical Commentary on the Philosophical Investigations*, Oxford: Blackwell 1996.
Hume, D.
  1738—*A Treatise of Human Nature*, 1738.
  1975—*Enquiries Concerning Human Understanding and Concerning the Principles of Morals*, 3rd ed., ed. L. A. Selby-Bigge and P. H. Nidditch, Oxford: Oxford University Press 1975.

References 163

Husserl, E.
 1913, 1921—*Logical Investigations (Logische Untersuchungen)* two vol. 2nd ed., 1913, 1921.

James, W.
 1890—*The Principles of Psychology*, 1890.

Kripke, S.
 1980—*Naming and Necessity*. Cambridge, MA: Harvard University Press, 1980.

Libet, B.
 1983—Libet, B., C. A. Gleason, E. W. Wright, and D. K, Pearl., "Time of Conscious Intention to Act in Relation to Onset of Cerebral Activity (Readiness-Potential)", *Brain* 106(3): 623–42.

Malcolm, N.
 1959—*Dreaming*, London: Routledge 1959.
 1977—*Thought and Knowledge*, Ithaca and London: Cornell University Press 1977.

Moore, G. E.
 1959—"Wittgenstein's Lectures in 1930–33", in his *Philosophical Papers,* London: Allen and Unwin 1959, 252–324.

Piaget, J.
 1955—*The Child's Construction of Reality*, trans. Margaret Cook, London: Routledge and Kegan Paul 1955.

Pidgen, C. R.
 2010—Pidgen, C. R., "Coercive Theories of Meaning or Why Language Shouldn't Matter (So Much) to Philosophy", *Logique & Analyse* 210: 151–8.

Plato
 The Theaetetus

Prior, A. N.
 1971—*Objects of Thought,* ed. P. T. Geach and A. Kenny, Oxford: Oxford University Press 1971.

Putnam, H.
 1985—"The Meaning of 'Meaning'", in *Philosophical Papers, Vol. 2: Mind, Language and Reality*, Cambridge: Cambridge University Press, 1985.
 1995—*Words and Life*, Cambridge, MA: Harvard University Press, 1995.

Quine, W. van O.
 1951—"Two Dogmas of Empiricism", *The Philosophical Review* 60: 20–43.
 1966—"Carnap's Views of Ontology", in *The Ways of Paradox and Other Essays*, rev. and enl. ed, Cambridge, MA: Harvard University Press 1966.
 1969—"Existence and Quantification", in *Ontological Relativity and Other Essays*, New York: Columbia University Press 1969.

Rhees, R.
 1981—(ed.) *Ludwig Wittgenstein: Personal Recollections*, Oxford: Basil Blackwell 1981.

Russell, B.
 1907—"Fundamentals", unpublished MS in the Russell archives.
 1912—*The Problems of Philosophy*, New York: Henry Holt 1912.
 1917—"Knowledge by Acquaintance and Knowledge by Description", in *Proceedings of the Aristotelian Society*, 1910–1911. Reprinted in his *Mysticism and Logic,* London: George Allen & Unwin Ltd. 1917.
 1918—*Mysticism and Logic*, London: Longmans Green 1918.
 1921—*The Analysis of Mind*, London: George Allen and Unwin 1921.
 1984—*Theory of Knowledge: the 1913 Manuscript*, in *The Collected Papers of Bertrand Russell, Vol. VII,* ed. E. R. Eames and K. Blackwell, London: Allen & Unwin 1984.

164 *References*

Schroeder, S.
   1997—"The Concept of Dreaming: On Three Theses by Malcolm", *Philosophical Investigations* 20 (1): 15–38.
   2001—"Are Reasons Causes? A Wittgensteinian Response to Davidson", in *Wittgenstein and Contemporary Philosophy of Mind*. ed. Schroeder, Houndmills, Basingstoke, Hampshire; New York: Palgrave 2001, 150–70.
   2006—*Wittgenstein: The Way Out of the Fly-Bottle*, Cambridge; Malden, MA: Polity Press 2006.
Searle, J.
   1967—"Proper Names" in *Philosophical Logic,* ed. P. F. Strawson, Oxford: Oxford University Press 1967.
Tallis, R.
   2004—*Why the Mind is Not a Computer: A Pocket Dictionary on Neuromythology*, 2nd ed., Exeter: Imprint Academic, 2004.
Teichmann, R.
   2008—*The Philosophy of Elizabeth Anscombe*, Oxford: Oxford University Press 2008.
   2011—*Nature, Reason and the Good Life*, Oxford: Oxford University Press 2011.
   2013—"The Importance of the Past", *Philosophy* 88 (1), 115–31.
Von Wright, G. H.
   1973—(ed.) *Letters to C. K. Ogden: With Comments on the English Translation of the Tractatus Logico-Philosophicus*, Oxford: Basil Blackwell, 1973.
Watson, J. B.
   1913—"Psychology as the Behaviorist Views It", *Psychological Review,* 20: 158–77.
Williamson, T.
   2000—*Knowledge and Its Limits*, Oxford: Oxford University Press, 2000.

Index

acts of will 19–20, 23, 61, 89
animals 21–2, 47–9, 54, 58n29,
    93–4, 113
Anscombe, G.E.M. xiii, 26n21,
    28n40, 53, 54, 58n26, 83,
    99n20, 99n23, 99n28, 106–7,
    111–12, 113, 142–6, 153,
    156, 157
Aquinas 122
Aristotle 19, 24, 122
aspect-perception 89
assertion 61, 93–7, 151
Austin, J.L. 59 n.36, 99n25
Ayer, A.J. 26n13

behaviourism 21–4, 61, 63, 89, 93
belief 18–19, 32–4, 91–7, 150–51
belief/desire model 1, 152, 154–6;
    see also dualism of thought
    and will
Bennett, M.R. 138
Ben-Yami, H. xiii
Berkeley, G. 7, 8–10, 13, 29, 33
Butler, J. 97n8

Carpendale, J. 138–9
Cassidy, D. 159n8
Castañeda, H.-N. 123n17
causation 7, 11–13, 24–5, 141, 146–50,
    152, 157–8; *see also* dubitability
    of causes and effects
Chihara, C. 134–6
Child, W. 58n29
Chomsky, N. 131–3
cognitive and conative 2, 17, 60,
    154–6; *see also* dualism of
    thought and will
Crane, T. 58n24
criteria 81–3, 94, 105, 113, 133–4

Davidson, D. xiii, 58n29, 93–4, 129,
    146–157
Descartes, R. 1, 2, 4, 17–18, 18–19, 21,
    25, 97n4, 103–4, 107
decision (stipulation) 8–10, 13–14, 16,
    33, 40
demonstratives 103–4, 106–7, 109–11
desire 20–24, 113, 154–5
dreaming 133–4
dualism of thought and will 1–2, 8, 14,
    17, 120–21, 154
dubitability of causes and effects 12–13,
    20, 37, 49–50

eliminativism 136
expressions of intention *see* intention
external relations *see* internal relations

falsity 3–4, 10–11
final causes 24–5
Finkelstein, D. 58n29
first-person authority 12, 64–6, 72–3,
    114, 133, 137, 147, 150–52
Fischer, E. xiii
Fodor, J. 134–6, 139–41
formal concepts 30–32, 36
Frege, G. 4, 5, 6, 13–16, 31, 33, 97n5

general ideas 8–10, 29
grammatical (proposition, enquiry)
    58n26, 69–70, 72, 119
"greebles" 44–5
Grice, P. 99n19, 159n10

Hacker, P.M.S. 43–5, 69, 98n17,
    99n19, 112, 138
human beings 101–4, 110–11, 120–22
Hume, D. 1, 2, 7, 19–20, 29, 49, 73,
    128, 136, 147, 158

166 *Index*

Husserl, E. 27n26
Hyman, J. xiii

"I" 4, 30, 103–4, 104–13, 117, 119, 120
"I was about to . . ." 75–7
identification 104–5
ineffability, 6, 10
intention, intentional 18, 20, 52–6, 77–9, 84–5, 99n25, 113, 117, 132–3, 137–8, 142–54; *see also* decision
internal relations 35–7, 40, 42, 48, 50–1, 132–3, 141, 149–50
introspection 64–5
involuntary *see* voluntary

James, W. 21, 23
Johnson, W.E. 158–9n2

knowledge/foreknowledge of one's actions 50, 144–5
Kripke, S. 123n12, 139

language-game 41–2, 53, 55
Lewis, C. 138–9
Lewis, D. 129
Libet, B. 137–8
Lichtenberg, G. 123n3
Locke, J. 6, 7, 26n13, 29, 128
logical pictures 30–3

Malcolm, N. 98n9, 131–2, 133–4
mental causes 144
mental states 78, 114–16, 119–20, 133
metaphysics 127, 129
misidentification *see* identification
Moore, G.E. 123n3
Moore's Paradox 58n27, 115–16, 119–20
motives 143–4

natural expressions 47, 54, 105, 113
nonsense 31, 48–9, 126–7

orders 38–9, 88

Parmenides, Parmenidean 3–4, 10, 17, 25
"peebles" 43–4
performative utterances 55–6, 115
Piaget, J. 92
pictures 7–8, 10, 39–40, 45, 62–3, 121–2; *see also* logical pictures

Pigden, C. 159n2
Plato 5, 10–11
Prior, A.N. 33
privacy (of the mental) 22, 35, 67
process 63–4, 73
proposition *see* thought
psychological state *see* mental state
Putnam, H. 123n12, 130, 139
putting your hand up 76–7

Quine, W. van O. 128–31, 157

reasons for action 53–4, 85, 142–4, 146–50, 151, 152–4
representation 7–11; *see also* pictures
resemblance 7, 9–10
Rimbaud, A. 49
Rogers, C.R. 131
Russell, B. 5, 11–12, 20–4, 32, 37, 67, 73, 128

sameness of meaning 41–5, 102–3, 116–17, 151
"same pain" 67–8, 69–72
saying and showing 31, 36
Schopenhauer, A. 1, 17
Schroeder, S. xiii, 99n19, 134, 152–3
scientism 128–31, 136
Searle, J.R. 109
self *see* "I"
Skinner, B.F. 131
Socrates 3, 10–11
soul 33, 121–2
Strawson, P.F. 159n10
Subject 4, 9, 13–14, 30, 33, 101, 103, 120; *see also* "I"
surprise (absence of) 85–6

Tallis, R. 138
Teichmann, R. 158n1, 159n11
Thorndike, E.L. 21
Thought (*Gedanke*) 4, 13–16
truth 4, 13–14, 155–6

volitions *see* acts of will
voluntary (acts, movements) 23, 85–9, 99n25, 156

Watson, J.B. 22
Whitman, W. 136
Williamson, T. 124n19
wishing 17–18, 156